D1074011

GREEN FIELDS
GAELIC SPORT IN IRELAND

GREEN FIELDS

GAELIC SPORT IN IRELAND

Tom Humphries

photographs by

Sportsfile, Dublin

Weidenfeld & Nicolson

LONDON

First published in 1996 by
George Weidenfeld & Nicolson
The Orion Publishing Group
Orion House
5 Upper St Martin's Lane
London
WC2H 9EA

Printed in Italy by Grafica Veneta S.p.A.

British Library Cataloguing-in-Publication Data

A catalogue record for this book is available
from the British Library

ISBN: 0 297 83566 1

Reprinted 2005

To Mary, Molly and Caitlín with love.

CONTENTS

ACKNOWLEDGEMENTS

Many thanks to everybody mentioned or quoted in these pages for their time and generosity. Thanks also to Malachy Logan, my editor at the Irish Times for his help and advice. To Sean Moran, Liam Ryan and Emmet Malone for advice and good company on so many trips. To Danny Lynch. To Liam McDowell in Belfast. To Tony and Pauline McSweeney in Killarney. To Danny and Catherine Quinn in Derry. To Pauric McShea in Donegal. To Muiris Bowler and Lillian Evans in Boston. To Dave Hughes and Jim Barron in New York for sorting the wheat from the chaff with regard to publishers. To Tommy Smith. To Mick Maguire and Fiachra O'Marcaigh in systems. To Brian, Eddie and Jason Sherlock. To Dave Clarke and his hurley in Kilmallock. To everybody in Achill. To my parents for encouraging me to become literate. To Beth Vaughan and Michael Dover at Weidenfeld for their patience and help. Most of all to Mary Hennessy for her encouragement and shared strength in everything. To anyone I've inadvertently left out. Many thanks also.

INTRODUCTION

Gaelic town

The waves are hissing the secrets of winter. They arrive here bearing a wind which has lost no sharpness since it left the west coast of Scotland. The roads are empty and frosted tonight. The moon is timid in a louring sky. The dressing-room lights are off. The floodlights have yet to be cranked up. The pitch is fringed with frost. There is nobody here. Why would anyone come?

The roads out from Newry take treacherous turns when they head eastward. Driving here you can collect a necklace of football towns, match the places with the great names who sprang from them and drive through the backways of the imagination. Past and present. The boys will be turning themselves out of those towns tonight – heading for the coast and hard work. Why will they come? For the love it. Only for the love of it.

February is a dark month for them. Blow on your hands. Warm yourselves with your daydreams, boys. The summer is a long time away. The imagination of the country hasn't yet reawakened to the possibilities of football and hurling.

Aye. February, and the weeks on either side of it, mean four in a car and a cup of stewed tea sipped in a wet-walled dressing-room after training. February means bitter nights under watery yellow floodlights, the cold catching in your throat and the fog of your breath coming fast. February is an ache in every muscle, a regret in every step, and a constant wondering about the sense of it all.

And yet February brings its comforts, too. At no other time is the Gaelic Athletics Association (GAA) world so united and so classless. In every county, in every town, and on every pitch, players are erasing Christmas excesses and the winter slackness from their guts, re-acquainting themselves with old aches and new twinges, monitoring themselves, making sure the hunger is still there.

February is the most democratic of months. Everybody is equal again at the bottom of the ladder. In the realm of pub talk, just briefly, a Jack might aspire to being a King. One muddy field is much like any other on a night like tonight, one shapeless bunch of players fairly indistinguishable from another.

A player's every movement is well lit in his own home-place but, in the heart of winter, he seems only marginally more luminous than everyone else, getting by on low-wattage celebrity. The excitement of the championship, be it club or inter-county, hasn't taken us by the throat yet. In the months before the daylight lengthens, that's when you earn the right to be a local hero come summertime.

Something in the soul of the game and the disposition of the country gives this time of year its pleasant feel of slowly mounting expectation. The Championship, the essential ceremony around which the GAA is structured, has romance sewn into its centre. Every team starts with one chance. Lose and the summer is over, the year is over. Win and you take all the glory. All these nights in the cold, the wet, and the dark they might just be for seventy minutes of football. One chance for every part of Gaelic Town.

Ballykinlar, county Down, and the arc of a flaming flare creates a brief buttermilk sky above the army camp. Flares usually mean that the British army boys are about to start their shooting practice. Tonight, though, the familiar rat-a-tat-tat of gunfire never comes. Too cold. Too damn cold.

Tommy McGivern has arrived in his jeep with Mickey Linden in the passenger seat. Mickey Linden was the footballer of the year the last time the weather was warm, the man who piggy-backed Down to their All Ireland title in 1994. Now he sits in Tommy's jeep, and the dial on the dashboard tells him that it is one degree above freezing. That's before he steps out and takes a sample of the mean wind that is whipping in from the sea. That wind will be embedded in your bones if you spend time standing around tonight. Mickey hops back into the jeep and pulls his knees up to his chest.

Mickey is a driving instructor. The boys he's been with through thick and thin over the last few years each have their own lives and their own worries, too. There's a couple of teachers, a supermarket manager, an engineer, a publican, a dentist, a pharmacist, a promoter, an accountant, a bunch of students. They've all fixed up their business for the day and driven out here to the wilds of county Down. All over the country in windswept fields, boys, girls, men and women, are making the same sacrifice, making similar journeys.

Gaelic Town. When seven men sat down in the billiards room of Hayes Hotel in county Tipperary, on the 1 November 1884, to formally found the GAA, can they really have envisaged this? Possibly. One of them, Michael Cusack, felt that the 'Association could organize the whole country within the year 1885'. Yet, well over a century later, the country is still in thrall to the games.

That the Gaelic Athletic Association succeeded at all is due to the manner in which the fare it offered fitted perfectly within the culture, rituals and aspirations of our society. On an island where native culture had for centuries been subordinated to political imperatives, the games became a passionate and rugged expression of a people's soul. When all other forms of Irishness had been stamped out, the spirit burst out of captivity in the form of play.

Almost immediately that play assumed a political complexion. Everything on this island does.

The culture of Gaelic games has been built upon the Irish need for collective self-expression, the desperate hankering after something indigenous and Irish in a world which formerly repressed such forms of articulation, a world which latterly has become increasingly and depressingly homogenized. Through a long history, during which native language and native law were driven underground, the door to freedom always remained ajar for a people who could express themselves through play. Throughout the time when a small island nation on the western periphery of Europe has been looking for an identity, the games have been something we have drawn confidence from. Our distinctiveness no longer shames us.

Today, three-quarters of a million Irish people are members of the GAA, but that figure represents only a fraction of the Irish people who are touched by the games of football and hurling in their regular daily lives. The influence of the GAA cannot be measured in units of membership or revenue, through attendances or viewing figures. Its impact is emotional, visceral.

Even those Irish people who devote their lives to turning their faces away from the games are touched by them. The games have enmeshed themselves in Irish life in a manner that nobody in that billiard hall just over a hundred years ago could have foreseen. The GAA is more than a sports' organization, it is a national trust, an entity which we feel we hold in common ownership. It is there to administer to our shared passion.

Passion. In a perverse way these boys tonight in Ballykinlar relish it all. The early arrivals keep on counting their own number, knowing that this is a night when their faith and commitment will be tested. They know that, come the dizziness of high summer when they are being talked about in bars, living rooms and TV studios around the country, this investment of time and energy in the dead of winter will have welded them together as a team. They will have earned their celebrity, sorted the hangers-on from the real football people. Bad nights in Ballykinlar have more to do with the soul of the GAA than bright days in Croke Park.

'There's been nights,' says Tommy McGivern, 'like last Wednesday night when the wind and the rain was so bad that you could have lain back into it and if it stopped suddenly you'd have fallen over.'

Tommy is retired now, departed from a successful career selling tyres. He can remember days when he drove from Down to Cork and back in a day, because it had to be done. In retirement, though, coming out here and helping the county team is his pleasure. He picks up a handful of Ballykinlar earth, lets it run through his fingers. 'Sand and loam. That's why we come here in the winter.'

For others, the draw to Ballykinlar is a gravitational thing, the pull made stronger through habit and friendship. Take Ross Carr. This is his eleventh winter. Leaving his pub, The Brass Monkey in Newry, and getting into the car and driving east towards Ballykinlar doesn't get any more appealing as the years take their toll on the legs.

'The hardest part,' says Ross, 'is thinking about it, just getting up out of a warm house on a cold night to drive out here and do this. I've never liked it, but I've grown to accept it. This is the hardest time of year. It's not easy after a day's work.'

'Don't let Carr tell you that he knows what a day's work is,' roars his friend and travelling companion D.J. Kane. 'Teaching kids is a day's work. What Ross Carr does is something different. He's glad to get out here for the bit of exercise.'

The two have been friends for virtually all their Senior football careers and they knew each other by reputation long before that. Sons of football families – DNA crossed somewhere back in the Mourne Mountains.

Ross Carr's uncle, Barney, trained the great Down team of the 1960s, his father and most of his uncles played in the county colours at some grade or other back through the 1940s and 1950s. Just in case there was ever a chance that he himself mightn't play, Ross was reared in Hilltown playing in the parish colours of Clonduff. Hilltown, a tiny little spot with its face turned to the purple Mourne Mountains, is a football hotbed.

There is a story told in the town which sums up Hilltown. An elderly villager died one Thursday evening not long after midnight. As the mourners gathered, the implications of the time of death dawned quickly. A death after midnight on Thursday would be deemed to have occurred on Friday and would consequently push back the time of the ceremonies to coincide unhelpfully with an inter-county game on Sunday. Time of death, it was therefore agreed, had been not long before midnight on Thursday. Assent came almost telepathically. The deceased would have wanted it that way.

D.J. Kane also springs from one of the great Down footballing families, a scion of one of the tribes who dominate and shape the game here. Drenched in the traditions of Down football specifically, and the GAA generally, D.J.'s professional life as a teacher in Lagan College, a fully integrated school perched on a hill above Belfast city, is devoted to dissolving the prejudices which surround the Association. There, he takes children from nationalist and Loyalist families out to the playing fields on a daily basis and teaches them Gaelic football as a mere game, not a way of life or a badge or a statement. Just a game. Not the feral, atavistic business that football in south Down can sometimes be.

'It's a strange time of year this,' says D.J. 'I don't know how hard it is for teams that never win anything. You just know that they are out there somewhere doing the same work that we are doing on freezing nights like this. Then you plan to beat them.'

There is always this feeling about the GAA, this knowledge that it has its arms wrapped around the entire country and the culture. There is a comfort in knowing that people elsewhere on the island are doing the same exercises, playing the same games, hoping for the same summer. Every village partaking in the things which define us a different race and yet bind us Irish together across class and territory.

The games cut through almost all the things which divide and separate us. Hurling, football and camogie are played throughout the thirty-two counties, and in almost every country where the Irish have gathered to live and work. News drifts on to the sports desks of Irish papers from time to time of the flowering of a hurling club in Argentina or challenge games played in Saudi Arabia, or a row at a match in the Bronx, New York. Often those taking up the games in foreign fields bypassed the games when at home. But away from home, Ireland becomes greener and the language, the music and the games clench the heart.

When it comes to this expression of Irishness, the only bar against playing is one which is an anachronistic echo of our own history. If you wear the uniform of the security forces in the six counties of Northern Ireland you cannot wear a GAA jersey. The rule is an embarrassment to some and a comfort to others. It has survived for decades as a last remnant of the fact that the playing of Gaelic games is more than just play. It is politics, too.

The games of football and hurling have existed for many centuries. Hurling's history stretches back to documented games in the thirteenth century. Football or its rough-and-tumble predecessor, caid, is first referred to in the Statutes of Galway written in 1527. When the Gaelic Athletic Association sprung to life in the latter part of the last century, however, it codified and promoted the games as a form of nationalistic self-expression.

The early GAA rode the crest of a wave of revived Irish political and cultural self-awareness, tapping into the new feeling of collective identity designed to put a spiritual if not physical gulf between Ireland and its British rulers. The Association was Catholic and nationalistic, and unashamedly so when it was born. The men of the Irish Republican Brotherhood marched with hurleys on their shoulders instead of guns. The divorce of Charles Stewart Parnell almost split the organization into two. The IRA man, Dan Breen, threw the ball in to begin the 1920 All Ireland Football final. Whatever happened in the country affected the GAA and vice versa. It has never quite managed to become merely a sporting organization.

These ties between Irish nationalism and the playing of Gaelic games have never been severed. Nor will they be. As the sharp political edge of Irish nationalism recedes and is replaced by a softer but equally intense interest in the culture and language, the games of hurling and football are increasingly cherished as part of the national character. They come as part-and-parcel of a softer less threatening nationalism. As every yard of fibre optic cable and every bounced satellite beam shrinks the world, a small place without a vigorous language of its own can be pervious to every form of global blandness. Hurling and football are elements in which we preserve the root of ourselves.

For those who regard the popularity of football and hurling as a sign that the country will never be quite sophisticated enough to take its place in polite society, there is the occasional suggestion that the games are about to die. Mirthless smiles, too. During the great years of success enjoyed by the Irish soccer team, when the country dizzied itself with excitement at the sight of an Irish team and its supporters at two successive World Cups, it became popular to assess the impact of soccer on the playing of Gaelic games.

If the entire country watched Ireland playing Italy in Giant's Stadium, New York, well surely that was a critical cut to the body of the GAA? Perhaps it was. Yet the very social dynamic, which made the pot-bellied legions of Irish soccer fans so unique a spectacle on the world stage, is the dynamic which is at work within the GAA all the time. That is, the need to use sport as an advertisement for our own home-place and for our own virtues, the need to celebrate ourselves and appreciate ourselves through song, music and sport.

The GAA was always too big and too firmly rooted in the Irish imagination to ever get itself washed away by the tides of a soccer team's fortunes. Gaelic games are more than mere sport, they are politics and culture, recreation and entertainment. They are the unifying force and the identifying force throughout our country. The games are the thread which runs through all our lives. As surely as being a small island nation has defined our character, so the playing of Gaelic games has become an expression of that character.

In Ballykinlar, the boys are arriving in dribs and drabs now, the pale glow of their car headlights visible from about half-a-mile away. At the gable end of the little clubhouse, they guess the occupants of each car. Who'll arrive with whom? There'll not be a full shout out tonight, the students on the team are busying preparing for the annual bout of warfare that is the colleges competition, the Sigerson Cup.

Two floodlights shed a grudging ghostly light on one end of the pitch. A handful of All Ireland medal-winners huddle together in the warmth of the dressing-rooms awaiting the arrival of Pete McGrath, sharpening the barbs with which they will punish their manager for his uncharacteristic lack of punctuality.

Everybody has a day's work under their belts, yet that part of life is off limits in the dressing-room. The talk is of football, talk broken down into little mock-angry arguments over the new rules of the game and their impact; about how fucking thick you'd have to be to ask a question like that; and, sorry boys, but the Queen didn't give me the same education as she gave you. Where's McGrath anyway?

They've known Pete McGrath a long time, many of them have grown from boys to men in his company. Pete is an old corner-forward. He tried to prosper in that position back in the 1970s when the Dublin and Kerry teams of that era had made Gaelic football a big man's game. Pete was no big man, but he scraped a few years out of wearing the county jersey.

Up in Rostrevor, in St Bronagh's club, they'll talk all night about Pete McGrath, the schoolteacher who lives down in Colman's Gardens with his mother.

Rostrevor is football heartland. Twice Pete has brought an All Ireland winning team up the hill into Rostrevor on the night after the final in Dublin, the pubs staying open all night, the men, women and children lighting bonfires, singing songs and shedding tears as they wait to offer their welcome. Back in 1991, they stopped the bus specially in the middle of the little row of houses just short of the village. Pete got out and hugged his mother. Not a dry eye in Rostrevor. Or a dry throat.

Pete McGrath teaches in St Colman's College in Newry and there, in the nursery of the county's footballing ambitions, he and Ray Morgan have processed most of the talent which has made its way on to the Senior team here tonight. They have known these players since they were boys. They are stars now – successful men, yet they haven't grown away.

When the GAA first ordered itself, almost by accident, it stumbled on the key to its own success. Every player represents his own place: his school, club, county. The county, a concept born as an English administrative convenience, became the defining mark of place in the Irish mind. So, it goes still. School. Club. County. Your own place.

The schools' system lies at the heart of the machinery of the GAA. As the nation struggled to assert its own identity and values in the years after independence, the running of the schools was handed over to the religious orders. The sport of choice in most Catholic schools was GAA.

St Colman's, north of the border and technically part of the United Kingdom, is no exception. The school imparts the sports and culture from which a swathe of this community derives its political ambitions and aspirations. St Colman's is at the heart of football here in Down. Pete McGrath is at the heart of Colman's. A man of substance and reliability. 'Where's McGrath? He's never late. Well, fuck him anyway. Fuck boys, but it's cold.'

Everywhere has history to it in the GAA. Ballykinlar has plenty of it. The adjacent camp, where the British army is still installed, served as an internment camp back in the 1920s and men from the four corners of Ireland were rounded up and brought here for detention without trial. They played their own games and sorted their own teams on a county-by-county basis. The Ulster council of the GAA even sent medals in to the boys inside. Tadhg Barry, a GAA writer with the Cork Free Press, was shot dead trying to escape from here in 1920.

The camp somehow got absorbed into the life of the place around it and became so renowned as a source of IRA weapons (stolen or blackmarket) that it was known colloquially as 'the stores'. Just last year, in an effort to build some bridges with the local population and to score a few easy public relations points into the bargain, the British Army battalion billeted here offered to play a Gaelic football game against a local side. The offer was refused, but the British Army took its PR points anyway. By trespassing in the very heart of nationalist culture the point had been made yet again that football and hurling aren't just games. They are a part of life and a part of history.

History. When Down football had at last tasted some good times, Paddy

Doherty, the great Paddy Doherty, sprang from the little cottages between the army camp and the Down training pitch. As captain, Paddy brought the Sam Maguire Cup back here to Ballykinlar in 1961, the middle of his three All Ireland wins. That's one of the first things people tell you about when Ballykinlar comes up in conversation – Paddy Doherty and the loamy soil.

Ballykinlar, Paddy Doherty and the loamy soil. That coalition seems to say something about the impact of the games on our consciousness. In every town and suburb there is a celebrated player of past or present, somebody who has brought pride to the area, somebody whose name and club are as integral to the character of a place as loamy soil, stony mountains or raging sea. When you have been reared in the GAA place-names are never meaningless. Even the stingiest hamlet will be the home of some hero who has given the people there cause for communal celebration. Whole places are defined by the games and the way they are played there.

Ballykinlar is out on the eastern edge of the football territory that is South Down. Across on the southern tip of the windswept Ards peninsula they play hurling with a passion and determination that is frightening. They wear the same black-and-red jerseys as these Down footballers, but they are another tribe entirely.

The geography of county Down is such that, given a person's address, you could guess what sport they are devoted to. Across the south of the county, from Newry to Warrenpoint, Rostrevor, Hilltown, Mayobridge and Castle-wellan, right out to Downpatrick and Newcastle, all this is football land. The proximity to the Republic, and the density of the nationalist population in south Down, has always given teams from the county the generously confident swagger of city sides.

There are little patches of hostility, of course, even in the south of the county, where the glamour and self-confident success of the Down footballers have been an irritant. When the minor All Ireland team of 1987 passed through Clough on the way to Downpatrick on the night after their win, their bus was stoned by Loyalists. When the Senior team passed through with the Sam Maguire four years later, all lights were dimmed in the team bus and in the town. No point in doing anything else. In Newry earlier on that evening, as the crowds gathered to welcome the first Sam Maguire win for the six counties since the troubles had started, somebody planted a bomb not more than a couple of hundred yards away. As the crowds celebrated deliriously, the car carrying the bomb was destroyed in a controlled explosion.

Elsewhere around the county there have been difficulties. The hurling community out on the Ards peninsula have their troubles with clubhouses burning down regularly. Some of the football folk have faced the same problem. Both Gary Mason's club in Loughinisland and Bryan Burn's club out in Bryansford have been burned out. Further up the county, where a little oasis of football exists just outside the Antrim border at Belfast city, Greg Blaney, Neill Collins and John Kelly line out with Carryduff – three All Ireland medal winners playing for a club without a pitch. Once in the early 1970s, they got themselves a place, but the posts got ripped down and the field got sown with broken glass so they abandoned the idea and kept their heads down ever after.

The expression of a distinctive Irish culture, through the playing of Gaelic games, has always been a little too much for others to take. Cultural supremacy is as threatening as political supremacy. It is so much harder to articulate the cogent arguments against playing football games on green fields, though.

Tonight the boys are all here in Ballykinlar, under the flares from the British Army post, huddled in the wind waiting for Pete McGrath to arrive. The most glamorous team in the country, the All Ireland football champions twice already this decade, standing in the rain – their bodies petrifying in the face of all that cold – wondering about an afternoon in May when they will play Donegal; wondering if the boys in Donegal are doing the same thing, concentrating on the same afternoon, peeking at the fixtures beyond that.

They know that September is big time. September is luxury coaches, big hotel rooms, television cameras, popping flashbulbs and the swarm of the press. September is fine hard pitches, huge throaty crowds and a throbbing excitement in your head. September days are glory days when everybody knows your name.

The All Ireland finals in football and hurling are events which define autumn in our culture, great gatherings of the clans, afternoons when a farmer in Mayo will sit down to watch the same game as a labourer in the Bronx or a displaced schoolteacher in Sydney. Once upon a time, winning an All Ireland medal in September virtually guaranteed you a seat if you ran for Parliament the next time there was an election. That era has passed maybe, but the social phenomenon of the All Ireland series continues to grow.

An All Ireland win is a wave which breaks over the lives of people in the county involved. The trophy passes for months in a triumphant procession through the schools and clubs of that county. Nothing else brings a community to blossom in quite the same manner. To chart the travels of the hurling and football trophies, from September to December, through the highways and byways of the winning counties, through the halls of the emigrant communities, through the crowded schoolyards, is to chart the celebration of a tribe. Dreaming of September is what brings the most accomplished stars of the game out on to the same fields as the most humble hoofers in the depths of winter.

By February, all that separates an All Ireland team from the also-rans is the entry in the history books and a residual of tribal confidence which beating the rest of the country leaves behind. By February, the All Ireland champions are just another group of men desperately searching for the next breath on a cold dark night, measuring their progress against summer expectations.

Just another group of men. At one level they are merely that, but on another they are a cultural constant; the memory of them at their peak in their finest hour, that memory dims slowly. While they search for the near perfect version of themselves, which they managed to turn out last season, they are discussed in public houses, workplaces and living-rooms up and down the country because, in late winter and early spring, Gaelic town springs to life again like a slave of nature and conversation is the breeze that circulates through its streets.

By the time they say their goodbyes and head off towards their homes or nightshifts, white freezing rain has begun to fall. Headlights cut the night and cars roll out across the countryside. February. Home and September seem a long way away. They have come out here tonight for nothing but the hope of glory and self-fulfilment. The last of the amateurs, the last great sports people to do it all purely for the love of it. The metal shutters are pulled down over the dressing-room doors. Fumbling of keys. 'Ack boys but it's cold,' somebody says again.

In thirty-two counties, they are locking up dressing-rooms, storing hurleys, counting footballs and saying the same things.

CHAPTER ONE

Football people

Major and Paddy are setting out the flags, rigging the nets, getting things ready. Stout fingers bent to familiar tasks. It's the thick of the murky city winter, the sky is inky, but the ground is holding firm. 'Thank God for that anyway,' says Paddy.

No complaints. So long as the match goes ahead, no complaints. The pitch is bounded by a crumbling graffiti-splashed grey wall. Near the sixty-one metre (twenty-one yard) line somebody has had a Halloween bonfire and the grass hasn't even started to recover. The ball hops freakishly when it lands in the scarred circle where the fire has burned the green away.

Major and Paddy are waiting on the lads. The bus is doing the rounds at the moment and all the boys are being bundled in. Up first to the site at the Grand Canal Harbour, across to Finglas, and Coolock, and then Dunsink. They have the use of the bus till January. This is December and the passage of time is beginning to weigh on their minds.

They don't know what they'll do when they lose the bus, but they know they'll continue somehow. Pavee have been playing football for twenty-five years now and they've never missed a match, never left a fixture unfulfilled, never given anybody the satisfaction of saying that the Travellers didn't turn up. It's a matter of simple pride for Paddy, Major and the boys, their reliability confounding the glib prejudices of settled people. Bus or no bus they'll get to their games in January and beyond.

Major and Paddy have known each other since they were twelve years old. Down all the days together, thick and thin, good times and bad. Paddy is tall, fair and big boned, Major is smaller and dark with quick eyes, a sharp sense of humour and the ability to suck the life out of a cigarette in one or two drags. Major has another name, Martin Joyce, but when he was a young fella he wore a cap and was in the habit of greeting people by tipping his index finger to his forehead and making a little salute. They christened him Major and nobody ever calls him anything else now.

Names are a complex business within the travelling community. The Pavee Senior football team once had so many Joyces playing for it that Bill Shelley, the manager, wanted to put them in the Guinness Book of Records. Between the Collinses, the Joyces and the McDonaghs there is plenty of room for confusion so they have their own names for each other. Coppers. Blue Eyes. Bimby. Doodle. Booey. Even straightforward names have trapdoors. Over there with the beard, that's John Rhattigan. His real name is John Collins, but he's known as John Rhattigan. Makes it easier.

There is a dirty smog hanging over Phibsboro this afternoon as Paddy and Major make the pitch ready. The sun, already waning, has to make an effort to peak through the off-white clouds. Up past the shopping centre the flood-lights in Dalymount Park dip their grey heads like wading cranes, their tapered bodies disappearing into a pool of grimy urban decay down below. The canal drifts by silently. Thirty years now, traveller teams have been playing on this field, lots of wins, lots of losses, a few fights and the odd tear. Paddy and Major hear the growl of the bus engine and perk up. They're here.

This is the first year of activity for the Pavee Under-Thirteen team. All summer long Paddy McDonnell and Major have been out on this little pitch teaching them the fundamentals of Gaelic football, introducing them to the arts of catching and kicking and solo running. Gaelic football isn't something that is indigenous to traveller culture. Ireland's largest ethnic minority gets the sharp end of the more brutal prejudices which sweep the land of saints and scholars. Travellers have learned to keep themselves and their culture invisible. Playing football is a means of shaking hands with settled culture; that and the best craic a bunch of fellas can have without a roof over their heads.

The first year of activity for the Under-Thirteens and another landmark in the travellers' football history. The travellers' team first started playing football back in the late 1960s with the help of a settled person, Bill Shelley, some schoolboys from St Paul's school in Raheny, and a Christian Brother by the name of O'Neill.

The team played challenge games around Dublin for some years until the novelty wore thin and Major, who was seventeen at the time, proposed entering a competitive team in the Dublin leagues. The team was called Avila Gaels originally, taking its name from Avila Park, the little cluster of houses and chalets in which a core group of the team have been settled for some time. Avila Park is mainly populated by Collinses, McDonaghs and McDonalds, and those names along with the Joyces form the core of the senior team today.

Today is the second last game before Christmas for the Under-Thirteens, maybe the last if things keeping going the way they are with the rain and the waterlogged pitches. The weather has turned bad, the evenings have grown shorter, and Paddy and Major haven't been able to get them for training as often as they would have liked. Maybe the break will do the boys good. If they beat Whitehall today they'll be top of their league table when it is published in the paper on Wednesday. Not many people will notice, but it will be there. Pavee tops! There is a dizzy buzz of anticipation from the youngsters as they jig about trying to get warm, looking for some focus.

'Major, Major,' roars Paddy from behind the nets, 'would ya sort them out.'
A couple of lads are swinging their legs at each other, fooling around.

'C'mere the pair of you,' says Major and the whole group moves towards him.

They mill around Major looking for words of instruction and influence with which to calm themselves down. Major knows what football can provide them with, knows what the game has given him. The boys can learn things here. A few weeks ago the lads had problems with another team, just some name-calling which started on the sideline and spread to the children on the field until, pretty soon, small fists were raised.

Major went to the referee afterwards and spoke softly.

'Don't write anything in your report until you have had your lunch and thought about it all,' said Major.

Such sweet reason worked its magic. One child muttering the word 'knacker' to another child will always escape unpunished on the football pitch. The wounded traveller-child who raises his fist in red-faced retaliation won't usually be so lucky. 'When there is a choice,' says Major, 'we are always second in line.'

Later that day Major and Paddy sat the young lads down in the dressing-room and explained things slowly and gently. 'We told them that there is always a small minority of people that will do this to them, but that when they put on their jersey they are representing the travelling community. When name-calling happens they have to put down the ball and walk away. We know how hard it is. When we started playing years ago we were like sticks of dynamite waiting to go off as soon as the first name was called. Now we just play our football.'

These boys will be Major's and Paddy's interest and diversion in the years to come. They are the future of traveller football. Major and Paddy don't know what they'd do without the thread of football running through their lives. They have shaped traveller football and, in its turn, football has shaped them.

For a while they tried cold turkey.

In the late 1980s, Avila Gaels disbanded for a year or so after a row over refereeing at a match. Bill Shelley was recovering from an operation, the lads were disheartened, their break-up having come after a run of nine successive wins, and the team just went their separate ways for a year or so. Major switched clubs, but missed the camaraderie of playing with fellow travellers.

'I loved the football and I missed the lads. There's not much we can do together as travelling people. I kept on at Paddy about the team.'

So, in the end, Paddy McDonald with his friend Major prompting him incessantly decided to take responsibility for the foundation of a new team. Pavee was born. Bill Shelley moved gracefully to the periphery of things and the lads learned to look after themselves. Major had a traveller team to play with again.

These days, for Paddy McDonald and Major Joyce, the GAA is a seven-day a week commitment, a non-stop journey into the settled world. Monday: Junior Board meeting. Tuesday: Training for adult teams. Wednesday: Training for Under-Thirteen teams. Thursday: Training for Division Three team. Friday: Training for Division Nine team. Saturday: Under-Thirteen match. Sunday: Senior games. Monday: Begin again.

Paddy doesn't play at all. Sometimes if the adult Division Nine team is stuck for numbers he'll put on a jersey at the behest of his brother Davy and fill a spot, but generally he likes to watch and to organize. 'If I could have played the game as well as I can understand it, I would have been grand,' he says with a laugh, 'but I couldn't, so here I am.'

Major could always play the game and could always understand it. He started going to Croke Park when he was a wee splinter of a kid back in 1963. Born in Newry, but reared in a tent on a campsite in Finglas, young Major had his head turned by the glamorous exploits of the Dublin football team of 1963.

Des Foley with his golden head of hair, his brother Lar with his relentless bustling effectiveness, Ferguson, Fox and Behan with their cut and thrust, all combined to seduce him.

From then on, Major was to be found within Croke Park every time it opened its gates. Other travellers thought he was half-daft but he stuck with the Gaelic football, started kicking a ball himself, liked it and finally screwed up his courage, struck out on his own and joined a team.

'I played with teams of settled people first. Teams like Fergal's and Gabriel's and Erin's Isle. I did that for four or five years and made a lot of friends.'

As the only traveller playing on a team of settled people, it was tough and lonely at the beginning. The volume of prejudice might have been turned down to the level of a whisper, but it was there somewhere.

'As the only traveller, I was ashamed,' says Major, 'but in the end I overcame it. Getting through the early part of it was the worst of it. I was sixteen when I started and I can still remember the shame. If I got picked on a settled team I always knew there were five or six settled players on the line who hadn't got picked. I would think about that all the time. If I made a mistake I'd know they were saying: 'Well, the knacker made the mistake. What's he doing playing?'. I'd be red in the face if I made a mistake at all. You can't play football if you're afraid of making mistakes.'

Who can say what prejudice has deprived Major of? His best football memory is of playing in Croke Park in 1974 in a league game against Erin's Isle. Major, a small player but one with brains and feet made for football, played at midfield and scored 1–11. Avila was beaten by a handful of points, but it ranks as the day-of-days for Major.

'Playing there after all those years of going up every Sunday to see whatever was on, that was a day. That was my greatest experience in playing football.'

For three years running, he was called out for trials for the Dublin Minor football team. Each year he knew he was as good as anything on view, and each year he knew nobody would have the guts to pick him. So Major never got to wear the blue Dublin jersey.

Some of these lads might be good enough for it yet, though. Paddy's son Paul, fair-headed like his father, has a handy way with the ball. Young Martin Maughan is tall for his age and sees things on the field that the other lads don't see. When things are going badly they look to Martin to pull his weight and that of a few others out on the field. James Wilson can play a little, too, and has a good eye for goals. Joe Collins has the cut of his father about him. Little Michael McDonagh needs a bit of meat on him, but he has football bred into his bones. His father, Bernard, and his uncle, Martin, both play with Major.

'Look,' says Martin Maughan, tugging at his own green, white and gold jersey with one hand and pointing at Whitehall's red-banded jersey with the other, 'it's Derry against Offaly.'

Derry against Offaly. Martin Maughan has been watching TV, has been absorbing Croke Park, the blur of colours and all the excitement it has to offer a child. Television! When Paddy and Major were growing up, watching football on television would have been unthinkable.

'I used to go to Croke Park and see these teams and I'd be on me own,' says Major, 'now the boys watch them on television and they know all the counties and all the players. By the time we get them out here, they're all mad for a bit of football. Travellers' teams have always worn Offaly or Meath colours. The lads love playing against a jersey they know. They look up to all those.'

The boys are buzzing now. Paddy and Major have given them their team talk, sorted the players from the subs. Buzzing. They scarcely notice when their opponents for the day, Whitehall Colmcilles, emerge from the dressing-room kitted out but with all their possessions zipped up in kit-bags which they solemnly deposit behind one goal.

Major stalks the sideline from the time the ball is thrown in. Often in his excitement he finds himself inside the perimeter of the pitch, trying to get lads to mark up, to stick to their positions.

'Major, Major, will ya get off the pitch before the ref puts you off,' shouts Paddy.

Major rolls his eyes and starts walking backwards towards the touchline. After three decades of football, this is almost his pitch. Who'd put him off it?

Football is his game, but he played hurling for four or five years with clubs about the place. He got his nose broken so many times he decided to give it up. After that he refereed for a while and loved it, travelling with a Dublin referee's team to all parts of the country to play other referees' teams. He enjoyed the camaraderie, but when he was refereeing the heckling voices from the sideline were always in his ear.

'The abuse wore me down. Both sides might be roaring at you, and you'd feel on your own. I gave it up in the end, but playing with the referees on their teams was some of the best football I ever had. I met some great people.'

* * *

Whitehall start well. Their boys are bigger and look better drilled. They pile up a couple points early on, their shouts of celebration bouncing off the graffiti'd walls and scalding Major's ears. Major and Paddy are beside themselves with anxiety. The Pavee lads look a little lost out on the spread of the pitch. The backs are wandering out of position and the forwards are clinging together for comfort. Sometimes when they look up field, James Wilson's Pavee jersey is the only one they can see. Major directs remedial operations at one end.

'James, James. Come out a little bit, son, and somebody'll put it down to you – Bend your back to the ball – Martin will ye get rid it of it, son, you should have done that twenty yards ago – Oh, give it to him, give it to him – Ah, bend your back to the ball – Hi, don't be hittin' him. C'mon play your game there. Don't be hittin' him – '

He has fears for these young fellas, fears that put lines on his forehead. Short-term and long-term fears. He worries about losing them to soccer. He worries about losing them to drugs. He worries about what will happen to them when they grow older.

'It's hard for a traveller to get jobs. The future's not too bright for the boys. They'll make a living the way their fathers done it. A bit of scrap here, a bit of something there, anything that'll turn a few bob. It doesn't look bright for them. Travellers always get the worst end of the stick. They'll learn that the hard way. I tell them, we're second in line for anything.

'They'll end up scraping a living, pulling scrap out of heaps, maybe sifting through garbage with the seagulls and the smell out in Dunsink. They'll end up dead too early, or depressed too easily. Lots of turnings their still folded lives might take, but no yellow brick roads.'

He dreams of a job himself, can't imagine anything better than himself and Paddy ending up as development officers for the GAA, working among the travelling community, spreading the love of the game. Nothing gives him more pleasure than going home on a weekend evening and telling his people that Pavee beat Vincent's or Kilmacud or one of the big settled teams. The pride in their faces. It's like looking into a mirror.

For twenty-five years he has been playing in the Dublin leagues. He is a corner-forward now, his energetic mid-field days long behind him. Since the spring went from his legs, he's been using his head to pay his way. Fooling unwary corner-backs. Major knows the game, see.

Major thinks that at the end of the season he will drop from the Division Three team down to the Division Nine team. The tax the fags have extracted from his lungs won't seem so heavy down there in the basement of Division Nine. Anyway he's forty-two in March, time to let a younger lad have a crack.

The Pavee boys are pulling back now as the half-time break looms. Major smokes a cigarette and loiters nearer the sideline now, content that the boys have the measure of things at last. They can't kick the ball far, but they have the hang of moving it quickly among themselves and then hoofing it into space for one of their number to chase down.

Between themselves, the youngsters often lapse into Cant, their own traveller dialect. From the time a traveller can speak, he can speak Cant. Major often listens with amusement as his own little fellows shout: 'Here's Muskers,' or 'Here's shades,' when Gardai approach.

Football is for building bridges and for mixing with settled people, but aspects of traveller culture are carried into every battle. When Major's own team play against Colaiste Mhuire up in Long Meadow, the Colaiste Mhuire boys speak Irish, the Pavee lads speak Cant, and scarcely a word of English is heard all afternoon.

At half-time the boys are losing by two points, but they've let in a silly goal and generally had the better of it for the last ten minutes. They gather around Paddy and Major, and several sets of instructions are bawled out at once. The lads swing their arms behind their backs and in front of their chests to keep warm. Some of the more distracted players gaze up at the Whitehall lads gathered in a knot around their own coach. The Whitehall boys gaze back, staring across the field. For the Whitehall boys this is the first time they have encountered travellers in the flesh.

Major is charitable about his early days and the raw bigotry, and the hard words, and the call from the Dublin minors that never came. Little point, though, in dwelling on this. 'Football always got my head clear,' he says. 'I always put away the bad thoughts and tried to play better. Most people come to accept us – if not as travellers then as footballers. Sure that's a start. No need to dwell on these things. If you love the game nobody will put you off of it.'

Life is changing so slowly for travellers. Out of the tents and into the leaky caravans has been the leap of a generation. The 25,000 men women and children who make up the traveller population still know the hard road. Travellers have the highest infant mortality rate, the lowest life expectancy, the highest unemployment and illiteracy rates, the biggest alcohol and family problems of any group in Ireland. In any given year of his life, a traveller man is twice as likely to die as a settled man.

Major and Paddy and the boys are members of the only ethnic group who are routinely banned from places of public entertainment in Ireland. On a Sunday sometimes when the game is over, and there are a few hours to be put down, it would be nice to share a drink with the team you have just played. Publicans don't see it that way. The lads shake hands and head for home. Home! For years the county councils have boundaried off potential halting sites with boulders. Settled residents have hunted travellers out of their areas with threats and occasional violence. Home is sometimes wherever the semblance of home can be erected and maintained for a while.

The future doesn't hold a lot for the Pavee Under-Thirteens. Paddy and Major use football to keep the young lads in school. Leave school and you can't play, they tell the boys. They are in the process of starting a girls' team.

They tell the girls the same thing. Stay in school. Be proud of yourself.

Martin Maughan has the ball and suddenly looks bigger than anybody else on the field. He carries it and carries it, past the tackles and beyond the despairing shouts from Major. Suddenly uncoiling himself, Maughan releases the ball in a high and elegant arc. Waiting underneath at the far end is James Wilson. With a little of the insouciance he has picked up from television he turns and deposits the ball into the Whitehall net. In the late winter air a great cheer goes up.

Paddy and Major begin throwing in their substitutes. The skinnier faster lads have been held back. The team has only fifteen jerseys, so each replacement runs in bare-chested and stands fiddling in the cold while the deposed player reluctantly takes off his jersey and hands it to the replacement and then races off. He has to find the substitute's jumper or jacket along the sidelines somewhere before the cold starts nibbling him.

The second-half progress of Pavee is as unstoppable as the tide. Whitehall fails to score again. James Wilson scores another goal and Martin Maughan grabs one for himself. After each score the lads perform a little unselfconscious ritual of celebration, hands raised like soccer stars, embracing each other fiercely. They win by eleven points. Top of the league. Christmas will be good. In January, Paddy and Major will start worrying in earnest about what they'll do when the bus is taken back from them.

When the sun wanes over MacCumhail Park in Ballybofey, it still drops behind the great wall of firs and pines to the west and its orange blaze makes a brief chaos of colour out of the greens and browns in the tangled woodlands. The Finn river still rolls in wise tranquillity onwards and onwards behind the concrete terracing, down from Lough Finn, moving on in its own sweet time from past the back of Jackson's Hotel, under the little humped bridge which separates Stranorlar from Ballybofey, and onwards heedless of borders until it eases itself into the Foyle and heads to Lough Swilly many miles to the north. Tonight, on a warm yellow hued evening in early May, its body is a promising trouty brown and a million summer-flies jig on its placid surface.

On the heaped banking around the field, small boys chase down stray footballs and return them faithfully to the hands of their heroes. In the car park, fashioned from dried mud and chipped stones, the vehicles are scattered higgledy-piggledy. The faces in the dressing-room are largely the same as they were when Donegal broke through in 1992.

Brian Murray drives all the way from Dublin to be here most nights, while a clutch of his comrades sweep in on the narrow roads from Killybegs and Kilcar. Others emerge from The Rosses and Gweedore. Martin Shovlin red-haired and wiry yet, still drifts in from Dunkineely. Afterwards when their sweat has been shed, they'll wander down to the U Drop Inn just off the main street and eat together before they spread out again on the roads. Same old story.

In MacCumhail Park the county football heroes are wrapped in sweatshirts and tracksuits which have come as gifts from sponsors. Some players wear the jerseys of other counties like trophies from unforgotten battles. There is a confidence about them all which was lacking in Donegal several years ago. They look taller and better groomed, more intense. Brian McEniff, the hotelier from Bundoran, has given them this new dimension. After a lifetime of striving he took a Donegal team to the pinnacle in 1992. It changed the whole complexion of a county.

'When I began playing for Donegal,' says Brian McEniff in Bundoran, 'even the cows in the field would turn their backs if Donegal came out to play. I remember a time in the sixties when we were invited to play a nine-a-side tournament across in the village of Belcoo in county Fermanagh, and we set off full of ourselves for the day out. We had five Railway Cup players on the side that day.

'Well! Were we treated poorly that day. We got dressed and undressed in the rain at the side of the pitch. At the end of the day, things got a bit uncouth and a few of the lads got a thumping. Out of the melée there was a roar from a Belcoo man: "Fuck you, McEniff. I got bad spuds at a wedding in the Holyrood last month".

'The game ended and we were all a bit sore about the sort of day we'd had, so Pauric McShea our full-back lifted the match ball and slipped it into the bag of Father Liam McDaid who was playing for us that day. There was a roaring match afterwards with Belcoo looking for their ball, but nobody had the guts to search the priest's bag. We got away with it. Turned out, though, to be a cheap old ball!'

The stories of the bad old days are legion, and are recounted in tragi-comic tones by a people who can now afford to turn them into sentiment. In a league play-off game in Croke Park once, Donegal was awarded a penalty kick which would decide the match. The ball was placed, the player stepped back and, just before he made contact with the ball, it blew off the spot and was sliced gloriously wide. Game over. God on the other side. As usual.

Once when Bundoran played Downings in a county semi-final, a Bundoran player was forced to dive into a river to retrieve the match ball after a careless kick. He played on.

They all played on – through the bad years and the years of promise – a small race playing their short hand-passing game, hopeful rather than confident that their day would come. In Donegal as much as any place in Ireland, the game is tied to the land, is an expression of the character of the people who play it.

Tonight as the sun slips away behind the woods in Ballybofey, McEniff's face has been replaced by that of his old friend and comrade P.J. McGowan, a schoolteacher, from just down the road here. With two weeks remaining before Donegal play Down in the championship, McGowan is doing a little tinkering with his side.

It is three years since the All Ireland win, but the effect of it on the broad community in Donegal is still evident. On every street from Lifford, through Castlefin and Killygordon, and into Stranorlar and over to Ballybofey, youngsters worshipfully wear the county jersey. Among the adult population, there is a bounce in the step; and for every person in the county entitled to vote there is a different opinion about how the county should proceed from here.

In MacCumhail Park, Manus Boyle, a special hero in this place, has the ball in his hands, all alone, bearing down on goal. He's shouting, supplying his own commentary for the actions he is unspooling: 'And Manus Boyle, Manus from Killybegs, all alone on the twenty-one – Manus – '.

Manus is one of the new breed of Donegal footballers from a club which, although still in its infancy, epitomizes what football here in Donegal is all about. Manus is confident, and quick, and a winner. A boy who goes well when he has the roar of a crowd at his back and something worthwhile to play for. Manus is a Killybegs' man.

Killybegs, replete with its mackerel millionaires and its new footballing superstars, represents something central in Donegal life. It's a busy jumbled little town, stuck fast to the sea with the Donegal hills rising up all around it. Without the fleet, which pushes off from the battered pier, this corner of the country would have been left to the wilds long ago. From Rossan Point to Inver, from Kilcar to Ardara, this chunky peninsula of north-west Ireland draws its breath from Killybegs and the sea.

In Killybegs, fish and football are the mainstays of life – in that order. Killybegs has been here for a long time, but in the last couple of decades a large part of the town's view of itself has sprung from football. In Donegal, people resent Killybegs with its supply of jobs and fine footballers. They resent Killybegs, but concede that Killybegs is necessary. They understand, too, that for all the wealth the big ship- skippers in the town might possess, the boys who play football know the bite of hard times and the dread of winter.

'Sometimes when you are away you can feel a little lost,' says Conor White, tying the football into some context with the fishing as everyone must do here. 'If you have an old ball with you on the boat you can get a game going when you put ashore and you don't feel so far away from home.'

Thus it is that the west coast of Norway reverberates with the sounds of Donegal men playing football during the winter months. When they play, and when they fish, the thoughts of Killybegs' folk are with them always. Every now and then a boat goes out of Killybegs and never comes home again. The bad times which death brings, and the good times which football brings, are what ties the town together. That, and the necessity of fishing.

Four of the crew of the *Sheanne*, for instance, have other lives as members of the Killybegs' Senior football team. All of the fleet has some connection or other to football in the town. The skippers give money to the training fund, the boats give up players and supporters. Everything is funnelled back towards the pursuit of excellence.

During the winter, the fishermen chase the mackerel southwards from

Norway to Castletown Bere, sailing against the gulf stream from frosty winter to gentle springtime. When they tie up somewhere, a soccer pitch will be found, teams will be mustered, football will be played and distances will be diminished. With the wind biting and the sea singing they could be at home on their beloved field in Fintra.

The football and the fishing don't always mix so easily, however. When the Donegal league is played out during the winter, the club plays on sometimes without one-quarter of its squad who are off at sea. Conor White can remember a league final Killybegs played which he never saw.

'We were in a tiny town in Norway and we rang Radio Na Gaeltachta, who were covering the game half-a-dozen times for reports. We won that day and we had a good old time of it in Norway that night.'

Conor's brother Jimmy is responsible for this extraordinary devotion to football. Jimmy started the first Under-Twelve side that Killybegs ever had. Jimmy was just seventeen at the time, but his charisma fed the cult. His brother Conor was his first recruit, then the two Cunningham cousins, Barry and John, enlisted, as did Barry McGowan. Manus Boyle was a little over the age limit, but Denis Carbery played; so did Tony Hegarty and David Meehan and Flipper Gallagher. Flipper? Size thirteen feet, see.

Ten of that Under-Twelve team went on to win Senior medals playing football for Killybegs. From Under-Twelve right through to Senior level the team never lost a single game in the championship at its own grade. It lost an Under-Fourteen final once, but then they were all playing Under-Thirteen at the time, so mentally they don't really factor that afternoon.

The sense of adventure had a binding effect on the whole town. Killybegs is a small town in a large sprawling county. Thirty of the town's youngsters would be stuffed into a couple of vans every Saturday and driven off to various pitches around the wilds of Donegal. Most weekends they came home with a win under their belts. Putting it up to Ardara, and Naomh Columba, and Aodh Ruadhs, and St Eunans, and Kilcar. Putting it up to the best of them and winning. In Killybegs when that happens, the whole town takes notice.

For a place populated by about 1,500 people the response was remarkable. As the team matured, it won two Ulster Minor titles in a row and, in 1988, graduated to win the club's first-ever Senior football title, beating local rivals Kilcar in one of those games which instantly enters the storehouses of local legend. Jimmy White had the satisfaction of winning his first Senior football medal in the company of a team which he had almost reared himself.

The success has been unremitting. The team that Jimmy started has won another three county titles and lost two finals. Four of the boys have gone on to take All Ireland Senior medals playing in the Donegal colours. More Killybegs' men have All Ireland Senior medals in Donegal than any other club or parish.

The fishing has defined and moulded Killybegs, but the football has given the town cause for celebration and joy. Still, through the seasons and the heady summers, the sea is the master and it defines the limits of Killybegs' footballing progress through the winter.

When Killybegs wins a county title and proceeds to battle through the Ulster club championship, it does so with fingers crossed that some bad weather will keep the boats in port for a round or two. The skippers of the big mackerel boats apply for licences to fish from October onwards. The county championship is usually wrapped up by then, but any time beyond that is difficult to plan for. In the early 1990s, for instance, when Killybegs was involved in a provincial final against Castleblaney of Monaghan, four of the crew of the *Sheanne* were flown home from Norway at the ship's expense to play.

'It's the time of the year when the lads make a fair pound,' says Jimmy White, 'and so there is nothing really we can do. We are a small club and we can't afford to take players off the boats every time we have a match. It's only for very big games that we can afford to have them home.'

Nobody even considers the possibility of developing a team without fishermen on it, a team which wouldn't be disrupted during the winter months when bigger prizes beckoned. The Killybegs' team is as much a part of Killybegs as is fishing. They take what comes their way as a community.

Sometimes it can break your heart. The war in the former Yugoslavia has taken away a great mackerel market. An eastern European country, tearing itself apart, hits the football in little Killybegs. Things have dried up a bit lately on the football front as well. Jimmy isn't sure why exactly, but the players aren't coming through, not like the ones he reared.

'Nine years ago in 1986 we had an Under-Twelve team that won the county championship. Seven years ago they won an Under-Fourteen championship. Two years later the Under-Sixteen championship. This year we could barely field an Under-Twenty-One team for the club. Only three of those boys are left playing. They leave school early, get fishing on the bog boats, or get jobs in the processing places, and they are gone. They phase out the football. They have to if they're to make a living.'

The club lost perhaps its greatest prospect ever not to fishing, funnily enough, but to soccer and Glasgow Celtic FC. Declan Boyle is twenty-one and a reserve centre-back at Parkhead. If a Donegal team is to lose somebody to soccer, they would wish it to be Celtic. Two of the Celtic Senior squad have played Senior football for Donegal, but the connections are deeper again. Glasgow has always been a destination for Donegal emigrants, from Patrick Magill's Children of the Dead End to the post-graduate techno kids of the 1990s. They lost Declan Boyle, but only in the strict physical sense. Maybe not even that much.

This summer he will come home to watch the county final, watch his brother play for and his father manage the team. He will travel with the boys and 'just to get him in' have his name added to the subs' list so he can sit in his gear on the sidelines and catch the atmosphere. Suddenly caught up in the drama of the breathtaking last five minutes, he will urge his father to bring

(*above*) Croke Park people (*below*) Comrades: Dublin footballers

Dublin fans on the hill

(*right*) Dublin v Meath, Leinster football final 1995

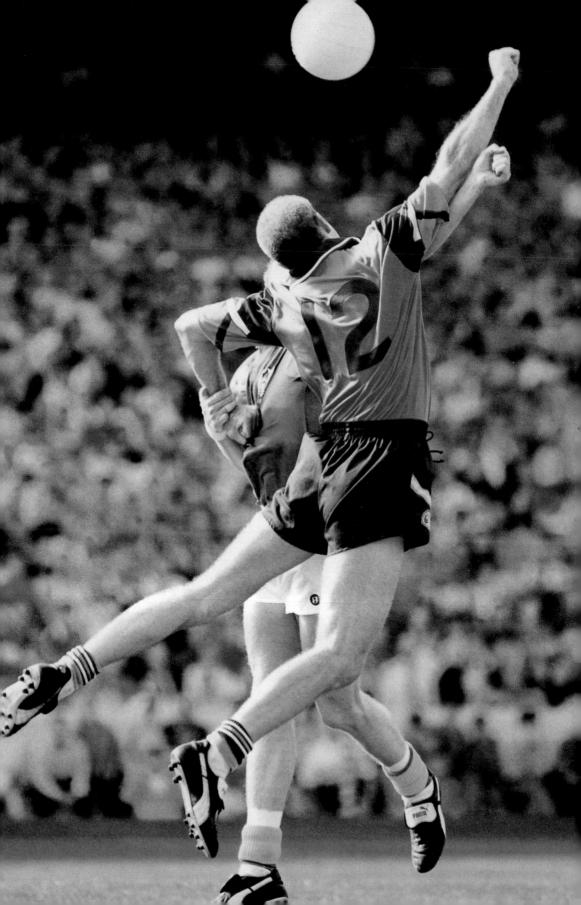

Kerry v Cork, Munster football final 1995, San Francisco's Danny Culloty soars on home fields

Band at Derry v Tyrone, Ulster Championship 1995

(*above & next page*) Munster final 1995, Niall Cahalane and Billy Morgan

All Ireland club semi-final 1995, town and country, Kilmacud Crokes v Castlehaven

(*above*) Kilmacud Crokes v Castlehaven (*below*) All Ireland club-final March 1995, Bellaghy v Kilmacud Crokes

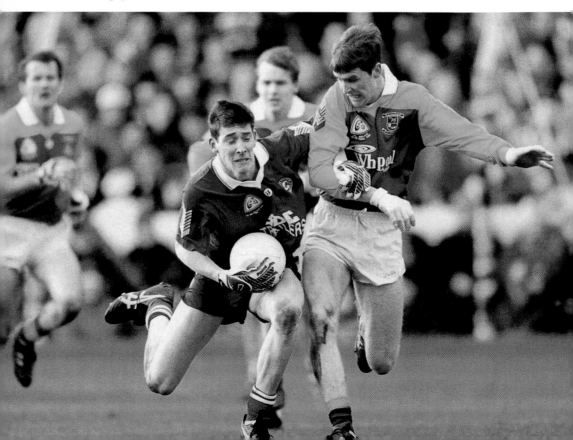

All Ireland club-final March 1995, Bellaghy v Kilmacud Crokes

(*above & left*)
All Ireland club-final
March 1995, Bellaghy
v Kilmacud Crokes

(*right*) Town and
country, Kilmacud
Crokes

All Ireland football final 1995, Tyrone fans

(*above*) North: Ulster final day

(*left*) Munster football final 1995, fans at Kerry v Cork

Last words to the boys

him on to the field. And? Inevitably, he scores the winning point against Naomh Columbas. A professional soccer player with Glasgow Celtic scoring the decisive point with his only kick of the ball in the entire Donegal Senior football championship?

'Ach, sure that's Declan and the sort of fella he is,' says Jimmy White. 'Killybegs is in his heart. He knows if he doesn't make it at the soccer he'll be back here playing for us.'

Some things roll on forever. Where a younger version of Jimmy White, unmarried and energetic, once rounded up the boys of the town and whipped them into footballers who would backbone an All Ireland winning team, so Joe McBrearty, seventeen years old himself, does the same job today.

'We have a young Senior team,' says Jimmy, 'and with the work Joe does with the wee boys around town, we'll have players coming through again, good players in the next few years. Killybegs will always be a football town now.'

Killybegs is a phenomenon within a county which remains a law unto itself, a little independent state where time pours itself out more slowly than it does elsewhere. Its geographical isolation provides the county with a mood of friendly mischief and constant introspection. A county with one set of traffic lights at the bottom of the hill in Letterkenny and no real need for them. Bounded by the Atlantic ocean on one side, by the border with the north on another, and allowing access to the south only through a little strip of shared border with Leitrim, Donegal is self-contained, self-sustaining and self-absorbed.

They celebrated the All Ireland win of 1992 as fervently as any tribe delivered by its leader unto the promised land, and when they had had enough the bickering began and lasted for two years afterwards. For many Donegal people, McEniff's face had never quite fitted, but it had suited them that his passion brought him out to look after the county team in years when nobody wanted the job. Suddenly, though, Donegal were All Ireland champions and the county had as many opinions as it had people.

The arguments bubbled and boiled. The team had no place to train. The team was bitter about certain players getting money to bring the All Ireland trophy to commercial functions. Finn Harps, the soccer club in Ballybofey, was miffed about a perceived slight which slipped in jest from McEniff's mouth (that McEniff was a keen soccer man himself was forgotten) one night in training. County board fund-rasing efforts were questioned.

Various players were whispering that the credit for the win was theirs, that they had masterminded tactics and seized the moment to give inspirational team talks. A National lottery grant caused a bit of a stir. On it went, just like the old days. McEniff packed it all in two years later and his good friend P.J. McGowan accepted the chalice in the interests of continuity. Now P.J. is just days away from his first championship game. Playing Down, the All Ireland champions, in Clones. Mountains don't come much steeper.

Towards the end of this training session, a strange thing happens. A large, giggling man, who has had a gallon or so too much to drink, shambles out towards the middle of the pitch. He makes for an amusing sight and yet his presence lends some tension to the evening. On the sidelines, those who have gathered to watch the team train watch in fascination to see if the training session will lurch towards anarchy, if minds looking for a distraction will seize their moment. The players are unconcerned, though, playing around the drunk as if he were invisible. Finally P.J. McGowan bears down on the interloper and sends him packing. Through the haze of drink, the steely voice of authority cuts, an authority which football has granted weight to. The heads along the sideline nod approvingly. The football continues and Manus Boyle breaks free, all alone bearing down on goal.

The session ends with the shrill of a whistle which sharply interrupts Manus Boyle's stream-of-consciousness commentary. The goalkeeper is spared the final humiliation, the picador's last jab. Manus Boyle kicks the ball skywards, a huge celebratory kick aimed at nowhere except the heavens, marking nothing but the fact that another evening on the training pitch is dead and the championship and Down are a day nearer. One afternoon in May. One chance.

Cooraclare. Cuar an Chláir. The curve of the plain. At the cross in the road, there is a sign. Community Alert it says. Somebody has taken a shotgun to the sign and blasted a hole right through the centre. The mangled metal gleams in the summer sun. The rest of the sign is pockmarked with shot. It serves as a local landmark. 'Take a left when you get to the Community Alert sign that somebody took a shotgun to. That'll get you to Tom Morrissey's place.'

The little tar roads of west Clare have turned treacly with the heat. The sun is burning up the grass, turning whole fields yellow. Tom Morrissey, bare to the waist and tight-packed with wiry muscle, is working with his brother, Noel, in the deep cool shade of the haggard. The house, the haggard and the little football field are at the centre of 130 rolling acres. Morrissey land.

Ah, the little football field! Holy Thursday, seventeen years ago now, can you believe, they built it. A burning hot day like this one. Tom Morrissey senior went to the mart to sell some cattle. His son, Tom Morrissey junior, was seven at the time, somewhere in the middle of the tribe of thirteen children. Young Tom likes to remember those balmy days. This yarn is well thumbed, part of family folklore. Over the kitchen table, above the mounds of ham and hospitality, it gets another airing.

'There was Holy War that day. AW! Holy War.' He throws his head back, his laughter bouncing off the walls and filling the house. 'There's a wood down below. John, Martin, Michael, Joe and meself, anyone of us that could walk, really *really* was involved that day. John decided to cut down four lovely straight trees. We went and dug the holes in the field. A day's work in it there was.

'The father came home and noticed the new goalposts on the way in. A roar out of him. "Where's my grand trees?" Four trees he'd grown from saplings. Gone. Nothing he could do. They were gone, sure.

'There was a priest staying at home at the time. An uncle. He helped us put the posts up so we were saved the worst of it. The mother was all for it anyway. After that, any chance we got we'd be over the field kicking ball. Nothing being done on the farm. The father would see the ball being kicked in the air and he'd come roaring, and we'd hide in the ditch till he'd go again.'

Picture postcards from childhood. All of them sepia, all of them shot on this little pitch, with the posts made from trees, which takes up the field hard by the little house here in Cooraclare.

'We'd great games. All the neighbours' children would come in, twenty or twenty-five garsuns playing football. It seemed like such a massive field, back then when we were all six or seven years old. Now I go out there and kick the ball from one end of the field to the other, but it stood to us. Last year there were seven of us, four Morrisseys and three Downeses playing football for Cooraclare. All played football in that little field.'

Last year the Cooraclare Seniors had four of the Morrisseys wearing the light blue jersey when they lost to Kilrush in the first round. The game took its toll on the family. Pat Morrissey 'a glorious full-forward with great hands' took a nine-month suspension out of the game. Pat had just made the Clare Senior panel and the suspension broke his heart. Tom's, too. Pat is working away in Chicago now, still playing a bit of football, biding his time. Martin took a suspension out of that Kilrush game. It was lighter than Pat's, but as hard to bear because it was meant for Tom. The referee got mixed up with all the excitement.

So, Tom perseveres and his is, the name which springs to mind when one thinks of Cooraclare and its 400 houses shaken over this lovely parcel of land. These times, Tom will tell you, football is his life. These times Tom? Hard to remember a time when it wasn't. 'There's more to life than football,' he says with a smirk, 'there's work, too.'

Great games across in the little field by the house. It stood to them all. Marie, the eldest girl, arrived after the births of six boys. 'Poor cratur,' says Tom, 'six big brothers. We weren't going to play no dolls' houses!'

So Marie played football. If she got hit there wasn't much point in marching away crying. So she learned to hit back and she got good at it. Now there are six All Ireland medals in the Morrissey household, all of them for football and all of them won by the sisters. Marie has two Under-Sixteen, two Junior and a Minor medal. Eithne is captain of the Clare Minors this year, having captained the team to an All Ireland last year.

'In this house,' says Tom Senior, 'we're all football mad. Football mad. We're waiting on Tom to start catching up with his sisters in the medals. We've spent enough on petrol bringing him around to matches, to be due that at least.'

'Ha,' says Tom, 'there's the problem with Clare football. Four brothers, three of them priests, and one as blind as a bat.'

Tom senior has poor sight and wears glasses with lenses as thick as the bottoms of Coke bottles. The sight makes him something of an aberration in a family tree which has blossomed with football talent. Sean Morrissey, the grandfather of the Morrissey's, was a sturdy corner-back who won three county championships many, many years ago. Sean was in and around the famous Clare team of 1917, the last great Clare side before Tom's team emerged in 1992.

Sean had four sons – John, Martin, Michael and Tom – and nine daughters. The first three sons were fine footballers, but poor eyesight held Tom back. John and Martin famously played mid-field together for Cooraclare in the 1956 county final. They were seventeen and eighteen years old at the time. John scored a goal from forty metres (forty-five yards). Cooraclare won, and the legend was set. The boys won medals again in 1964 and 1965. The Morrisseys were at the heart of it all.

The bloodline almost stopped there, however. John, Martin and Michael were all claimed for the priesthood. It fell to Tom to look after the land and produce the next generation of footballers. He served the land and football well, producing nine sons and four daughters. The Morrissey dynasty looks safe and sound.

As for Cooraclare, the emigration stills nibbles away at the parish's potential. Nine years ago, back in 1986, they won the Clare championship with a fine team. Only six of the fifteen are left in Cooraclare now. The Morrisseys themselves are emblematic of both the football and the difficulties that beset it. John and Mike went to England in 1986. Joe followed a few years later. Pat is in Chicago. Dan is in the army at Baldonnel. Noel is just back from England and is away to college in the winter. Marie is in England studying accountancy. Eithne, Anne, Paul and Nora are too young to have moved anywhere. The football has brought Tom some extra work so he has been able to stay, working the farm by day and selling some insurance in the evening. Martin is still knocking around, too.

Today the family is bundling itself off to Ennis to see Nora, the youngest of the tribe, play in a football final for the Leitrim club. Same old story, wherever there is football to be watched or played the Morrisseys will tag along. The boys and a couple of the sisters were playing hide-and-seek behind the goals in Milltown Malbay back in the 1970s on the day when Kerry put nine goals in the Clare net. The lowest point ever for Clare football.

The Morrisseys were there, too, on the best day when Clare beat Kerry in the 1992 Munster final. The old West Clare railway was still running the previous time such a thing had happened. The county celebrated for a week, and Tom, the county mid-fielder, celebrated with them. He remembers waking up in a house in Quilty on the Thursday after the final, having celebrated right across west Clare, through all the football land. He headed into Ennis for training that night and had to excuse himself for twenty minutes till he got his guts and his head in sync.

A month later the procession to Dublin started. Cooraclare, Doonbeg, Corofin, Kilrush, Lissycasey, Kilkee, all the little football satellites drained themselves of their population and headed to Croke Park. Tom, second Clare man to leave the tunnel and drown in that sea of saffron and blue, remembers his legs going as he looked around him, remembers his co-ordination deserting him. To calm himself he stood still for a minute 'and took it all in, north, south, east and west'.

The whole family – missionary priests, auditing sisters and hard-working brothers – was together that day, summoned back from whatever parts of the globe. All in Croke Park to watch Tom play.

In Cooraclare they dream of having another day like it. This Sunday, they travel south to play Cork in the championship. Big Tom at mid-field again. It's all they've talked about all week.

Tom stirs himself from the seat. The house is quiet now. Nobody is left, except Tom and Anne, his sister. Another day lost to football. Tom stretches his limbs. Acres of good grass won't turn into hay by themselves. Work to be done, horses to be watered, energy to be spent.

After 1992, the excitement of it was in his blood for maybe twenty-four months. He reckons he went soft. Shy of work and fond of celebrating. Then he woke in the summer of 1994 in the last minute of a football game and the ball was dropping through his fingers and into the Clare net, and Tipperary had just beaten Clare in the Munster championship. Cured him.

'I'd give anything to get back to Croke Park on a big day with a Clare jersey on my back. You know the way of it. You have been there once and you want it again.'

He strides out. The sun is still beating down. He ties the straps of his dungarees around his waist, announces that Cooraclare needs a win on Sunday, that Clare football needs it. He sticks out his hand to say goodbye.

'So,' he says, 'that's me. Tom Morrissey. Stone mad. With the football anyway.'

We stand and gaze at the little home-made football pitch which the Morrissey boys once built on a Holy Thursday afternoon long ago, a chapter in the legend which still grows in the curve of the plain.

Here's a story. Returning to work late one Friday afternoon, Niall Cahalane, footballer and working man, became aware of a little voice whispering in his ear. *Echo*. Don't forget the *Evening Echo*. A short way from his house he pulled in. Get the *Echo* now before you forget, the little voice told him. Get the *Echo* now and you won't be in the doghouse with Ailish later.

Now then. He doesn't know whether the situation could be described as an arrangement or an understanding, but Niall Cahalane thought that he would be the last man on his estate who would ever have his car stolen. There was 'mutual respect'. Under the terms of this arrangement or understanding, Niall

Cahalane, busy estate agent and famous footballer, often left the keys in his car's ignition while performing errands. Sometimes, he thinks, he may even have left the keys in his car overnight. There was an understanding, maybe even an arrangement. Certainly there was mutual respect.

So, on this particular Friday evening when he emerged from the local newsagents with a bottle of Lucozade in one hand and the *Evening Echo* in the other, he was a little surprised but not unduly alarmed to see a man climbing into the front seat of his Saab 9000.

The Saab 9000 was the sort of weapon which a man might describe as his pride and joy. After years of working for himself and then beavering away in estate agents, the Saab 9000 represented a sort of arrival for Niall Cahalane, two time all-star award winner, busy estate agent and footballer. The first car he ever owned outright. No loans. No leases. His.

Until he heard the low familiar growl of ignition, responding to the turn of the key, he doubted that anybody would be climbing into the front seat for anything other than a respectful look at the dashboard.

Vroom! He leapt out in front of the vehicle and, for a second or two, there was a stand-off – eyeball-to-eyeball through the windscreen. Niall Cahalane remembers addressing the car-thief in his mind: 'Now then, you can get out of the car and we will shake hands and both walk away from this. I won't kill you. You can walk away. We both can'.

However, as he was thinking these reasonable thoughts, it became apparent that no hands were going to be shaken. He raised the bottle of Lucozade to fire it through the windscreen, but the thought of all that shattered glass and sticky Lucozade inside his car paralysed him. He made to fire the *Echo* instead but, but the car almost knocked him down. 'Not a nice feeling to see your car flying down the Sarsfield Road and you not behind the wheel.'

The car was recovered undamaged. The thief, poor foolish man, realizing whose car it was he had stolen 'got out and walked away while he was ahead'. The guards, who had seen Niall Cahalane's car leave the road for a brief period at a roundabout on the Togher Road, had assumed that Cahalane had chased a little way to no avail.

Later Niall Cahalane sought to reopen the lines of mutual respect which had served so well in the past. He adopts the vernacular of our learned friends.

'Finding out that this individual frequented a certain licensed premises which I had never before been in, I proceeded to that premises. I walked in cool enough, but still in a fairly bad mood. I had got a fix on who this individual might be, and it was who I had thought it was. Well, I don't know if the individual was there or not, but he wasn't pointed out to me. So, I left my calling card, said I was looking for him and went on my way. A few funny things have happened in this same licensed premises since to give it, well, local and national prominence. Some might say I was lucky to come out of it alive but, sure, there you are.'

The public house involved has indeed become famous for reasons too unsavoury to detail. What illuminates the story of Niall Cahalane and his car, however, is the phenomenon of the star Gaelic footballer sharing the same world as the rest of us, recognized by all participants in the story, respected by them all, living among them, scarcely conscious of his celebrity.

No problems with the car since. Niall Cahalane hasn't seen hide-nor-hair since of the individual who nearly ran him down with his own Saab 9000. 'I believe,' says Niall, 'that it's not something he boasts about.' Mutual respect has been restored.

Niall Cahalane doesn't think that he is 'any tougher than any other player' he has played against. He 'has given' and he 'has taken', and when the whistle has blown, he has walked away. Not tough he says. Not tough.

In many ways he's right, although this summer he has already finished a championship match with Clare, and refused to eat, just gone straight into fasting for a cartilage operation twenty-four hours later. Not tough. Not the guy who often cycles the thirty miles or so from Castletownshend to Cork city. Not tough. Not the guy who has broken his leg twice, shattered a cheekbone, shredded the ligaments of his knees and ankles, the guy who has dislocated shoulders, broken fingers and injured his back and ribs, the guy who has done all this and kept going, for the love of the game and the love of the place.

He has played through it all. Endured the intensity of an All Ireland final with a hairline fracture in his right leg, played with the fracture and a useless torn muscle all around it. He did it because Cork needed him. He did all the damage originally because Castlehaven needed him. Having taken the fracture in a county championship game against Muskerry, he kept going till the end, until after the cause was lost and only honour was left to be chased. He chased it.

Nothing new either. In 1989, he won a county final with Castlehaven while playing with torn ligaments in his knee. Not just torn ligaments, but a finger which had been crushed the night before by an iron bar. Mr Cortisone. He knows that, later in life, there will be a price to be paid, in arthritic joints and cruel winter pains. But, in the summer of his youth, with football in his blood, what else could he do?

Not tough. Sledgehammer shoulders and cast-iron challenges don't make a footballer. Cahalane has powerful skills of accumulation and distribution which ornament his game. Cahalane is a do-what-you-have-to-do footballer. Maybe this resilience comes from Castlehaven, the wee club made up from the populations of the neighbouring villages of Union Hall and Castletownshend. There, all native pragmatism was forged into football success – do what you have to do.

Founded in 1941, Castlehaven's success waxed briefly in the 1940s and waned drastically in the 1950s to the point where the club was abandoned entirely. In 1957, Castlehaven was reconstituted and, through the subsequent decades, clawed its way to national prominence, its journey from being a lowly Division Two Junior side to being the champions of Munster made all the more remarkable by the scarcity of their resources.

'We have about 700 people in the parish,' says Cahalane. 'No choice of players. We try to keep it going by having big families and making footballers out of half of them.'

That's how it is, that's how it was, and that's how it will be. Cahalane won his first medal playing for the Castlehaven Under-Twelves. He was seven at the time. 'Not a good seven-year-old either. It was always a case of being one short and togging the next young fella out. I was the next young fella.'

The Cahalanes are the foremost football tribe of their area, their prominence being copper-fastened by sheer weight of numbers. The presence of Niall, Francis, Patsy, John and Dinny in Castlehaven squads tends to outweigh the fraternal contributions of the Clearys, the Collins and the O'Mahonys. When it comes to making the next generation of footballers, Cahalane is primed well. He has married into the Clearys. Castlehaven awaits.

The five Cahalane boys each took medals out of Castlehaven's two county championship wins so far. Dinny, the youngest, was just a fifteen-year-old substitute back in 1989. In 1994 he was the team's left corner-back.

Ah, 1994! Niall Cahalane, the man and the footballer can't be placed in context without an excursion to the fishing village of Union Hall and the little town on the steep hill that is Castletownshend. This is from where he sprung, the place that shaped him and the place to which he hopes to return someday, 'to the farm. Away from phones. Out in the fields. Just you and the elements'.

The year, 1994, was the great watershed in Castlehaven's history, beating Skibbereen's O'Donovan Rossa in the county final (in a replay) at Pairc Ui Chaoimh. Cahalane took a week away from work as an auctioneer to swim in the celebrations of the town. You have to understand that Castlehaven and Skibbereen exist cheek by jowl, and that football is all that separates the tribes, giving them their identity and markings.

They hit the two villages on Sunday night, Union Hall and Castletownshend. They took most of the population to Blarney for the man-of-the-match award on Tuesday and then ended up in Larry Tompkin's old pub on the Lower Glanmire Road. By the time they got back home they found their own pubs still packed and had to drink on the streets.

Tuesday, they took the cup to Skibbereen, back to the old school and then passed the evening in Paddy and Angela Hurley's pub. Wednesday was put down in Castletownshend in Christy Collin's pub, Thursday Cahalane took a break, Friday was a night in the club house and Saturday – well, Saturday he forgets.

'Nothing ever has or ever could compare with beating Skibbereen last year. That's not to have a go at Skibbereen. It's just the way the local rivalry is between us. We all went to the same school, St Fachtna's and grew up with each other, and the rivalry is intense and healthy. Beating them was just marvellous, unforgettable for our people.'

The blue-and-white hoops of Castlehaven are what makes him most animated. His face brightens as he talks about growing up between Union Hall and Castletownshend, about cycling down the astoundingly steep hill in the latter village, about family and friends and the club house in Moneyvoulihane, about kicking a football in the black field in Union Hall until darkness fell almost every day of his youth.

In this talk, he's not an estate agent or a tough customer any longer, he's passionate and animated. He's not a city man, but a country man. Country men don't often confuse the qualities of pride and pragmatism with the business of just being a tough customer.

'That's where the passion and the love comes from. You never want to lose when you are representing Castlehaven. And you always represent the place you come home to. Always.'

That's Niall Cahalane. A hero to his people.

Hero! People shower abuse on him. From the bank of the hill at winter club matches, from the stand in inter-county games. Sometimes he hears abuse when he is on crowded streets in his suit, ready to go to see some property or other. The price of being a legend.

'I get abuse about games I played fifteen years ago,' he says, 'so it's not really surprising that I get abuse about 1993. That's still fresh.'

The year, 1993, and the All Ireland final. His fifth final and the well-spring of so much regret in his sporting life. One of the most calamitous afternoons he has spent on a football pitch. People remember his contribution as being a flailing haymaker of a punch directed at Enda Gormley. And more.

The punch wasn't spotted by Tommy Howard, the referee, for the day, but was noted by a linesman. Amidst much baying from the stands, Cahalane escaped with a booking and a bit of finger-wagging.

Howling public opinion expressed from the stands, however, demanded that the next Cork player to think about crossing the line should get sent off. So Tony Davis took the long walk for a foul on Dermot Heaney. Harsh badly applied justice. People remember that incident and the tide of sympathy for Davis who was recovering at the time from a personal tragedy. Cahalane is the fall-guy for those who need a man to blame. People judge him by that incident, he says.

He has been judged now, but there was more to it and he wants to tell you.

'I don't think I have ever been so pumped up for a game. I was very psyched up, very emotional about it. I don't really know why. It seemed especially important. I had had an injury and they had got me a special caste and several injections. People thought perhaps that I would be the weak link. That pumped me up.

'We got motoring anyway and suddenly I was being hit from all sides. I got a lot of punishment. My shoulder ligaments got torn away in a challenge. Then I lost two teeth. I was getting taken out on the ball and off the ball. Well, if you keep beating the dog he'll bite back. That's what happened. I swung. I didn't connect properly – my ligaments were gone. At half-time I got four or five injections and played on. I should have come off. My strength was gone. It was a terrible day. The only time in my life that I have wanted to walk away from football.'

In Cork, feelings were mixed. He felt some pressure to stand down from inter-county football, but people he respected told him to hang in there, that good days would come around again. Cork needed him anyway, needed dogs that would bite back if they were beaten. Every team needs that pedigree.

Here he is thirty-two years old and in the throes of another championship summer. Where football is talked about in summertime, Cahalane is talked about. Is he gone? Does he still have it? His stature can be measured by the hours of speculation that his name provokes.

In Castletownshend and Union Hall, and around the hills of West Cork, they know the answers, they know their man still has the pride and the pragmatism, that he can still do what he has to do. They know that toughness is a veneer, but pride runs right through. They'll refuse to believe he's lost an inch, or pace, or an ounce of courage, until he tells them he has.

If Cahalane is gone, Cork and Castlehaven are probably gone, too. That's the mark of the man. The reason why his own people celebrate him so.

CHAPTER TWO

Hurling folk

On Seefin Hill, near Craughwell, county Galway, stands a monument to a man who it might be said was hung because of his successes in the hurling field. He was Anthony Daly, a Kilreakle man.

Seventeen-years-old and life is harsh already. The sky is glowering with threats. The teacher is pacing the sidelines. The game is up. The boys of Callan CBS are being beaten by the boys of St Kieran's. These boys in the black-and-white are the heirs to Kilkenny's hurling kingdom. Brahmins already. Same as it ever was. Callan CBS never had a ghost of a chance.

In early September, St Kieran's comes to life once more. Schoolboys fall silent as schoolteachers sweep into high-ceilinged rooms. The reverberating bell divides the day into classes, breaks and recesses. Sticks of white dusty chalk scratch out ancient theorems on virgin blackboards. More sacred truths are imparted, too. Out back, most characteristically of all, studded boots are clacking along the concrete pathways once more as hurlers make their way to the pitches. Sliotars go whickering past, timber crashes on timber. September, and St Kieran's is open for business again.

There is a broad slash of green hanging on the wall over by the two tennis courts. 'Tennis: The Swedish Way!' says the slogan. Nobody cares how pupils here play their tennis. Nobody cares whether or not they play their tennis. St Kieran's dedicates itself to hurling, the Kilkenny way. You don't come here to play tennis.

Nicky Cashin teaches here. He used to play in defence for Waterford. Every now and then he sees Kilkenny on the big stage and sees something happen in front of thousands of people, some movement which has the shimmering look of lovely spontaneity about it but which was worked out on these fields. Once, for instance, just a few years back in an All Ireland semi-final, he saw a ball sprayed out low to D.J. Carey in the left corner. D.J. killed it, turned and delivered it low towards Eamon Morrissey who arrived swinging his stick just a fraction of a second too late. The crowd gasped. They had almost seen the goal of the year.

'It would have been the goal of the year, too,' says Nicky, 'but it would have been a St Kieran's goal, two Kieran's boys playing in the style they were taught here.'

In September, a hundred boys turn out for trials for the school hurling team. St Kieran's has a population of about 700 boys, so a hundred represents practically the entire first-year intake. If you aspire to wear the stripes of Kilkenny, this is your academy.

About twenty per cent of the boys are boarders here. Again this helps in the separation of wheat from chaff. A boarder has long evenings to himself. His game improves just by virtue of being a boarder. Pat O'Neill, the current Kilkenny centre-back, boarded. Nicky reckons it made him.

'Pat O'Neill would have had little else to do in the evenings here other than practise out on the back pitch there. If he had been travelling home every evening I'm not sure he would have developed as well as he has. Boarding puts discipline into a young fella as regards practising. They've no choice in the matter.'

Kilkenny isn't a large county, there is no real need for a boy living within thirty or forty miles of the school to board there, but if he has work to do on his hurling and parents who appreciate that fact, well why not? Hurling will sometimes do as much for a boy in Kilkenny as a good school-leaving certificate will.

There are those in Kilkenny hurling who, to this day, would quibble with the school's decision to abandon the system of seven-day boarding back in the late 1970s. The Monday-to-Friday residency system has nibbled at the game here. Little erosions in the pursuit of perfection. Tut-tut. In the time of the seven-day boarders, hurling was a passport out of the place at weekends.

'They'd eat you without salt for a chance to get out of the school,' says Nicky.

An illustrious hurling graduate confirms this: 'We were boarders there in my time,' says Eddie Kehir. 'I was in the college from 1954 to 1959. It was great to get outside to play a match. Being a hurler conferred certain privileges on you. On the night of a match you would be allowed out down the town to see a picture. That was an incredible bonus for us at the time. That view of things meant that hurling predominated in the college.'

Not all the hurling gods were boarders, though. D.J. Carey arrived in the school in 1983 all the way from Gowran. A skinny wraith of a boy, already freckled with greatness, and known to all-and-sundry as Dodger. Even at twelve years old, his legend had preceded him to the school. By then, he was spending his evenings out the back of his house in Gowran, banging a sliotar relentlessly against the gable of his house, seeing how many strokes he could go without handling the seamed sphere. D.J. won two schools' All Irelands in his final years at St Kieran's, ample reward for the difficulties which hurling imposed.

'We would train Monday to Thursday. I lived about ten miles from the school and the bus would be gone when we finished. Some of the lads would cycle off home. Others would put out their thumb and hitch their way home.

For some reason, I could never do that, could never get around to the idea of hitching home. My mother would drive in and collect me every single evening and bring me off to handball games if I was playing.'

Younger Carey boys began passing through St Kieran's. Useful players, too. The school gave D.J.'s mother a job. Saved on the trips.

In the end, a good hurler here should go on to wear the black-and-amber of Kilkenny, should become an idol whom the next generation of Kieran's boys will emulate. The connections with the county team, and the marginally more ephemeral business of the Kilkenny-style of hurling, are worth documenting.

Father Tommy Maher, who recommended the school to D.J. Carey and countless other talents, arrived on the teaching staff in 1955, his brain teeming with ideas. Eddie Kehir takes up the story.

'He revolutionized hurling coaching in this country. Previously, players would go out into a field to practise – he introduced the idea of coaching. He was very scientific about the whole thing. I remember going to his room and seeing him weighing hurling balls and calculating distances for frees. He was responsible for the style of play that Kieran's and Kilkenny evolved.'

The schools' 1957 All Ireland triumph over St Flannan's of Ennis is still held up as a triumph of coaching. St Kieran's scored three goals in the final ten minutes to turn a losing game around. All three goals were the result of set-piece routines practised on the back pitch at Kieran's. That year, Father Tommy Maher took over the running of the Kilkenny Senior hurling team. The wedding of styles and influences was immediate. Kilkenny won a handful of All Ireland's before the rest of the country even cottoned on to the notion of coaching.

Years later, generations of hurlers have passed through here, boots clacking on the walkways as they step out under classroom windows and move towards the grass and the realm of play. Hurling can still do more for a boy than a leaving cert can. Watching them open their shoulders and strike a sliotar cleanly and freshly, watching their hungry eyes follow the game around them, it's hard not to envy them. Hurling greatness lies ahead of them waiting to be claimed. They can be the high kings of their own culture if they want it well enough. Who wouldn't rather excel with the ash wand than the fountain pen?

The rain is slanting down now. It's a dreary Saturday afternoon, late in the game, and the boys from Callan CBS have almost stopped trying. It is as they expected it to be, as it always will be. Hurling matters more in St Kieran's. The boys in the black-and-white play with an exuberance and will which expresses the confidence they bring to the seizing of their own heritage.

The school and its history have a grey elegance about it. Slate stone, green fields and hurling postulants. St Kieran's is, perhaps, the finest place to learn hurling, but not the only place. St Kieran's is not unusual. Every hurling county has at least one school which lays down its life for the benefit of the old game, which passes the secrets, the skills and the wonder onwards, down through the years. North Mon. St Flannan's. Birr CBS. St Peter's. St Mary's. St Finbarr's. All cradles of the game, nurturers of the art.

'My name is Noel Shanahan and I'm a hurley-maker. Sometimes I'd go to a hurling match and I'd know just how many hurleys had been broken, but if a man asked me I wouldn't know the right score to tell him. You know how it is. You'd see the broken sticks flying up in the air and fellas would nudge me and say: "Hey, Shanahan, that's good for business". It's not good at all. After all the work, after all the pride, you'd have in it you'd never like to see a hurley broken. No hurley-maker, with pride in his work, likes to see that.

'See this wood here. This has come up from Charleville. A farmer was reclaiming some land and, well, word got round and I high-tailed it down to Charleville, found the farmer and made a deal. I always pay cash up front as soon as I see the ash. If you don't pay up-front people won't ask you to buy the ash anymore. If there's any doubt that you're the sort that won't pay, you won't ever get told about the ash. The longer you're at this game the quicker people will let you know about ash.

'I like rooting out the ash the best, although it makes for the hardest work. I enjoy getting out and making a deal with the farmer, hiring a few lads to help me and then cutting into the trees down near the root, taking away about two metres (seven foot) of the tree just where the root starts. It's hard work, but it's in the open air and you have good company out there, the best of company. Talking hurling is what we do mostly.

'Aye, the hardest thing is rooting out the wood but it's the most enjoyable thing, too, getting a good piece of ash out of the ground and seeing the earth fall away from her. I like that and meeting fellas, getting the people to help me. There are lots of fellas out there rooting it out and selling it. They are a breed in themselves. There are thousands of trees around the place still. They'll do the looking for you.

'If the ash is bad, the hurleys that come from it will be bad. I dread getting stuck with a big bunch of bad ash, where the grain doesn't run right and too many frosty winters have made the wood all tight and mean. The best place to find good ash trees, I reckon, is in a county without much hurling in it.

'At £350 pounds per cubic metre, ash is the most expensive hardwood in the world these days, can you believe, ahead of brazil and mahogany. Other good woods sell at £150 or so for a cubic metre. That's standing, before anything has been done. Often, when getting rid of the waste blocks, the off-cuts from the hurleys, I'd say to the lads "That's the dearest firewood in the world boys, the dearest firewood in the world".

'Lads have started bringing ash in from Wales. That's a good idea. The hurley-maker only needs the butt of the tree, the Welsh can keep the rest. We wouldn't take much of what they would consider good wood. They haven't been cutting ash there at all. We have been cutting all the ash down for a hundred years here because of the hurling.

'People always said to me long ago that ash grown on poor ground was good ash. That's not true. Bad ash is as much use to you as a man without food. People only used to say that about ash trees because poor land was the only place they found them. The trees survived on river banks and ditches and deserted patches of bare ground.

'People have a lot of funny old ideas about ash trees. A huge big tree is of very little use, for instance. We call what comes from those big trees gross wood. The hurleys from them are no good to any man. They get a tip and fly up in the air. Broken. Once the trees have gone over thirty-five or forty-years-old, they are on the way back to the earth. You get an old brown tinge inside the log itself and the grain gets light and thin. You could get fifteen hurleys out of it and none of them would be worth a candle. I get the butts of those old trees and split them down in two and maybe make a few small hurleys for children out of them. A butt of a tree with four or five hurleys is what I like. Best thing is if the tree is exposed facing the south, getting the sun, then it will have a nice grain.

'When the word came from Charleville, we headed straight away to collect the haul of ash. We saw into the butt of the trees at a forty-five degrees angles until all the cuts meet in the middle, then go in all around with the chainsaw to get the root out. Hard men in the old days used to go at this job with a hatchet – harder men and better hurlers in those days, some would say.

'I have a friend in county Clare who cuts the wood up into planks four or five feet long for me. I used to do that myself. All night long out here at the saw, turning them over. I was younger then. I do all the travelling. I go down to Clare to collect the ash. Right now, there are the guts of ninety trees or so here in the drying shed. They'll be there for nine months or so, stacked in huge towers with the air circulating in and out of the planks.

'It's a slow process, but they have to be dried. You're dealing with a different stick after three weeks if it isn't dried properly before it's made. If the sap's in it, it'll warp. If there's too much moisture, it'll lose some weight as it dries out. You'll end up with a different stick if it hasn't been dried. No hurler wants that.'

Different strokes, different yardsticks.

An echoing call from the stands.

'How long was that cut, Eddie?'

'A 105 yards at least,' calls back Eddie smiling.

Long ago, Eddie's father was famous in the territory of a neighbouring superpower. Willie 'long puc' Murphy of Cork. Then young Eddie went and spliced the Tipperary posts with an extraordinary twenty-one metre (seventy-yard) sideline cut in a championship game in 1987 and the nickname suggested itself.

'Now we have Eddie Sideline Cut Murphy here in Kerry.'

Ah, 1987! The great glory years of Kerry football had just ended and the tight little hurling community in the north of the county raised its head in hope. The county hurling squad, a black hole of anonymity in a galaxy of footballing celebrity, emerged from the twilight zone of 'B' Grade hurling with nothing but a little momentum and some loopy optimism to fuel their ambitions. They were tossed in as meat to a slowly reawakening Tipperary team on the opening day of the championship.

No romance that day. No happy ending. Kerry was shredded. Pat Fox scored 1–10 and Tipperary stretched a long unbeaten record against Kerry into another era. Tipperary went home with twelve points to spare and, in all likelihood, never looked back on that afternoon again. In Kerry, they mulled over the lessons.

Hurling is ghettoized in some counties. The very fact of its frailty and neglect is a cause of tenderness in the sensibilities of the GAA nabobs. Speak softly here and use double-edged words. The areas where the neglect has been most acute are referred to as 'so-called weaker counties', as if their poor showing is an illusion created by dastardly media liberals.

The game's roots and its complex knotting of history and tradition have been at the cause of its own neglect. Hurling people are distinctly different to football people – quieter, bonded together like a family which has spread itself across county borders.

Clannish, too. There are those in the hurling world who would rather watch a monster truck rally than attend a Gaelic football match. Love of hurling sometimes runs to chafing resentment at the game's neglect before gaining altitude and becoming a fully-fledged snobbery which, in itself, contributes to the neglect. It's an old Irish failing to become precious about these things. You can only speak Irish if born to it. Irish dancing isn't Irish dancing unless the participants are standing ramrod straight and stiff as corpses. Sean nós isn't sean nós unless it's boring.

In the hurling world, these are the same satisfied souls who are content to watch a half-dozen or so thoroughbred hurling counties joust annually for the All Ireland title. The game is a yardstick of Celtic purity. Nothing in the future can compare to Tipperary and Cork in Semple Stadium anytime in the past, so why not just have an eternity of Tipperary and Cork games? By and large, the weaker counties (so-called, that is) have been left to fend for themselves.

In Kerry, the struggle has been long and heroic and the odd missionary has come to its aid from the developed hurling world elsewhere in Munster. Out in the north of the county, the hurling community has always gone about its business stoically, large families filling out teams in little clubs and passing the game on to the next generation.

Little towns that football had historically bypassed – Ardfert, Kilmoyley, Ballyheigue, Crotta, Lixnaw, Bennettsbridge, Abbeydorney, Causeway, Ballyduff, and so on. Out in the north of the county, a little cluster of nine parishes send out nine Senior hurling teams. In the south of the county, hurling survived in patches – Kenmare, Killarney and Kilgarvan being the noted centres of activity. They played their championships and kept their pride and passion burning quietly.

They struggled away in the same backwaters as Down and Antrim for many years. A famous tale told in the bar, in McSweeney's Hotel in Killarney, concerns Kerry hurling and Bracker Regan. Bracker is a porter in the hotel across the road and an old Kerry hurling goalkeeper. When he drops in for a late pint of porter in the evenings, his friends are wont to remind him of an instant late in the game in a promotion play-off with Antrim many moons ago. Michael O'Muircheartaigh relayed news of the Bracker's mishap to the world by means of a little commentary couplet.

And the Bracker saved but failed to clear, and Kerry must wait for another year.

Waiting for the good times. In 1986, the county imported a hurling coach from Cork, the notion being that the excellence of that aristocratic hurling breed might be contagious. Con Roche came and went, taking the secrets of championship hurling with him. He was replaced by Tom Nott. Still Kerry laboured.

Maurice Leahy, who was one of half-a-dozen or so Kerrymen who never missed a training session through all these winters of hope and summers of capitulation, took over the team himself for a little while in the early 1990s. Finally, just when Maurice grew tired of it, the county board decided that it had found its man.

John Meyler, he who is called the messiah, answered the call in the autumn of 1992. Originally from Wexford, Meyler's hurling life has brought him westwards as inexorably as the sun. After several years of hurling for his native county, he grew weary of the 130-mile drives to and from training and transferred to Cork, where he had been a resident since his student days began in 1974. If it was incessant hurling and football that his body demanded, well, he fell in with a good crowd for it. For the rest of his playing days he wore the blue jerseys of St Finbarr's.

The decades away from Wexford have taken their toll on his accent. Today he gets as much hurling and football as he could want, working through winter and spring as a development officer for the GAA in the regional technical college in Cork and spreading his wings to the summer schools throughout the sunshine months.

One night in the autumn of 1992, he travelled to Tralee to talk to the Kerry county board. One delegate, sated by the unremitting success of the county footballers and a little dubious at the prospect of another hurling saviour being shipped across the border for the benefit of the ne'er-do-wells on the hurling squad, took on a tired tone and posed a question.

'And what are you going to do on the nights when four or five players turn up for training?'

'That's my problem, isn't it,' said John Meyler briskly and, at that instant, assumed all moral responsibility for hurling evangelization in Kerry.

The nights duly came when only five or six hurlers turned up. It was Meyler's problem and he dealt with it. Most of his adult life had been devoted to spreading the gospel of hurling. So, if one night, there were more selectors than players turned out for training, well, then, the mountain was all the more challenging.

He knew they would come around eventually and when they did, they put the work in, training against the unforgiving bleep tests until they were fitter than they imagined hurlers could be. On 23 May 1993 they won their first inter-county championship match in sixty-seven years: Kerry 4–13, Waterford 3–13. They'd put in 120 sessions before that game – farmers abandoning the land early in the evening, teachers leaving homework uncorrected and spinning off, three or four to a car usually, through winter nights and on into spring and summer in the hope that humiliation might be avoided.

One championship win in sixty-seven years? They have been selling the game feverishly since it happened. Soccer has made huge in-roads in Kerry, and hurling has been the first of the Gaelic sports to go about aggressively reclaiming the old allegiances and hammering out new ones.

Maurice Leahy, a full-time hurling coach, has been spending his days in the schoolyards of Dingle and Castlegregory and hopes to work his way west from there, leaving behind a trail of Junior leagues and new coaches.

'The young fellows who were ten and eleven when we started are fourteen and fifteen now,' he says, 'more kids of that age than ever before are playing the game. Gives you some hope.'

Somewhere in Maurice Leahy's DNA is the original hurling gene. In that, he is an unusual species of Kerryman. He takes a quiet and cussed pride in it, too. 'I have been to every All Ireland hurling final for as far back as I can remember. I've never been to an All Ireland football final.'

Maurice played through the dark years when clubs and parishes let their rivalries fester to such an extent that the county team almost withered and died. He wore the Kerry green-and-gold for a couple of bad, bad beatings but always came back for more. The team even abandoned the idea of playing in the Munster Senior hurling championship after debilitating defeats in 1977 and 1978. Waterford inflicted the damage both times: 'Eighteen points they beat us by the first year,' says Maurice.

There were little landmarks of hope. A useful coaching course run by Ned Power in the late 1970s gave a jump-start to a few lads. And a famous draw, hewn out of a bad day against mighty Kilkenny in 1980, when Maurice Leahy marked the great Christy Heffernan into oblivion, still lives in the memory.

Consolation was hard to find, though. They had to strip the game down to its most basic elements to find cause to continue. Maurice's brother D.J. is the optimist of the family. The Leahy boys put down over thirty years between them, hurling for Kerry when it was neither profitable nor popular. D.J. knows just why they stuck in there. You don't choose to be a Kerry hurling man, it is the life you are assigned. Being neutral or half-hearted about it isn't the way to a full life.

'I always say to myself that playing for the Kerry hurlers gets you around the place. We yo-yo up and down between Divisions Two and Three. One year we might get Kilkenny, Tipperary or Cork to play, then the next year we'd be off to Mayo, Fermanagh and Roscommon.

'You have friends everywhere if you play hurling for Kerry. If I'd played for Tipperary I'd only know half-a-dozen counties. With Kerry, I've been everywhere that hurling is played. I've been to New York, and Chicago, and all over the place with the hurling. There hasn't been much success, but the crack has been good.'

There hasn't been much success, but the outlook is good for the hurling folk of Kerry. In the days when the county football team ruled the land, the hurlers used to get life hard. County coach, Mick O'Dwyer, wouldn't let the hurlers out on to the pitch in Fitzgerald Stadium until the footballers had finished their business. The hurlers would sit in the stand and watch the footballers train, keeping an eye on the waning daylight and wondering about the drive home. Some nights, when spirits were low, only five or six hurlers would turn up.

For the Leahy boys, however, there was never any question of quitting.

Kerry re-entered the Senior hurling championship in 1986 and took a few more hammerings, one at the hands of Limerick has left a few scars. Things started to improve, however. They won a trip to London when they beat Clare in a league play-off; they won the All Ireland 'B' championship when the corner was being turned, but got knocked about a bit by Galway in the subsequent All Ireland hurling quarter final. They persevered.

Hope is the staple of the season here. They tell the story of a summer long ago when Eddie Kehir, the hurling god from Kilkenny, holidayed in the football territory of Killarney. He played a little hurling with three local boys every evening, tipping around in the dwindling daylight. From the football heart-land of Killarney sprung Sean O'Shea, one of those three boys. He served Kerry well at corner-back. From little seeds – Persevere.

'I have had the machine for the past few years now,' Noel Shanahan says. 'It's an old Italian model that I worked with, oh forty-five years ago I'd say, making pick-axe handles and broom handles on it. It can cut out four hurleys in twenty minutes. Then I take the hurleys and give each of them their per-sonality, sanding and grooving the handle just right. Every hurley-maker has his way with a stick. I take them off the machine and know by the weight and the run of the grain, and the feel of it, what is needed. The machine gives me more time for the finishing of each stick. Some fellas wouldn't like the machine, but I don't think the machine takes anything away. Your wood is the same, and, if you have the feel, your finished hurley is the same.

'I designed the master pattern myself, cut an old hurley, took it to a foundry and got it cast in aluminium. You could be trying that for months but, as luck had it, I got it right first time. Now I just have to draw the shape of the hurley on a plank and make a rough-cut of it. I check that the wood has no warp in it and place the four rough-cuts into the machine, switch on the blue button and these four grinding wheels cut away at the rough-cuts of the hurleys from handles to bás. Twenty minutes and four hurleys. I can adjust them for any style or size I want.

'Afterwards I like to feel the weight of each hurley in my hand. What sort of stick are you? Light, heavy, big bás? I can adjust the machine to determine the outcome. Then I finish them. I get more time for that, as I say. When I was making them all by hand it was tougher.

'I had a friend down the road in those days. We used to go fishing together. He would come over here every day and stand above and I'd be making the hurleys and we'd talk about fishing, nothin' else but fishing, getting ready for the weekend again. We'd talk all day. I said nothing to him about getting the machine. He came over one day and I put the four hurleys in it and just switched it on.'

'What did you do that for?' he said. 'That's no good.'

'Paddy, that'll take a lot of work off me,' I said. 'That'll make four hurleys in twenty minutes.

'You'd make a hurley faster than that with your hands,' he said. 'Make one there for me. I'll bet you five pounds you'll be faster.'

'So I made a hurley, not hurrying myself and made it in five minutes. What he didn't realize, of course, was that I could work the bandsaw or the sander to finish the hurleys while the machine was making four new hurleys. I suppose that wasn't the point. He came once or twice more, then never came any more after that. I lost my friend over it.

'Machines can give you a bit of friendship, too. The one I used to work on in MacMahon's was like my left hand. I got so fond of working with it over the years, knew the personality of it, knew its moods and all its noises. Then things changed in the business.

'All of a sudden there were white lines on the floor and good machines being taken out and thrown away, forklifts lifting them up and throwing the old machines into the dump. I just couldn't wear it anymore. It sickened me to the stomach so, after twenty-seven years, I packed up and walked out. Everyone thought I was mad.

'I'd been making hurleys in MacMahon's from as far back as 1960. I had the privilege as a young man of knowing a great hurley-maker by the name of Paddy O'Neill. Paddy was a Limerick man and a gentleman. There was a great friendship between the two of us. He was in his seventies back then, thirty years ago. I used to run the hurleys off on the machine for him and he'd finish them off, give them the bit of personality. He taught me a lot about hurleys.

'Anyway, when I hadn't the job, I was like a man with his legs cut off. We went off to the seaside for a fortnight. Wonder we didn't drown ourselves. I had to come back anyway and face it up after the two weeks at the seaside. Coming in the Tipperary Road, down at the roundabout, on to a field, I saw about forty young girls going out to play and everyone of them had a hurley. I looked at them and said that's what I'll do. I'll make hurleys. I always made a pound at it. Making hurleys, and fishing, and hunting, is not a bad life for any fella.

'For people involved in hurling, it's a labour of love really. I love it. Fellas walk in, and they are all characters. They all have their own ideas about hurleys. They want light ones mostly, then a fella will want a heavy one. Once a little fella about nine stone walked in here and left with a little latt that had no weight in it at all. Taught me a lesson. Every hurler knows what he wants. Some fellas want a round handle, some want an oval handle. I thought about that a lot and now I try and shape it like one of the small hammers that the Stanley Tools' people make. They've been around for a long time, they're at tools all their life, there's a lot of thought gone into how they shape their handles. You take a bit of notice of what they'd be doing.

Concentrate. Concentrate.

'I see where Michael got married,' comes the voice.

'Mmm, yeah. Michael?'

Crowd roars. Smack of sticks. Dave Clarke, beaten to the ball, watches the outcome.

'Michael? Who the fuck is Michael?' says Dave.

In front, his man just shrugs his shoulders. Free tutorial over. Concentrate.

The long drum-roll for the Munster final has begun. On the fruit markets the talk is of little else. The job takes Davey about the place a bit: Limerick on Mondays, Wednesdays, Fridays and Saturdays; Macroom on a Tuesday; Mitchelstown on a Thursday. A long early-morning run to Smithfield in Dublin early in the week. You'd be in Portlaoise before the cold gets out of your bones sometimes. Out on the stall meanwhile, the world goes by and bids Davey Clarke good luck on Sunday.

He's the Limerick fruit-and-veg man, the Limerick hurler. Not in that order, though. It's Thursday afternoon in Mitchelstown. The old square is singing with the sounds of the market. It's a typical Thursday, same traffic, same people, but it's the Thursday of Munster Hurling final week, and for Davey Clarke there is no escape.

In the GAA, everything comes down to where you are from. The square has three fruit-and-veg stalls arrayed at the bottom of the slope near the main road. Three stalls. Three proprietors. Three counties. Simple set-up. Limerick folk buy from their man Davey Clarke right in the middle, near the statue. Tipperary folk go to his left for their produce, and Cork folk find their man located in the corner down to Dave's right. It always amazes Dave that some people in a marketplace will buy their fruit and vegetable on the basis of county allegiances and not prices or quality. That's how things are, though, and how they ever will be. So the banter about the hurling goes around all day, circulating like a summer breeze.

'Good luck to you on Sunday, boy.' And that's from a Cork man. 'You'll beat them, surely.'

Davey smiles on all who smile. You'll beat them, surely. And Michael got married there recently. Concentrate.

'Hey! Who are you playing on, on Sunday, Davey?'

'Jamesie O'Connor again, looks like.'

'Tell us, Davey, any chance of Jamesie slowing down to make you look a bit faster this time?'

Concentrate.

He knows the sensation of drowning. Right there on a hurling pitch in front of 65,000 people, time whipping past for sixty-five minutes, and, click, suddenly he's not breathing air anymore. The world slows down. Slow-motion moments – desperate – heavy – slow-motion moments. And somewhere up there, above the surface, the world isn't opaque, the skies are blue and men are roaring while somebody else is winning the All Ireland title. Offaly is winning the All Ireland title.

He's been there, under the surface, gasping for the next breath. September 1994, the All Ireland final. You'll win, surely, he remembers thinking to himself. Five minutes left to play and five points ahead on the scoreboard. Click! And something dies. Sinking suddenly. Sucked under. Right down to the twilight zone. Wound up losing by a handful of points. Deadman.

'At the end, it was like you weren't there. People just blew past. Strangest thing. I've met so many people since who had moved down to the front of the stand to be the first person out to me when the whistle blew, and then – Offaly just blew past us all. There's not a day gone past since when somebody hasn't spoken to me about it. It won't be out of our system in Limerick until we win an All Ireland.'

You'll win surely. He remembers it all. Being four points up. Then five ahead and wondering if the fact that Offaly now needed two goals to win might just be a peril. Next thing, salt water in his mouth and the current dragging him under. Two goals and a few points to serve as exclamation marks in the hurling history books. Jesus wept!

'Hard. Hard. Hard. A very hard defeat,' he says.

He's been asked about it a million times. Hard.

In Limerick, the scars lingered of course. The team bickered with itself until Christmas. Got relegated in the spring. Didn't care too much for the sight of the coming summer.

The players could see that those final calamitous five minutes in Croke Park had robbed them of so much glory, so much confidence, so many good times. They wanted victim-support, not spring training. They asked the county board if the team would be having a holiday, having nearly brought the county an

All Ireland. The county board replied that 'nearly' was a horse that never won a race. There would be no holiday.

'And where is all the money that was collected right through the summer for the team?' they asked.

'We trained ye with it,' said the county board.

Tempers were lost. Resignation threats flared the Limerick sky. Eventually, late in March when the league was already a lost cause and the forthcoming championship was a pressing worry, they found a piece of their old selves. They located some ancient hunger in the gut when faced with Kilkenny's lordly stripes. They had thirteen wides and a disallowed goal in a thunderous first-half, but huffed and puffed right to the end. A one-point win took the bare look off their winter campaign and refurbished their sore hearts.

'That was the first time the experience of the All Ireland looked like it would stand to us,' says Davey.

So, here they are not many months afterwards in another Munster final, waiting to avenge history. Playing Clare on Sunday. Clare a county with a rich tradition of failure on the big day. You'll win, surely.

A Tipperary man sticks his head into Davey's van.

'Sean McMahon can't be right for Sunday, Davey.'

'They say he is. They say he's okay.'

'Not with a broken collarbone just a few weeks ago. That man can't be right, Davey.'

'Well, we'll wait and see.'

'He's some man. He'd have the beatin' of you with the collarbone or without it.'

'Sure, maybe he would. And wouldn't Tipp love that.'

The head withdraws, throwing an envelope into the van as it goes. A card. Good Luck, Davey, it says.

Another summer. July drawing in. A Munster final waiting and Tipp already beaten. Rehabilitation doesn't come any quicker.

'Beating Tipp. If we never won another match, that was something special,' sighs Davey with satisfaction. 'The way it is with us, is that Tipp are the enemy of everyone and the friend of nobody. When we beat them, it was something special. You could see it in the faces of our supporters even.'

Tipp beaten! Up till last year, Tipperary had beaten them four summers in a row, beaten them, filleted them, trimmed them and maddened them with their high fives and their cockiness. Beating Tipp, you could see the happiness in the supporters' faces all right. Neighbours and friends.

Supporters' faces. Davey knows them well. In Kilmallock, he grew up among them and lives with them still. His family weren't obsessive in the faith, but they knew where they stood. There was a little hurling tradition on both sides of the house but Dave, the only child, can't tick off the Munster hurling finals of his youth and claim to have watched them all. Appreciation of that aspect of the faith came later on. The family followed Limerick in fits-and-starts, and if there was a Kilmallock man on the team it made it twice as likely that the Clarkes would be in attendance.

Growing up in Kilmallock, though, there was never much chance that the ash wouldn't find its way to his palm. He lives in a little bungalow on the Charleville Road not far from the tiny hurling field. In Kilmallock the hurling field is the pool hall, the bowling alley, the coffee shop, the meeting place. Davey is in the garage now, rooting amongst his hurleys, and nods his head in the direction of town.

'We're one hundred yards away from the hurling pitch in my house now. There she is just over there. Of an evening that's where we all meet. Some towns would have an arcade or something. In Kilmallock that's where we meet, rambling down there of an evening. Town lads, country lads, fellas off the Senior team and young fellas. You might just talk, but most of the time you'd be pucking a ball about and talking, too. Just paying your dues to the hurling.'

Kilmallock is in thrall to the hurling. Back in the days when Kilmallock was going well and heading towards an All Ireland club final, there was a man who became famous in the town. After each successive round, which Kilmallock would win on their march to the final, he would round up several head of cattle, sell them at the Monday fair and drink the proceeds for the rest of the week in homage to the boys with the green-banded jerseys. All year it went on, through the county championship, through the five games of the Munster championship and then the All Ireland semi-final and final. Eventually, he almost went broke. Broke, but reasonably happy.

Hurling is the lifeblood of conversation in Kilmallock – through good days and bad. In the months after Offaly came back from the dead and pipped Limerick in that memorable All Ireland final, Kilmallock lost to the Offaly champions, Birr, in the club hurling championship. Reaction in Kilmallock was bad. People had been expecting the boys to go all the way and atone for the county's loss of the year before. Instead they got another sackful of defeat.

'Them Offaly fellas put one over on ye again.' All day and all evening people getting in their ears. Seven of the team packed it in eventually. The pressure was getting too great for ordinary club hurlers to handle. Offaly pulling another one over on Limerick, on Kilmallock. Who needs that sort of grief?

Dave is made for it, though, designed for the banter and the chat. He was a stout young fellow when he first ventured out into this neighbourhood of hurling. He'd tip about with ball and stick on the farmland of his neighbour and friend, Mike Houlihan, and when the time came he journeyed to the Christian Brothers' school in Limerick where the old Offaly corner-back, Pat Fleury, and his assistants 'bate some bit of courage into him'.

The weight fell away from him in secondary school and he found the legs and the touch that would carry him through an hour's hurling and usually bring him out on top. He made the county Minor team when he was seventeen and that same season got called out for the Seniors.

Cork, fresh from its coronation as All Ireland champions, was graciously playing Limerick for the opening of some field or other. Limerick was scraping up the numbers. Dave Clarke played for fifty minutes, flailing after Pat Buckley for most of them. Called ashore ten minutes from time, he was told to come back 'when you're two years older, two stone lighter and about two foot taller'. He wasn't discouraged.

He kept two-thirds of the bargain, made the Senior team in time and has entered the pantheon in Kilmallock. Not that Kilmallock ever expected anything less. Nobody there can recall seeing Davey Clarke skinned in a game of hurling. Even in Munster finals, he's kept his head when a young lad like him would be forgiven for ducking out.

They'd know if he was skinned and they'd be quick to tell him, too. In Kilmallock, you measure yourself and others measure you against the best. Hurlers grow from boys to men hearing songs of the heroes – Mossie Dowling, Paddy Kelly, Tom O'Donnell, Tony Moloney, Bernie Savage and other giants. On the day when Davey first played Senior hurling for Kilmallock as a fierce-willed fifteen-year-old, Bernie Savage, aged forty-three, was playing full-forward in his final game for the club. 'I can always say I played with him,' says Davey. It means a lot around Kilmallock to be able to say such a thing. Davey has paid his dues. In one corner of the family kitchen, there is an old picture of himself and Mike Houlihan. Standing between them is Paddy Kelly. Davey played with him, too. Played with Paddy Kelly.

This Sunday, Kilmallock will be emptying itself out. The town will pack itself into a fleet of cars and head to Thurles for the Munster final. Monday. Tuesday. Wednesday. Thursday. Friday. Saturday. The week limps past. The game bangs about in Dave Clarke's brain.

He knows his own routine by now. Out on the Thurles' pitch, out there in sacred Semple Stadium walking around in the parade of teams before the game, he'll hear the dizzying dementia of the crowd. His brain will keep asking him the same question. 'Jesus, Davey boy, what are you doing here? What are you doing here?' He'll study the blades of grass disappearing under his feet in case he catches sight of a face from home.

He knows how it will go. Before the team get out on the pitch, he'll head into a toilet stall on his own and talk to himself for a few minutes. Then he'll change and burst out into the riot of experiences that is a Munster hurling final.

He'll have an old friend in his hand. Every hurler has their preferences when it comes to sticks. Most like something light, handy and reliable. Dave remembers his first stick, 'Just a little play hurley and I went mad, just mad, till the oul fella hooped it for me. He put two hoops on it and I never looked back.'

Never looked back. For big days now, he takes out the good hurley – the Excalibur of sticks. He knows every twist in the grain of her now, every contour, the comforting feel of her lightness. Mike Houlihan had six of them made one time. Dave took one off him and has been smitten ever since.

'I've never played a bad game with it yet. Three years and it's like my own arm now. I won't use it in training or in challenges. Only championships. I took a chip off her recently, and she's being repaired at the moment. He's trying to make two the same for me at the same time. You can get the brothers, but you'll never get the bloodline quite right I'd say.'

He takes good care of his wand of ash. For hurlers, the things they carry bring comfort to the soul and routine to the most turbulent of days. Recently Kilmallock played the first round of the club hurling championship. Rough enough. Dave had a decision to make.

'We were going into a place where there was going to be a bit of slagging off. Fair old rivals now. It'd be a shame to come back with the best part of a fella's hand stuck to it, so I left it at home. I'd sleep with my hurleys before I'd sleep with my girlfriend, you know.'

This last comment will be his epitaph around Kilmallock.

Sunday. He knows what else it will hold. It will start early. He'll wander over to Mike Houlihan's and, together, they will take a walk down to catch early Mass in the big church at the edge of town. If there's time afterwards, they'll walk out on to the Houlihan land, not much talk between them. They might look at a few cattle and just chew the fat. After scrambled eggs and toast, they will be summoned to the Clarke family benediction: 'The mother always has a splash of the Holy Water. Houlihan will come in for a drop, too. Superstitious, you might say. Then we'll head off.'

Afterwards, in defeat or victory, it will be back to Kilmallock. No matter how Limerick strives together as a team, Davey comes home to Kilmallock when the sun goes down. Straight to Dermot O'Rourke's bar on Lord Edward Street. Dermot's bar is a haven for hurlers. 'Not all the team comes in here,' says Dave, 'only them that drinks.' The walls of the saloon bar are decorated with pictures of Kilmallock teams that have brought the town nine county championships since 1960. One end of the bar, down past the pool table, houses a big mural which pays homage to the team. Somebody has tracked the team's progress to the 1993 All Ireland hurling final, here on the wall of Dermot's bar. County Champions. Munster Champions. All Ireland?

On Sunday night, whether they beat Clare or get beaten, Dave Clarke will take refuge in here with Houlihan and a few other friends and watch the highlights of the game again. They'll have a laugh at the commentators and the studio experts. They usually mix Dave up with Steve McDonagh. Dave either plays with the heart of two men or makes the mistakes of two men. Television boys live on another planet.

Monday morning then, and it will be finished for another year. Another Munster championship for the memory. The frenzy of the faithful reduced to an echo in his ear as he gets up in the darkness, turns the key in the ignition of the puncture-prone old lorry and turns towards the markets. Monday morning, and it will be finished. Concentrate.

* * *

'I played under age,' Noel Shanahan said, 'then I got very sick when I was around fifteen or sixteen years old. I got a bad dose of pneumonia. Sometimes in winter I think it's still in my lungs. I had good hands, good wrists but after being sick I had no wind. So now I make hurleys and it keeps me in the game.

When the sticks come off the machine I take them over here, trim off the handle and the bit below the heel with the bandsaw. There's a bit of history in this bandsaw, too.

'It's a small bandsaw, a nice one. I got it from a fella who was sawing hurleys and making them. He got old and came along one evening and told me it was for sale. Some other bits and pieces, too. I bought the whole lot for £1200.

'The wood you start off with is important when you're making a hurley. You have to be able to see the nice curve of the grain where the hurley will be shaped. A tree that has grown in good conditions without much frost is your best man. The rings of the grain will be spaced evenly and the wood will be strong. The bark on the outside gives you the clues. You like to see a nice bit of healthy skin, light green, not rough at all. If wood is old, the skin is rough and gnarled, and there'll be old scars on it. You might as well be working with a bit of a loaf bread for all the good that wood will be.

'Every county has a different hurley. I prefer the Tipperary hurley, but I'll be killed for saying that. Ted Loughman on the Limerick Road in Tipperary Town gave me a few tips on this. I listen to anyone when it comes to hurleys. I like to make a good Tipperary hurley. They are beautiful to handle, lovely to see. The handle drops back in a curve. The top hurlers in Tipperary use a lovely hurley, with a narrow handle. It's light and delicate up the top, but lovely balance. In Offaly, they like something similar, but in Kilkenny they have something heavier with a different bás. Tipperary hurleys take more wood and only a certain plank will make them. They're not popular with the hurley-maker always. You have to get a piece of wood with a sweep at the top.

'I can look at a match and see the hurleys of other makers, recognize them out on the field. Little signatures of the maker. Daly, up the road, cuts his hurley across square at the top. Kilkenny boys make them bigger at the bás. Jimmy Ryan down in Killenaule makes a lovely hurley. I'd know his. He used to make the hurleys for us here in Ballybrown. Some hurleys are desperate things to see in front of your eye, and yet good hurlers could hurl with them.

'It's nice to see a fella playing a good game with one of mine. Jamesie O' Connor of Clare used one of mine in the All Ireland this year. He got it through another lad. Now, a fella in Ballybrown might say to me "What's wrong with this hurley, Shanahan?" I'd say to him "If it's good enough for Jamesie O'Connor, boy, it's good enough for you".

'I know what I like in a stick. When I bring it across here to finish it, I know the things I like. I finish the handle a certain way. What I like is a nice heel. The pole, underneath the heel, should be about an inch in breadth. There should be a good true grain running from bás up along the handle. A knot in the wood and you can throw the stick away. You want a slight bend in it when you put pressure on it. Not too much bend or flexibility. It has to strike true, you don't want the bás flicking back a bit when a fella really opens his shoulders. What I call the bone runs along the front edge of the hurley up to the handle. I pare that a little bit in places. It's like a shin-bone.

'When the hurley is about the right weight a lot of lads put a bit of linseed oil on. This'll seal in the weight and keep it that way. Some fellas put a bit of creosote on the hurleys, but I can't understand that. It'll keep the weight in, but there'll be no beauty left.

'When it's finished I put two hoops on it. I usually get a young lad in for that. I get the tin for the hoops from a lad up in Dublin. He has it just right. You need the right temper in the metal – soft so a boy can put it on the hurley without cutting his fingers. It's not meant for hurleys at all, so you have to look around to get the right stuff. We put three tacks in either side, keeping the tacks away from the run of the grain. I always worry about the tacks. If a hurley was still drying out, say, the wood tightens around the tacks until it's ready to crack. The wood clenches around those tacks like it was alive. That's why you take the time with the drying and take care of the hurley afterwards.

'You never know where the hurleys will end up. I like that. A friend of mine was in a bar in Perth, down in Australia, and saw a hurley leaning against a bar there with my stamp on it. He stopped me in O'Connell Street to tell me about it as soon as he got back. Others I know have gone off to America or England.

'I love the hurling. When I watch I'm taken out of this world. Great hurlers are like a good gun-dog, they only last a few years. If you are going to win, you have to spend yourself on the game. They give it everything.

'I don't choose between hurlers, though. If a young fella is lucky enough to come in when I've made a nice hurley, then that's his good luck. I consider all hurlers the same. County hurlers have their own ideas, the bigger they get the more finicky they get. So I consider them all the same. Players like a lighter hurley now, more flicking in the game. Hurling is more scientific for them. They don't always open the shoulders up and hurl.

'I repair hurleys as well – put pins going up through the bás, long countersunk screws. A lad will come in and the heel will be gone. I'll put a whole new piece in. There's not a lot of money in that, but some lads love their hurleys, have to have the same one so long as there's life in it.

'Usually around February each year, they start to look for the sticks. Lads wander in with their own ideas of what a hurley should feel like in their hands, looking to buy a couple the same. No two are the same really. County secretaries might come in and buy a few for the county team. The top players just choose from a range the county will have for them. Then, all summer people are in and out.

'I look forward to the summer every year. Watching the lads in the club have a go at the championship, meeting all the characters. It's love really, a love of the game, the outdoors and the trees and the wood. I see a game and I know who made each stick and maybe where the trees came from. Then, again, when Limerick is playing, I hardly see anything. It carries me away to another world.

CHAPTER THREE

Places: town and country

The sounds of traffic never quite get blocked out. Double-decker buses heave up the hill past the shopping centre. 'Think blue-and-white,' roars Tommy Lyons somewhere below the din. 'Think blue-and-white.' A car screams to a halt to a cacophony of horns. On the pitch the boys yomp through a mess of puddles, the borders of which are fringed with ice. The grass is feeling the first breath of the night's frost. It will be crunchy underfoot by the morning. 'Cold enough for ya,' bawls Tommy. 'Cold enough?'

Ostensibly the pitch is sheltered from the wind by a wall of trees planted long ago in a neat line over near the car park, but right now in the depths of March the breezes cut in between the semi-detached houses and insinuate themselves under the collar. Tommy Lyons is wearing his woolly hat pulled right down to his eyebrows, and his padded anorak is zipped up above his chin.

'Think blue-and-white,' he shouts again as his boys trudge past him, picking a path from the dim sodium light thrown from the car park. They disappear in a pack, away out into the darkness again, their aggregated breath forming short-lived clouds in the cold night air above them. It's cold, but the boys are thinking blue-and-white.

Through the north of the country the roads are banked with dirty grey snow and the tar surfaces are untrustworthy. To make matters worse the clouds are hanging out a heavy curtain of rain, and from Armagh onwards the roads get tighter and more serpentine. You could nearly miss Bellaghy altogether on a night like this, shooting through the place on the way to somewhere bigger. From the main street, though, you can just about see thirty footballers chuntering around in their muddy floodlit field. That's the only sign that this is the epicentre of Derry football.

Nothing strange down there, nothing odd about thirty grown men hacking about in the worst of winter for nothing but the enjoyment of representing Bellaghy. Tonight, or virtually any other weekday night, there are footballers training down here for the same reward. This week, though, the road leads to Dublin and the All Ireland club final on Friday.

People in the village glance down at the distant tracksuited figures and know that all is well with the world. The boys are training and Bellaghy is on its way to the big time once more. It's been more than twenty years, but the surnames of the boys on the team are still the same. You can't recruit footballers here, you have to breed them.

In the city, the population shuffles itself all the time. Upwardly mobile. Downwardly mobile. Bored. Restless. Evicted. Unemployed. Bereaved. Inheriting. Dispossessed. Lucky. Leaving town or being run out of it. Any reason to keep on shifting about. Amidst all the impermanence and all the insecurity, people aren't relaxed with each other any more. Nobody leaves their front door open for neighbours to drift in and out of, everybody walks with darting eyes and the wary hunch of the city animal.

Once upon a time the outskirts of Dublin consisted of a necklace of small villages, each with a separate identity of its own, strung together around the same city. As the city grew, the population just filled in the gaps leaving the city surrounded by one great amorphous suburb.

The movement to the city caught us by surprise. De Valera and his notions of comely maidens dancing at the crossroads haunted us till long after he was laid in the grave. We saw ourselves as a small agrarian society right through till the end. Only when the eternity of Dublin housing estates was finally complete did we import fantastic notions such as civic planning and green-belt areas.

Children grew up being taught that Ireland was an agricultural country, busy feeding its generations, with only patchy success, mind, from the larder of the land. Then those same children grabbed their leaving certs and headed off for the city. Through the 1960s and 1970s Dublin grew phenomenally, bursting out beyond its natural borders, gobbling up the green spaces to the west, south and north of the city. On and on, absorbing the influx until one-third of the population of the country lived in the same place.

In an area such as Kilmacud, a place without edges or a shawl of green fields wrapped around it, the sense of local identity can be difficult to find. People migrate here from all over, settling down in semi-detached units from which they can commute and make school-runs and totter home at their ease from the nearest saloon bar.

When people think of Kilmacud, they think of southside suburban supermarkets, bowling alleys, fast-food joints and the chattering middle-classes. If people in places like this ever strive together as a community, it is usually inadvertently, unwillingly and in negative circumstances. Objections against planning applications, Neighbourhood Watch meetings, parents combatting the threat of hissing drug-dealers and so on. Always fighting fires, never putting anything together.

All the things which make the GAA strong and sturdy, all the conditions which provide the grass-roots' nourishment for the Association, all those things are missing here. The sense of identification is gone, the notion of territory has been broken down to the smallest conceivable unit. Trespassers prosecuted. 'Out of my face.' 'See you in court.' If a hurling and football club is to be at the centre of the community out here in the concrete maze, it has first to fight to create the community and then take the time to identify the centre.

And who has time? The migrant to the great ribbon of suburbia must adapt to the sooty air, to the breeze-block buildings, to the noisy hum from the main roads leading back to the roots of the country. Most of all, the widely depersonalized nature of city life needs adapting to.

Some never try. Hurling or football players traditionally bind themselves to their home-place through the GAA. Travelling home every weekend while they are still fit enough and young enough and keen enough to play. When the playing ends, the only links with the home-community will be the family unit.

For others, the links just never break. Not far from here, for instance, lives Frank Darcy and his family. Frank came to Dublin from emigration-ravaged Leitrim. When he left his home-town of Ballinamore and his beloved club of Aughawillan, Frank began making the pilgrimage home every weekend to play and put something back. By the time his playing days had ended, Frank had a young family and a young wife, but he wanted to keep putting more back into Aughawillan. He began driving the children down every weekend to line out in juvenile games. They then grew old enough to drive themselves and continued making the journey. Declan Darcy grew good enough to play for and to captain Leitrim. That's Frank Darcy, though. Others just moved to the city and became lost instantly to the GAA.

The fabric of the city is different in so many ways. In small-town Ireland there are always times when a non-native can be made to feel like an outsider, but usually the warmth of a place wraps itself around all who live there. If you don't bring notions about yourself, you won't leave with hang-ups about yourself. In the city you can be a stranger for ever, though.

Even things which seem the same, work differently. Beneath the homogenous surface of the national curriculum, education imparts different things in the city. The teachers are another breed and the schools themselves are bigger and more crowded. Not being tied to the community, teachers don't feel that they represent the community or that they need to be judged by the hurling and football teams which they produce. The city school is a conveyor-belt with a different quality-control system in operation. The demographics of the teaching profession have altered and the priorities of the education system have changed, too.

Not too long ago, the religious orders had both hands wrapped around the Irish school system. When the state was founded in a frenzy of Catholic righteousness, a guarantee of sectarianism was built into the constitution and the institutions. Nuns, brothers and priests ran the schools, taught the faith and chose the teachers. The GAA was still considered part of the sacred trinity of Irish life and old-fashioned Irish nationalism – one of only three

Half-time break, Croke Park

Clones town on Ulster Day

(*right*) Croke Park people

(*above*) Ulster Championship 1995, Cavan fans

(*left*) Croke Park

(*above*) Big day (*below*) Sidelines

(*above*) Pre-match parade (*below*) Town and country, Declan Darcy leads out Leitrim, county of his father

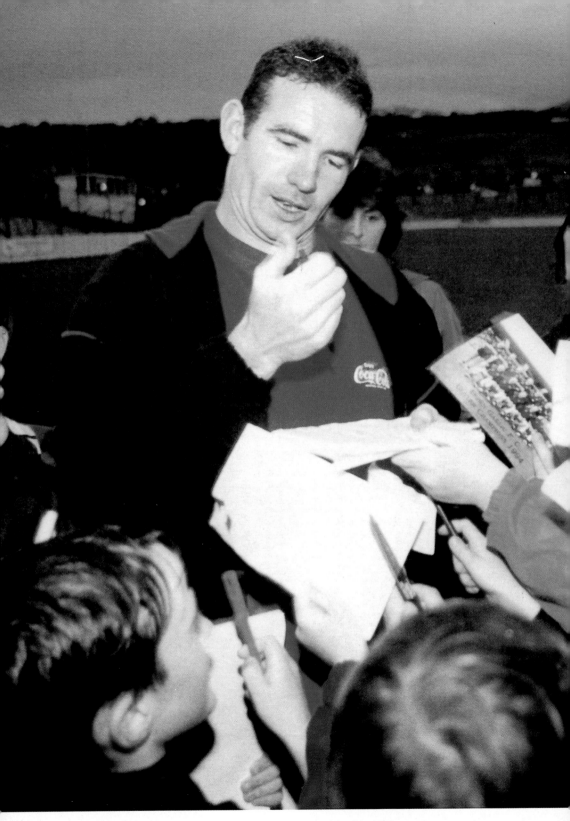

Ross Carr, Newry publican and footballer mobbed in his home town

Ross Carr in Newry

(*above*) Ulster football brings on the dancing girls (*below*) Green fields

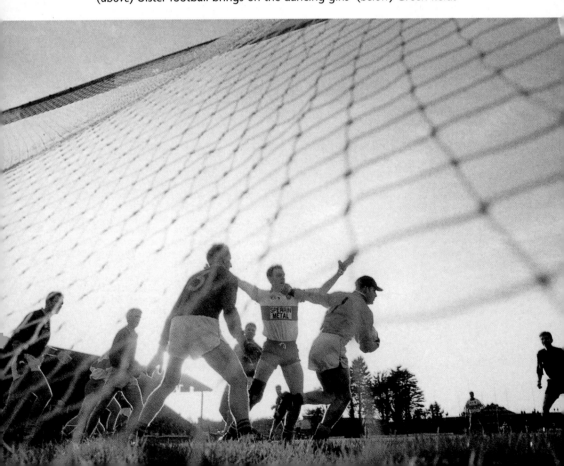

Schoolkids playing Gaelic football

Women's football is Ireland's fastest growing sport

Childhood

(*above*) Jason Sherlock and some fans (*below*) Jason Sherlock in action
(*right*) Jason Sherlock, Gaelic football's first superstar

New Croke Park takes shape

organizations a right-minded person could depend on. The Fianna Fail party, the church and the GAA: the moral equivalent of roughage in your diet.

Consequently, the GAA had the run of the school timetable if not of the schoolchild's imagination. Gaelic games were pencilled in as part of the prescription for all the modern ailments which might afflict a child, one part of the daily dosage of Catholic, nationalistic conservatism which would keep the country pure. Two hours of Gaelic games a week and soccer won't be a problem in the home, Madam.

Once upon a time, a boy passing through primary school had to fight hard if he was to avoid having Gaelic games drilled into him. The Christian Brothers produced rudimentary manuals on football and hurling, with the aid of which any child could turn himself into a Gaelic superstar. Girls could make the sandwiches and play camogie if they were big-boned. That caused resentments surely, but it created a conveyor-belt of players, too. The GAA was duly grateful to the schools and the religious orders, but the GAA missed the point. So many children (city children especially) grew to adulthood holding Irish sports in the same regard which they held castor oil, fried liver, bone-meal tablets and corrective shoes for flat feet.

The teaching profession has changed in the last twenty years and that change has impacted most directly upon the playing of hurling and football in Dublin. The first manifestation of the church losing its grip has been in the texture of the teaching profession itself. For every three male teachers in Dublin primary schools, there are now ten female teachers. This is no bad thing for the child, but the GAA has found itself having to work harder in the cities if Gaelic games are to be picked from the menu of leisure pursuits being offered to youngsters.

The grip is still strong enough. Most schools are still church-managed and somewhat GAA-oriented. Seven out of every twenty male teachers and one out of every twenty female teachers in Dublin schools are still involved in promoting football, hurling or camogie within their schools. It isn't enough, though, not enough to take a child's imagination by the scruff of the neck and make him or her sit bolt upright. Not in the city.

The GAA has always been complacent about the city, about Dublin especially. In the 1970s, when the game should have been declining rapidly, Dublin was enjoying the benefits of the last scrapings from an old-fashioned world. A team of Dublin footballers, drawn from the traditional clubs and the usual Christian Brothers' schools, somehow metamorphosed into the most glamorous team the game had yet seen, contesting six successive All Ireland finals. They filled the evening papers and touted their silverware around schools and so, quite by accident, the glamour of that team insulated the GAA from the worst effects of its own complacency.

That Dublin team was born just in time to save the city from the twin assaults of television and soccer. The 1966 World Cup had been the first to be broadcast into Irish homes. Its impact was small, but by 1970, when the miracle of colour was more than just a whisper and the magical Brazilians were there making poetry in a crystal box in the corner of the sitting room, the world was suddenly a different place and nothing could ever be new enough for us. We would grow our sideburns, wear our creased pants with the hint of a flare, and nod approvingly as the local publican tore down his old wooden bar and fitted some nice plastic and leatherette installations. Only the impossible glamour of the Dublin team of the 1970s kept the game alive in the city. Dublin people got behind their team with flags and scarves and songs – all the trappings borrowed from the denizens of the soccer terraces.

In the city, the child seldom had a context in which to place the forcibly imparted skills of hurling and football. Soccer spread itself ingeniously through the urban sprawl by usurping the GAA's oldest weapon, the sense of place, and creating a network of road and street leagues. When the Dublin team of the 1970s died its death, soccer had the imagination of a city full of children all to itself.

By 1995, the GAA in Dublin had gone twelve unprecedented years without winning an All Ireland title and had struggled dourly through the fun-soaked years brought to the population, courtesy of the Irish soccer team. When a quarter of a million people welcomed that Irish soccer team home from the World Cup in Italy in 1990, after three delirious weeks of endeavour, what starry-eyed youngster wouldn't have been dreaming of being up there with the well-paid lightly-tanned heroes of the soccer world? Gaelic games in the city needed a different blueprint.

The casualties were mounting. Five of the great Dublin teams, which saved the city for the GAA in the 1970s, went to the same Christian Brothers' school which looms above the traffic in Fairview Strand on the northside of Dublin. St Joseph's was a distinguished academy of Gaelic games, having become the first non-boarding school ever to have won an All Ireland title and having provided a steady stream of famous footballing talents for the service of the county team ever after.

In the 1990s St Joseph's found itself unable to field a first-year hurling team. The boys simply couldn't play the game. Brendan Leahy, the genial Kerryman who had run the games in the school for so long, found himself having to ask local soccer clubs for permission to use their players in games on Sunday afternoons. Dublin, as a county, was reduced to asking for permission to field a combined colleges' hurling outfit in the provincial schools championships, so disastrous had the outings of successive county champions from Dublin been. Finally, Brendan Leahy hauled in the local clubs, showed them the fruit of their complacency and demanded that they start playing their part. The county board chipped in with a couple of part-time coaches and the process of rehabilitation began.

'We couldn't do it anymore,' says Brendan. 'We couldn't just keep turning out players for the clubs. They had to come in and start helping us. Soccer deserved to have the success it was having because it was so well organized. We had to stop being complacent.'

Hurling and football are learning to present themselves in other ways, using the stars of the game, putting photographs of players in Cornflake packets, selling the message through the popular culture, turning the city into a string of communities again. Funnily enough, they learned all this out in middle-class, south Dublin first, learned it and applied it out in Kilmacud before anybody else did.

City children are more open to other influences than ever before. Television, which the GAA has never learned how to cope with, has beamed soccer into every home in the country, creating a pantheon of idols to be mimicked and adored. Youth culture reaches out its tentacles as quickly as TV moguls can spot opportunities. The airborne stars of the NBA, the Jordans, the Rodmans, the Shaqs, with their practised disrespect for authority and gravity, and their vigorously marketed lines of clothing, have tapped into a pop culture which the GAA has scarcely had time to identify. That's just the sporting competition. A million other fingers are crooked, beckoning the childish imagination to come hither.

So in Kilmacud in the heart of middle-class south Dublin, they just tilted the playing field and put the GAA club at the heart of the community, with a bar and tennis courts, snooker and swimming pools, and a community centre. They went into the schools and, instead of telling children that hurling and football would keep them pure in body and thought, proclaimed that hurling and football were fun.

They had their problems, of course. Those who find the GAA, with its rural conservative history and its classless social dimension, as indigestible as three-day-old liver, are congregated in the greatest numbers in southside Dublin. They fancied a tennis club with perhaps a GAA outlet attached. They fancied everything the GAA club had to offer except the GAA. But Kilmacud stuck in there, recreating the village right in the heart of the south city. They stuck in there and this week they are playing in the All Ireland club final for the first time.

Kilmacud and Bellaghy. The boys come round from another lap, looming suddenly out of the darkness like a great sixty-legged beast. Last lap of the night. They gather around Tommy Lyons, hands on the knees, bodies bent, breath elusive. 'Nobody will beat ye,' says Tommy. 'Nobody.'

'In Bellaghy,' says Danny Quinn, 'if you don't play football I don't know what you do.'

There is a momentary silence around the table as the thought of the area's rich contribution to the armed Republican struggle flickers through a few heads. Nobody says anything though. The point is well made.

Bellaghy Wolfe Tones is at the heart and soul of country football, a team named for the place it comes from and for the memory of a Republican patriot, a team which constantly regenerates itself from its own resources. Danny Quinn is one of those people whose life is one long journey in the arms of the GAA. From child to adult, from fumbling student to accomplished player, Danny has been in the blue-and-white of Bellaghy. He and his wife Catherine live right in the middle of the little village, down there in William Street.

'Football, football, football,' Catherine is wont to say of life in Bellaghy. 'Once in a while, a holiday from football would be nice.'

'When this final is over,' says Danny, 'we really don't know what we're going to talk about in Bellaghy for a while. We'll probably talk about beating Lavey in the championship next year.'

Danny Quinn, Tommy Doherty, Kevin O'Kane and Sean Browne are bunkered in one of the many little rooms dotted about the hive which is Bellaghy GAA club. Sean is the chairman of the club, Danny, a teacher, is the captain, Tommy Doherty, a civil engineer and building contractor, is the co-manager of the Senior team this year with Kevin, who works in the fuel-distribution business.

Danny, Tommy and Kevin played together on the last Bellaghy team to win a Derry championship, back in 1986 when Tommy was the captain and still an inter-county mid-fielder. If you met Tommy in another life altogether, you would mark him down as a potential mid-fielder with his hands as huge as shovels and his massive frame which tops out at about the six-foot five-inches mark.

Three nights a week, and most of the weekend, they spend down here getting the team right, talking about the team, fretting about the team.

Tonight all the work is finally done. Sean has the buses to Dublin to worry about, though. Who will be going, who'll drop out at the last minute? Who has paid and who hasn't paid? How will they get all the Bellaghy people rounded up again for the trip home if Bellaghy wins?

Down on the small junior pitch below the car park, the players have just finished their last training session together before their All Ireland final. Mud-splattered and cursing they have headed into the showers. Great gasps of steam and huge roars of excited conversation have escaped into the Derry night. Then onward towards the small kitchen, to mugs of steaming tea and handfuls of fresh sandwiches. Finally, they head off into the night with warnings about burning the candle at both ends ringing in their ears.

These fields and this building are at the centre of social and cultural life in Bellaghy. Out in the main hall, where the bar is, thirty or forty children are learning Irish dancing right now. Around the back is an even bigger hall which holds 2,000 at a time, a testimony to Bellaghy's ambitious nature. Bellaghy has a population of under 2,000. Sometimes the big hall gets used for indoor training, sometimes for basketball games, and sometimes for Bingo.

'The Chieftains came back from China and their first concert was in here on a bad night with about 150 people,' laughs Sean Brown. 'That was a wee bit of a culture shock for them.'

All this, the bricks and mortar and the tight sense of togetherness have sprung from the football. Twice in the last twenty years politics have come to the door here in south Derry and Loyalists have burned the club house down. Twice the whole place has been rebuilt. Bellaghy couldn't breathe without the GAA.

A small rural farming community lost in the heart of the south Derry countryside, these Bellaghy boys kick on the same soil and in the same dewy fields that one of Bellaghy's more famous sons, Seamus Heaney, has absorbed into his poetry. There is something here all right, something in the air, the trees and the land which stirs people, be it to war, poetry or football. Heaney has commented that growing up here, as part of the minority within that part of Ireland which Britain still claims as its own, 'emphasized rather than eroded' his sense of Irish identity.

His words find an echo in the GAA club where football is not just a sport but a non-violent expression of a cultural and obliquely political ideal. This is the case with most rural clubs on either side of the border. The pull of the city, and the shuffling, and the cosmopolitan pre-occupations of the mass media, have left people resentful of the slight paid to their home-place. There is a belated recognition that the value systems and cultural kinesis of small rural towns don't necessarily have to be crabbed and moralistic and the butt of citified humour. In a world which is shrinking itself so fast that it threatens to be homogenous, when the centre of Dublin looks the same as the centre of any mid-European city, the value of rural identity has belatedly been 'emphasized rather than eroded'. The local football and hurling teams have become expressions of diversity, symbols of identity.

Within the GAA club, the community can build a focal point for itself, a place where people might draw themselves together and draw down the energy given off by the passionate pride of place. This has been the run of the grain through late twentieth-century Ireland, the sense of local identity renewing itself, the sense of nationalism diffusing itself into culture, rather than repeatedly sharpening itself in politics.

It is fascinating and thrilling to stand on a muddy bank at a winter game somewhere in the country and listen to the cadences and accents of the local radio commentators feeding back live reports of the club's performance on the field.

Everything gets funnelled back in the vernacular, players described by their nicknames, with references to their jobs, family situations, where they drink. The next Thursday, the game might consume half a page of newsprint in the local paper. This growth in local radio and local media has fed off the resurgence in pride in small places, in the sense that any history is important, that there is more to life than bad land that wants escaping from. In Bellaghy, the whole process is given flavour by the political situation, but, at heart, Bellaghy Wolfe Tones is a country football club playing for the pride of a country place.

Bellaghy and the football territory that surrounds it is caught between two cities, between the bustle-and-buzz of Belfast to the east and the gentle beauty of Derry to the west. Neither Belfast nor Derry are good Gaelic football towns, both places having had their development hindered by the troubles and the GAA's own ban on Gaelic players playing soccer. Out here, though, around Bellaghy, football is the only game, the communal passion.

Around here, the football talent just teems. Just up the road, Lavey is watching broodingly as its great rivals from Bellaghy set about trying to win their second All Ireland club title. Lavey grasped the cup for the first and only time in its history in 1991. Another win for Bellaghy would set Lavey its target for another season.

Down the road a little way, the boys of Castledawson will be watching closely, as will the men of Newbridge and the lads in Dungiven, and so on. Twelve thriving clubs are condensed somehow into this tiny patch of rural Derry. Everybody is cautious about Bellaghy just now. The average age of its squad is just twenty-one. The club will need to be put in its place soon or it will rule the roost for a decade. Just two years ago, the Minor team won the Ulster championship for that grade. All those boys are now percolating through on to the club's Senior team. Some of them should go on to wear the red-banded jersey of Derry before the end of this year.

The other eleven clubs around here couldn't stomach another golden era of Bellaghy football. 'Aye t'would make a few people sick all right,' says Tommy Docherty when the prospect is mentioned.

Tommy grew up not long after the club. Founded in 1939, Bellaghy won its first county championship in 1956, discovered that it liked it and, having lost the following year, went on to win four in a row.

Since then, it's been mostly glory. Sixteen wins in forty years and plenty of finals. One Bellaghy man, Tom Scullion, has picked up a swag of twelve county championship medals. The good times on the football field have helped with the bad times off the field. In 1972, when the troubles were beginning to look as if they were long-term, a team from Bellaghy came down to Dublin on an Easter Monday and won the All Ireland championship for clubs, a competition which had previously been the domain of divisional and college sides. That warm memory lives on in more than just the photographs of the team which hang about the walls.

'They beat University College Cork that day,' says Danny Quinn, 'a gang of boys from the country up here going down to Dublin and beating UCC. They were so surprised that they hadn't even brought the cup up from Munster. They had to give them some sort of plaque to tide them over to the next day.'

The names on the team-sheet in March 1995 are much the same as the names back then in 1972: Diamond, Cassidy, Scullion, Mulholland, Donnelly, Quinn, Downey, Doherty. Football is a thread through life here, something which has tied families and friends together across the fields and across the shades of nationalist opinion and the strata of social class.

'Everybody here knows each other,' says Danny Quinn, the captain of this young team. 'Everyone knows each other, and everyone has rowed with each other. Families have married into each other and families have fallen out with each other. When it comes to football, though, we are all Bellaghy. At the end of the day, when the ball is thrown in, we're together. Through and through Bellaghy.'

They are tight, indeed. People tonight are wondering if Tommy Diamond will be able to make the final in Dublin. Tommy has been sick for some time, but his boys, Karl and Peter, will be playing in defence on Friday in Croke Park. It doesn't look as if Tommy will be there.

'Tommy married a woman from Ballymena,' says somebody, leaving the declaration hanging in the air as if it tells you all you need to know about what a unique family the Diamonds are.

The conversation in the little room twists and turns. Kevin O'Kane is a blow-in himself, having drifted here all the way from Ballerin. This is his second time to take a hand at managing the Senior team. He is talking about Kilmacud Crokes and its huge membership and the differences between city clubs. Once, a few years ago, at the sevens tournament, which the Kilmacud club organize every September, Kevin had the pleasure of introducing two Kilmacud members to each other for the first time.

'Two boys in the same club who never met each other,' says Kevin, still tickled at the thought

Club football and club hurling is the unrelenting heartbeat of the GAA. The year never ends for clubs in little towns like this. It is thirteen months since Bellaghy started out on the road that has brought it to Croke Park this weekend. Sean Brown and Danny Quinn drove to the county championship draw one night and, on the way home, decided that the Bellaghy boys were good enough to reach the final. That was thirteen months back. Thirteen months of life in a small rural town. Maybe 150 nights of training.

'One long adventure,' says Kevin O'Kane.

A couple of the men who founded the club in 1939 have passed on. Big Tommy Docherty has a new baby in the house. Injuries have hurt and injuries have healed. Tommy Diamond has been into hospital and out again. A county manager has been sacked. A few boys have headed off to college, and one or two more have packed in playing altogether. Life goes on. Dublin on Friday. 'What's these Kilmacud boys like anyways? Has anyone seen them?'

Tommy Lyons is from Mayo, Mick Leahy is from Wexford.

One day a couple of years ago, just before a big game, Tommy dropped a bombshell right into Mick Leahy's ear. Just called him over and told him he was dropped from the team. Dropped! Right there on the morning of a big game against Ballyboden. You could have scraped Leahy's jaw up off the ground. Dropped! He'd never known the tortures of the splintery bench before.

Wasn't he the epitome of what this club was all about? Big Mick Leahy. Dropped!

Lyons wanted more, though. Lyons wasn't listening to any arguments or encouraging any self-pity. Mick Leahy was instructed to go into the dressing-room and give the lads a little speech before the game. Told to just do it. With tears in his eyes, Leahy told a silent shocked dressing-room just how he felt, told the boys that he was gutted, torn apart, let down, destroyed. The lads stared at him, got up and went out. They won by a hatfull.

Big Mick Leahy laughs at the thought. Then he hammers home the message. This is life in Kilmacud.

'I'll tell you one thing. If you're around this club bad-mouthing Tommy Lyons, you're making a fool out of yourself. You're making one bad mistake.'

Kilmacud is a melting-pot club. Moments like that have welded them together.

Why else would a man from Tipperary, a man in his mid-thirties, a man with a family and a good career in the bank to escape to, put himself through the mill, go in and face his fellows with tears in his eyes and talk to them about what the jersey meant? Put the question another way, did it mean anything in Dublin to say you were from Kilmacud before this club blossomed into its glory?

The basis of the GAA, the identification with home-place, with tradition and history, the passing of the bloodlines, all those things dictate that Kilmacud Crokes shouldn't exist, yet here they are in their club house as close with each other as if they had all been born and reared together on these few acres hard by the shopping centre.

There's Tommy Lyons and Mick Leahy from Mayo and Tipp respectively. There's Mick Dillon from Wexford and Pat Burke from Clare, plus a handful of less accomplished blow-ins from around the country. Even the Dubliners are tagged by their country forbears. Niall Clancy's people come from Clare. Paul Walsh's hail from Galway. Displaced and dislocated, they have set themselves down here and built a GAA club, gotten themselves busy winning titles and evangelizing, knitted a community together.

It's unlikely soil from which to grow a thriving club. The members spring from an amalgamation, a marriage of desperation and convenience back in 1966 between the itinerant Crokes hurling club and the lowly Kilmacud football club.

The way of things in Dublin is such that they aren't entirely approved of. In fact, in most of the county, they are despised for their success and affluence and, damn it, their enlightenment. Once upon a time Dublin clubs were over-run by country people. The county teams were stuffed with country people. People from every corner of the nation pulled the sky-blue jersey of Dublin over their head. For instance, Dublin won six All Ireland hurling titles in better times. Only one native Dubliner, Jim Byrne, played on any of those winning teams. The rest were country men bound to the city by work and economic necessity, not by love. Nobody in the city could identify with these teams patchworked together with the remnants of thirty-one other counties. So they were scrapped and the era of Dublin people for Dublin teams was born.

The legislation worked because it suited the times. Clubs back then in the 1940s came from distinct places, villages. St Vincent's came from Marino and were as clannish as island folk. Erin's Isle came from Finglas. Parnells from Coolock with fishing rights in Donnycarney. Thomas Davis sprung from the little village of Tallaght. Ballyboden were mountain men. O'Tooles marched out from Seville Place. And so on, until one-third of the country decided to live in Dublin, and the boundaries and the villages disappeared.

Clubs stuck to the old racial-purity laws, however, and by and large they were successful. Through the 1970s, when the Dublin Senior team was winning All Ireland titles and lending a bit of swagger to the city, the traditional schools got by and GAA clubs blossomed in all sorts of new places. In leaner times, though, with the Irish soccer team cutting a swathe through the public imagination, football and hurling began to struggle.

Kilmacud recognized earlier than most that a suburban club needed to transform itself into something more than a leisure operator. Kilmacud turned itself into a community.

A couple of years back, Mick Pender, the goalie, and a couple of other players, sat themselves down and went through the lists of all the Minor teams to have represented the club in the previous ten years or so. They divided up the names and tracked down those who had dropped out of the club as relentlessly as loan-skip tracers. It is harder to escape from Kilmacud Crokes than it is to slip away from most small religious cults.

Evidence of the faith is everywhere. The schoolchildren of the area wear the Kilmacud jersey as much as a fashion statement as a sports' garment. Kilmacud have been among the pioneers in developing contacts between GAA clubs and local schools. A schools' officer, who somehow fits his duties in around a full-time job, visits the teacher in the local secondary schools and helps with the nurturing of young talents.

The primary schools in the area take the field wearing Kilmacud jerseys. There is a broad acceptance within the club as to what the future looks like. A full-time schools' officer will be appointed, the club house will be expanded again to provide a greater focal point for the community. These things will happen as something subordinate to the strength of the games. Everywhere you go within the club, somebody wants to make it clear that Kilmacud is a GAA club dragging a community along with it. A small part of country life blossoming in the city.

'I love the company of GAA people,' says Tommy Lyons, his good humour blossoming. 'I love it. Anytime, anywhere, give me a GAA person to talk to and we'll get on.'

Tommy is in the company of GAA people right now. He has just received a

December 1995 end-of-year award for managing Kilmacud to an All Ireland club title back on a rain-spoiled day in March.

'GAA people are the heart of what this country is all about,' says Tommy. 'Half my day I'm on the phone talking business, but I'm talking about Gaelic football, too, and hurling, with people from any county. We don't know what we have in this country with the GAA. I can't believe there is anything like it in the world.'

The talk ebbs and flows, who'll do well next year, who was hyped this year? Tommy is standing in the lobby of a Dublin hotel. He has given up managing the team. Bellaghy and Kilmacud, having tussled it out in a dour All Ireland final in March, rolled almost straight ahead into the new season.

Bellaghy became entangled with its near-neighbour Lavey, in the course of the county championship. As a result of the entanglement, some fifteen suspensions were handed out. The part of the punishment Lavey took cost the club its shot at another county title.

Kilmacud for its part just ran out of steam after its All Ireland win. Coming up against a team which had been lying in wait for it all summer, it lost. The club just took down the tents and went home.

That's only a small part of its story, though, winning and losing. Everywhere, in every village, suburb and small town, there is a story of the playing year. It can be told through statistics and league tables and matches won and lost. That's not the heart of it, though. That's not even the start of it.

CHAPTER FOUR

Places: far fields

December. They think the Scanlon Cup will happen this year. They meet on a Thursday night and gather the news. Men coming home from all parts of the island. It will, so it is hoped, happen. Set a date and they will come.

Achill Island has a long and proud history within the GAA, like most clubs in the west the theme is resourcefulness, struggle against the forces of nature and economics which have always ganged up to drive the people away.

They reckon hurling thrived here before football arrived. The islanders would hurl on the beaches with sticks cut from whin bushes around the island. Early this century, a baker from Westport or Kilmeena introduced Gaelic football to the island. It took a while for parish rivalries to consolidate into the formation of an actual club to represent the island. Achill GAA club was founded in 1941 and the following year won the first of five Mayo Junior Football championships.

The Junior championship was annexed again in 1949, but it was the Scanlon Cup, instituted in 1954, which caught the imagination of the island's people.

The Scanlon Cup, named for two brothers, Paddy and Jimmy Scanlon, who played together on the 1942 Junior championship winning team and were both dead within four years, has been the lynchpin of GAA activity on the island. The heyday of the competition was the years when the patterns of departure from the island were different from what they are today.

'We used to play the Scanlon Cup on Easter Sunday,' says Catherine Joyce. 'It was a highlight of the year on the island. People would come home in the springtime from their work in Scotland and England. Six teams from different parts of the island would play off. On the day after Easter Sunday they'd all leave the island again. Once the turf was cut here and the gardens set they'd go back, but for the pride of their parish and place they'd play the Scanlon Cup in Easter week.'

Catherine Joyce teaches in a one-teacher school. Her professional life has been an index of the island's problems. Having been reared in Achill Sound, she began working here in 1977. There were seventy-eight pupils in the school at the time and three teachers. Now she is the solitary staff-member looking after sixteen children. Her father, the late Padraig, was one of the primary forces behind Gaelic games on the island. Around Scanlon Cup time his memory comes alive, too.

Over the years the islanders from the individual villages, having made their way home from all corners of Ireland and the globe to take part in the thirteen-a-side Easter-week games, would fight it out for the Cup. The excitement generated was extraordinary. Talk would begin the previous Christmas as to who would be home and who mightn't be home, and the chatter wouldn't subside until summer.

The GAA provided the focal point for the year on the island. Funerals and weddings were the only other things which could draw people together in such numbers.

One of the schools on the island might need a teacher and they would be sure to hunt down one who was good at football. On match days, convoys of cars would cross the old bridge on to the island. People remember old Martin McGinty who would come home from London every year where he was doing well. Martin was fanatical about the Scanlon Cup and would arrive bearing a new set of jerseys for the Achill Sound team. That and Sound's run of successes made it the team to beat for many years.

The nature of emigration, which has shaped the life of the island, has also shaped the nature of the Scanlon Cup. Eventually the islanders stopped coming home in the springtime. In the old days a man might leave to find work and his wife and children would stay behind. The culture changed and the world of work changed. The jobs away from home were no longer land-oriented. Achill islanders were moving into construction, into third-level education, into everything. Entire families would take off from the island. At the end of the 1980s, the Scanlon Cup was moved to Christmas time. The competition survived. Achill is about surviving, about surviving and getting on with life. The history of this place is of loss and leaving, and the island's face carries the lines of its own sad history – lines left by grief, hard living, and a resilient determination to face it all down.

'We have had our troubles on Achill,' says Thomas Johnston, who has watched generations of youngsters pass through his school and his GAA club. He has chronicled them all, where they have ended up as little dots around the world. Thomas has a photograph of himself and the Achill team which won the Mayo Under-Fourteen championship in 1973. He is standing beside the tousle-headed boys, their coach on final day in McHale Park, Castlebar. The final is being played before a league game between Dublin and Mayo, and Achill's young team represents the island's hope for the future. Today, just three of the twenty-two boys in the photo are left living on the island.

'We have had our troubles, but we get on with life. It's not our way to moan or to get down about it,' says Thomas.

Yet history whispers in the ear always, the voices of the past carried on the winds that rake incessantly over the island. At Kildownet, in the graveyard, a monument commemorates thirty-two souls drowned in Clew Bay a 101 years ago – Achill people: men and women on their way to Scotland to Lanark, Ayr and Midlothian to eke out some migratory work.

They'd left the island at Darby's Point aboard an Achill hooker on a cool grey summer's morning with the potato fields as their destination. Near Westport quay, those on deck spied the wonder of a great steamer the *SS Elm*. From the hold, and from the other side of the hooker, the Achill islanders came running to take in the sight of it.

The boon, sail, and badly distributed weight of the passengers, turned the hooker over and tossed its cargo of emigrants into the sea. The majority of the passengers were saved – thirty-two drowned.

The names engraved on the memorial headstone in Kildownet are the same names as those above the shops and public houses of the people of Achill now. The tragedy still cuts into the consciousness of the island. A 101 years – not long in a place nourished by history. Last summer, when they held a memorial service, victim Mary Doogan's grand-daughter was the one to lay the wreath. Thomas Johnston's grand-uncle was pulled out of the water that day.

Here on Achill, all that Ireland has endured is magnified. Across the sound is the beach, at Mulranny, where, under the golden sands, lie the bones of the area's victims of the great famine.

The famine period of 1845 to 1847 saw Ireland's most noted wave of emigration occur, yet, long before the blight which took away the potatoes, the islanders were trickling out of Achill and hunting down work around the globe.

In America, islanders worked for eight years from 1817 onwards on the building of the Erie Canal, the slash of man-made waterway which links the Erie Lake at Buffalo to the Hudson River above Albany. When the islanders finished digging the big ditch they moved on to harvest the fruits of their work.

With the opening of the canal, Cleveland became a steel town, boats brought the iron ore down from Pennsylvania into the smelters of Cleveland. Achill islanders worked the barges, emptying the ore by hand ready for the belly of the smelter.

Thomas Johnston's own grandfather crossed the Atlantic twice for stints working there. Today, Cleveland is a colony of Achill. The islanders settled there and sent for their families and neighbours. They built Irish clubs, Irish pubs, and a GAA fabric at the American Irish club on the west side.

The people left Achill, but their hearts remained there. The churches of the island are filled with seats and pews bought with the contributions of Cleveland families. The schools have benefited from donations, a Cleveland scholarship exists in one school for the best Leaving Certificate student. A couple of years ago, Michael O'Malley, a journalist with the *Cleveland Plain Dealer*, went to the island and visited Thomas Johnston's classroom. He asked those among the twenty students to raise their hands if they had relations in

Cleveland. Seventeen of the children stuck their arms in the air.

Thomas Johnston remembers the visit he made to Cleveland in 1983, and the emotions which gripped him as, in this strange place, cousins, old neighbours and schoolfriends gathered around him. His arrival there was celebrated and long awaited. The welcome still stirs him.

'Our people, so many Achill people, all coming to greet you. I would be there still if I had accepted all their invitations. It was very moving, something which makes you appreciate how lucky those who stayed are. All those Achill people, first and second generation, starving for news of Achill. They get the *Mayo News* sent out every week. They know every single thing that happens on the island. I had a cousin who died here on the island a few years ago. One phonecall was made to Cleveland. The news got around the island from Cleveland people calling home to find out the details!'

They have spread out across the globe from this little west-coast island. The population here was never greater then the 6,000 recorded in the 1911 census. Emigration was even sponsored at one time. Fifty-nine Achill families were given assistance to emigrate to the US and Canada in 1883–84. Today, Thomas Johnston knows of Achill islanders involved in redevelopment work on the Falklands, in Gibraltar and Germany, and islanders who worked on the Olympics in Barcelona. Islanders everywhere.

'We are a people who will follow work. The Irish are like that and in Achill we were like that before anyone else was. We had to be.'

They put their faith in jobs around the world because their own land let them down so often. Into this century, they practised their version of communal farming, involving a system of transhumance known as 'booleying'. Communities of families or clachans (small hamlets) worked the land together as a huge co-operative.

The land was divided into three portions, an infield or tillage area adjacent to the clachan, an outfield used for pasture and, further away, poor upland grazing to which livestock would be sent for the summer months. The young would be dispatched during the summer to tend the cattle, returning only at harvest time.

This dispatch of the young to distant grazing areas was the element of the system known as 'booleying'. The testimony to its failure as a practice lies in the deserted village of Slievemore on the island – 128 houses left to go to ruin. They hope, one day soon, to turn Slievemore into something more than a crumbling relic to a failed farm system. The islanders have established a taskforce to bring an interpretive centre to Slievemore and bring people here to see a little of the poignant history of the last place in Ireland to practise 'booleying'.

Thomas hopes that 40,000 people a year could be attracted to the island. Tourism once boomed here, but Achill has fallen badly behind. The years before the turn of this century will determine whether Achill can get itself back on its feet.

Something is needed to bring people back here. It's Christmas now and the Scanlon Cup is in trouble. The St Patrick's team, from Lower Achill, hasn't enough players home this year. No team wants to field with a weakened panel and run the risk of humiliation. St Colman's, on the other hand, has such a clatter of talented players that it is suggested that it play the rest of the island for the Cup. Christmas has fallen awkwardly this year, the day itself being on a Monday. Emigrants have found it hard to build a holiday in Achill into their schedule. Some bickering and the shortage of players means the St Stephen's day preliminary round has to be scrapped. If the weather holds out the semi-final will be played on Saturday and the final will go ahead on Sunday.

The disappointment, however, has already set in for Catherine and Thomas and the handful of GAA people who keep the games going on the island. Things have been moving this way for some time. Emigrants have been finding it harder and harder to come home, no matter how much they might wish to. Some families have nothing left on the island to come home, too. It's a struggle to keep the fabric together. Next year is always a worry on Achill.

Catherine, though, has had a good year of it generally. Her fund-raising efforts for the club have been facilitated by the Senior team winning the Mayo Junior Championship for the fifth time. 'It's easy to raise the money when you win a championship. Next year will be hard. Even in a good year you never raise enough for all the stamps you buy and all the phonecalls you make from home. You wouldn't even begin to worry about that.'

The young team, which won the Mayo Junior championship, has been 'promising' since they were all youngsters.

'We matched Crossmolina all the way up,' says Catherine. 'It beat us narrowly at Under-Sixteen, beat us again in the Minor final of 1992 and beat us late in the Under-Twenty-One championship. Now Crossmolina is the county Senior champions and we are going to have to struggle to keep our team together for the Intermediate competition next year.'

A struggle it will be. Only four of the team who beat Lacken in the county Junior final this year live on the island. The rest come home from the cities of Ireland to train and play for Achill.

'The savage loves his native shore,' says Catherine. 'Thank God!'

They think the tide will turn, that Achill will reverse the trend of centuries and keep its children at home. The life here has qualities which no city can provide.

When Thomas goes to Dublin and stays with his daughter, the hustling city world assails him constantly. Getting into his daughter's house and having to switch off the burglar-alarm within two minutes, having to pay to park his car, is a culture shock. He thinks of Achill and wonders when people will begin putting a price on the quality of their lives.

'The world is getting smaller. We are only three hours' drive from Dublin now. Once it seemed a lifetime away. Our life here has so much to offer. The community, the air, the beauty of Achill, the links to the land and the sea, and our unique history. All we need is jobs. I am confident that the jobs will come. Then our people will come home.'

They will come. They have always done so in the past. They are a mobile people. Once for a while, back in the 1970s, there were three factories in Bunacurry. Catherine Joyce reckons that, for a while, up to forty per cent of her pupils were English born – the children of returned emigrants. Then the factories closed and she didn't have to take so much time explaining the Irish language to puzzled children.

It's 30 December. The road out to Achill from Westport onwards is thick with ice. The last town you pass through before hitting Achill Island is Tonragee. The town's name has a bitterly comic touch to it – Tonragee, Backside to the Wind. Today, the wind has ice in it.

On the little pitch, Davitt's Field (after Michael Davitt, founder of the land league and the man who got the bridge built to Achill) the ice around the goalmouths has refused to melt. The pitch is hard and dangerous.

They have played Scanlon Cup games in all weathers. Once in 1962, a Currane full-back scored two goals and a point against his own team from kick-outs which were lashed back at his goalkeeper in the face of a gale. Currane lost by three points. Today, though, the ice and the frost, and the disappointment at the numbers who have arrived home, have combined to deflate the spirit of the competition. Alice's Harbour Bar doesn't fill up early with spectators, no convoy arrives across the bridge, no old friends exchange shoulder-charges on the little field. Another little piece of Achill life is taken away.

'It's not an isolated thing,' says Thomas Johnston sadly. 'We can't separate the Scanlon Cup from the life of the community. It's a casualty of the problems we have right now. It was created for, and existed for, emigrants as a way of binding us together, bringing the island together, bringing out the pride in parishes. Now we can't sustain it because emigration has changed. We are sad. But we have other sadnesses. The death of the Scanlon Cup is just a symptom. We have to work to bring our people back to Achill. The GAA can hold a couple of people here, it can bring some people back, but it can't stand up to the problems we have. When we turn the corner, the Scanlon Cup will come back as part of the community. We go on in hope. We can't separate the GAA from the life of the people – one depends on the other.'

At the arrivals' carousel at JFK, the bundles of hurleys taped together for the flight attract little attention. The customs' men are used to seeing this sporting traffic pass through their gates all summer long. Hurlers saunter through and into America, where they are welcomed by beaming faces and whisked off to Irish homes in Yonkers, Woodside, Long Island and Riverdale, to be fêted and worshipped and then bundled out on to a hurling field above the Bronx to do their duty.

The Bronx: 'Special Games, special prices. $7'. The tatty notice, appended to the white-washed wall by the turnstiles, is the only suggestion that today is New York hurling final day.

It is late October and milky sunlight shafts down on to the silver carriages of the idle subway trains. The 1/9 line trundles from the southernmost tip of Manhattan northwards, right underneath Broadway, until the route terminates above ground in the broad bracing daylight at the heart of the Bronx, hard by Van Cortlen Park.

Those passengers, keeping their eyes peeled, who left between the stations at 238 Street and 242 Street on summer Sunday afternoons, will be startled by the sight of Gaelic games being played and fought out in the squat little compound that is Gaelic Park. It is an unlikely well from which to draw so much Irish passion but, here it is, a relic of 1950s' America, the old face of Irish emigration.

The Tannoy keeps up a constant chatter all afternoon. Play-by-play commentaries. A stream of announcements advertising benefit dances for emigrants fallen upon hard times. Lost children. News of forthcoming games. The results from home, read out in exhaustive detail from county Down to club level. They say that commentating here is one of the hardest jobs in sport. Nobody knows who half the players really are, nobody cares who the other half are. They have just come to see the stars imported from home.

Recent emigrant stock, those with the stubs of their boarding cards still crumpled in their back pockets, mix with first-, second- and third-generation Irish Americans on the makeshift stand. Those who are just dipping their toes in the great Irish American dream, intending to make some fast money and return home in triumph, queue at the bars with those who are broken and bowed by homesickness. They, in their turn, rub shoulders with those who have decided that this is their life – America with just a twist of home. Gaelic Park draws them all.

There are a couple of red-heads from Long Island wearing Jets' caps and half following the action. Their father, an O'Brien, came here from Meath in the early 1950s. They have never set foot on Irish soil, but every summer the games in Gaelic Park draw them along a couple of times. In September, they head into Manhattan on a couple of Sunday mornings to catch the All Ireland finals with the old man and his cronies on a big screen in a bar somewhere. They've never set foot in Ireland, but they've seen the games, drunk the beer, heard the talk, and watched the old man cry when Meath took an All Ireland or two in the 1980s.

It is hard to explain the role of Gaelic Park in New York-Irish life, hard to reconcile its existence with the new brand of emigrant which the last decade has produced. The mythology of the place plays tricks on the imagination. So many GAA stories are born in Gaelic Park, and inflated as they cross the Atlantic, that the sight of the place is a sore disappointment to most.

'Aye,' says John Byrne who came here from Kilkenny in 1936, 'there's always been a segment of Irish society who have come and said: "This isn't what we heard about". They'd steer clear. Then there would be others with a chip on their shoulder about Gaelic Park and the whole Irish scene as soon as they arrived. There have always been some like that, some who want to steer clear of Irish things once they were here. Gaelic Park is there for people who miss home and hope they might go home some day.'

John himself has had a finger on the pulse of the New York Irish community for most of this century. He has written for the *Irish Echo* since 1958 and has spent many summer Sundays in Gaelic Park commentating on games himself. He keeps in touch with home, too, is still immersed in the GAA. He hasn't missed an All Ireland hurling or football final in Dublin for over twenty years.

'The sad irony for those of us in New York,' says John, 'is that when things are good in Ireland we see so many good players leave New York and head home. We would be glad for any young fellow to be going home, but we know that the game they leave behind will suffer. When things are bad in Ireland, New York always has more to offer the GAA. People forget that when times are good.'

The GAA has been bound up with America for well over a century now, the bond knotted through nationalism, the want of cultural expression and the love of home.

Early in the Association's existence one of those brainwaves born out of the GAA's view of itself as a cultural lighthouse was born. The ancient Tailteann Games were to be revised on a five-yearly basis as a beacon to the Celtic World. Anybody with a drop of Irish or Celtic blood in them could attend or compete at this great gathering of the clans. In order to raise funds for this splendid endeavour, a team of Irish hurlers and athletes would depart for the United States on a fund-raising tour to gather the admission fees from the bedazzled emigrants.

In September 1888 a party of fifty sailed from Cork to the US, carrying with them 200 hurleys tagged with green labels and embossed with the words Gaelic American Invasion. In the States, a series of exhibition hurling games were played in Irish-hued towns such as Boston, New York, Philadelphia, Troy, Lawrence, Trenton, Newark, Patterson, Providence and Lowell.

Despite encountering some trouble with the weather, the five-week visit was a roaring success in all but the matter of fund-raising for the Tailteann Games.

By the time of this financially-unproductive American Invasion, the GAA was already putting down roots in America, The Wolfe Tones club had just been founded in Yonkers NY, and the Boston area already had four thriving hurling clubs. During the 'invasion', however, the games in Massachusetts were the only ones sufficiently well-attended to draw a profit.

The 'American Invasion' and its poor financial performance set the pattern for the GAA's strange relationship with its American emigrant communities. The games were well attended and the hurlers and athletes warmly received. The tour was promoted enthusiastically by the *Irish World* newspaper, the radical organ of one Patrick Ford, and yet financially the adventure was a disaster with free admissions being granted to large swathes of every attendance.

The travelling party had eventually to be bailed out in New York. Patrick Ford dipped into the 'Skirmishing Fund', a pool of money collected from Irish Americans for the purpose of funding the land-wars at home, and the bond between nationalist politics and nationalist culture became all the tighter.

Compounding the GAA's early problems with America and heralding future trends, was the unfortunate fact that, by the time the farewell banquet for the tourists was held at Tammammy Hall a couple of months later, seventeen of the Association's finest hurlers and athletes had opted to stay on in the US.

Several others members of the party came home to Ireland and subsequently returned to settle in the US. Among its number was one Willie Prendergast who had travelled to the US in 1888 as the newly-installed secretary of the GAA. He returned to America in the early 1890s and, after a period spent in the police force, went on to make a sizeable fortune dealing in real estate in Long Island.

It was Prendergast who was instrumental in securing a foothold for the GAA in New York city, and who purchased and equipped the first Gaelic Park. By the middle of the 1890s, New York had some twenty GAA clubs operating for the benefit of recent immigrants.

Of raw material for the GAA, there was plenty. The Irish in America had always either tugged against the pull of home or embraced it passionately. In the famine years, it is estimated that at least ninety per cent of those leaving the hard-pressed areas of Galway, Mayo and Clare were Irish speaking, seventy-four per cent of those leaving Cork spoke their own language. From the middle of the nineteenth century onwards Irish America was self-consciously Gaelic, a community trying to hold on to a vision of itself.

This cultural retentiveness represents something of a hidden history for the American Irish. Those who fled Ireland in desperation in the famine years and afterwards were driven only by a desire to escape hunger. In the New World they clung together and were slow to integrate. In exile, they found themselves homesick and experiencing a hardening of their nationalist feelings.

While many reluctant emigrants clung to the old ways, those who advanced quickest in the realms of politics and commerce were slow to concede that the impediment of a language barrier ever existed between the Irish and full and swift integration. This has become the official version, yet records show port officials of the time often complaining about the inability of entire shiploads of Irish emigrants to speak or understand English.

In 1852, the New York politician, David Nagle, urged his canvassers to approach Irish voters only through the medium of 'men who understand the Irish language and speak it fluently as it is the language best understood and most applicable to touch the feelings of the Irish heart, and is held in reverence by the great mass of the Catholics located in the eastern and mid-western states'.

Thus by the time the GAA had established itself and set off on its 1888 tour, it found Irish America most culturally receptive to the notion of any revival of Gaelic sports. The poor organization and planning which set the tour back, however, scared off many potential travelling teams in the years that followed, and it was the summer of 1934 before another official GAA party set foot in the States.

The 1934 tour, involving the All Ireland football champions, Cavan, was a huge success. The party was welcomed in New York by Mayor Furrillo La Guardia and played in front of 40,000 people in Yankee Stadium against New York. The tour proceeded successfully through New Jersey, Philadelphia and Boston before returning to New York for a return game with the home-side. This was marred by a spectacular and memorable shemozzle in the second half, when police, stewards and emergency services were required to clear the pitch of brawling spectators.

Since then, contact with the GAA branches in North America and Ireland has been sporadic. The 1950s, dark years of emigration at home, were boom years for the Association in New York. Hurling and football flourished. Top-quality players emigrated regularly. County teams followed in their wake to play the best that New York had to offer in competitions such as the St Brendan's Cup and the Cardinal Cushing Games.

By the 1870s, contact was institutionalized by the annual tours to America of All Stars footballing and hurling teams who would play the All Ireland champions in a series of exhibition games in various stateside venues. By the late 1980s this, too, had died out however, afflicted by the old failing on the financial front. Since then, the emigrant community has fended for itself in the matter of keeping the games going. Occasionally, the odd Transatlantic shouting match had broken out over player eligibility.

New York has paid little heed. Emigrants here separate their feelings about home from their feelings about the GAA. Talk of home is always doused in sentiment. Talk of the GAA as an institution is always tinged with resentment. For all New York's contributions to the GAA in the bad days, the GAA has continued to neglect and ignore its emigrants.

It has the feeling that, officially, it is on its own. Gaelic Park doesn't thrive as it once did, but it staggers on. The Irish have built themselves several centres in New York down through the years. Once there was a Celtic Park up in Sunnyside in Queens. That folded and two or three versions of the current Gaelic Park took its place. The GAA has been here in Riverdale, the Bronx, since 1928.

'Two men, Paddy Grimes from Offaly and Billy Snow from Cavan, had Gaelic Park for a while before the Second World War,' says John Byrne, whose experience of the place stretches back to the 1937 New York championship. 'They lost the license a couple of times for infractions and, after the war, John Kerry O'Donnell who had a few bars in New York at the time took over the license.'

The key to Gaelic Park existence is the bar and restaurant facility. The football pitch has traditionally come as an accessory. The autocratic O'Donnell was a figure of unceasing controversy within the GAA for half a century. As recently as the early 1990s, not long before he died, O'Donnell was found to be at loggerheads with the local GAA nabobs over his demand for a $300 fee for mid-week games in the park, $100 for meetings, plus a demand for forty per cent of gate receipts, plus the total take from the seating facility and advertising hoardings within the ground. GAA activity in the city almost came to a halt once more. Money has always been at the heart of the story with the GAA in North America.

Eventually, three years ago, economic reality meant that Manhattan College cut in ahead of the GAA when the city Transport Authority was looking for bonds from potential leaseholders. Now there is a softball pitch on one corner of the ground and Gaelic Park looks all the lonelier to the emigrant eye – less like home.

'John Kerry O'Donnell had Gaelic Park for many years,' says John Byrne. 'I think when he took over the lease and the license it was called Inisfail Park, but he changed the name to Croke Park. Pretty soon after that Dublin got in touch saying they didn't want the name Croke Park above a pub in the Bronx – the GAA, at home, was very anti-drink at the time – so John Kerry hit on Gaelic Park and there it has been ever since in one form or another.'

Gaelic Park. The pitch is so small that games must be limited to thirteen-a-side. At one end, the ground is bounded by the elevated parallels of the subway line, and all along the north flank of the ground the grimy railway sidings assist in creating the illusion of amphitheatre. When the commentator is giving his mouth a rest, and the Tannoy crackles gently with white noise, the clatter of the railworks and the occasional cursing of workmen blow across the field.

On the southside, there is uncovered seating for several hundred people on the flimsy-looking bleachers. Up at the west end, the ground is bounded by a steep and overgrown hill to which a sackful of sliotars are sacrificed every summer.

The New York Irish, who hunger so keenly after influence and power, have contented themselves with this surprisingly humble gathering place up here in the Bronx. At the entrance to Gaelic Park, the tricolour flies from the same pole as the stars and stripes, but the most startling reminder of the emigrants' tentative status here lies in that northwest corner of the ground where a great sand-surfaced softball diamond encroaches on to a large part of the pitch. The unenviable task of certain corner-backs and corner-forwards has been to play on two radically different surfaces in the course of the same game.

If the truth be told, between the diamond and the batting cage and the signs advertising the existence of the Manhattan College Jaspers, Gaelic Park carries more hallmarks of America than it does of Ireland.

Other accommodations with the New World have been made, too. The great green scoreboard underneath the railway sidings exists for keeping tally in baseball games, not hurling or football matches. With some ingenuity it is converted on Sunday afternoons for use during Gaelic games. It says now that Limerick are beating Westmeath by four points in the final minutes of this year's hurling final.

The game ends that way and there is some passionate cheering. Limerick is the power in New York hurling these times, phonecalls to Kilmallock and Patrickswell during the summer ensure a steady supply of good players throughout the summer.

Anthony Daly, the Clare captain, who just a few weeks ago spoke eloquently to nearly 70,000 people in Croke Park as the All Ireland wining captain, gets a slap or two on the back and is handed a can of beer when the game finishes. 'Thanks from Westmeath Anthony,' somebody calls. He makes his way from dressing-room to clubhouse. Home to Clarecastle on Monday.

The club house itself is a low-slung ramshackle affair, the cavernous interior consisting of a bar and a large dining hall. The walls are festooned with pictures of successful GAA teams from home, and with notices heralding forthcoming benefit events for ailing members of the Irish community.

Here, as among all emigrant communities, the GAA functions as a welfare and employment organization as much as a sporting body. There is a dance on Saturday night for the benefit of a man from the Falls Road who has fallen sick and can't work any more. The proceeds of other functions work their way back into the broader community also. On Sunday week, the Irish veterans of the Korean War, pensionless and forgotten, will be honoured and slipped a contribution. 'Ben Gilman will soon take their case to Washington,' says the script.

Irish people who keep their thoughts tethered to home gather here. The faces are ruddied or freckled and the atmosphere is light and social. It is October and the talk today is of the price of flights home at Christmas. Emigrants are solidly united in the view that, each festive season, they are fleeced by the airlines as systematically and remorselessly as turkeys are plucked by farmers.

Today, another New York championship has ended. The usual batch of big-name imports have disported themselves on the scrubby little field – Anthony Daly and Liam Doyle of Clare with fresh All Ireland medals in their pockets; Aengus O'Grady and Shane Dalton of Dublin; Joe Rabbitte of Galway. Graham Geraghty of Meath has just played in the Junior Football final. Next week, the football final takes place. Cars will be popping out to JFK to pick up James McCartan of Down, Kevin O'Brien and Robert McHugh of Wicklow, and Niall Cahalane and Larry Tompkins of Cork.

Life rolls on.

It has been a difficult year for hurling in the city. Back in the 1950s, New

York boasted some sixteen hurling clubs, all thriving with talent from home. At the beginning of 1995, that figure was down to six. Then in the spring, the Galway club ran out of breath and died having hurled in every championship since 1914. Only Westmeath, Limerick, Cork, Tipperary and Kilkenny are left to joust every summer now.

The death of Galway hurling has cut deep into the heart of the Irish community in New York. There is a certain loneliness, a heightened feeling of displacement in the knowledge that good hurlers can be fixed up with jobs in Ireland now, that the flow of grateful young talent has dried up, and that the city is coming to rely more and more on the trade in visiting star players jetting in for the weekend and being back at work in Ireland on Monday or Tuesday. The old consolation, which the lonely and homesick in New York made do with, was the thought that at least they were doing well, at least they were turning a buck. Now Ireland is booming and New York and its emigrants are left behind. The first-generation Americans, 'the narrowbacks', don't play much hurling. There is the odd exception – Seamus Carey is the name every-body mentions, but the odd exception won't fill a team or make a club.

Hurling is in trouble so, today, a few thousand Irish have gathered for the New York final to drink beer, renew acquaintances and watch a game together. No need for a wake as yet. History has taught them that when Ireland suffers again, New York GAA will be back on its feet.

The big names, whose exploits the emigrants have been reading about all summer long and whose faces they have been catching on cable TV, bring a lustre to today's proceedings which is contagious. But big names aren't the essence of what the day is about.

The traffic across the Atlantic may be a source of unceasing controversy at home in Ireland, but here they are just glad to see them and to welcome the players into their lives for the connection with home. There is a feeling of still belonging to the broader Irish community when fine young athletes are stepping off the plane every Friday to come and play in your jersey.

Sometimes the players come because they feel connections here in the US, a tightness between an American club and their own home-place. The Donegal club in New York is inextricably bound up with Castlehaven in Cork, for instance; the stars come for that sentimental reason, certainly, but mostly they come for the money.

Longer-term arrivals have changed their expectations as regards employ-ment, and the New York Irish are increasingly without influence as the world changes. They need the commerce with Ireland as much as they need Irish newspapers, letters and phonecalls home, and the Sunday night gatherings to watch footage of that day's GAA games, the get-togethers in the Hennessy Headquarters and the Characters bar and other Bronx watering-holes. They need it all just to keep sane.

'In the old days,' says John Byrne, 'a lad would be fixed up straight away. Donegal, Kilkenny and Mayo, all had influence with the Doormans Union or the Apartment Houses Union. (So much so, that the joke used to circulate about Donegal players hearing the referee's whistle and sprint to the sideline to hail a cab.) Tipperary was very much tied up with the Carpenters Union, The Six Oh Eight.

Other clubs had influence with the city unions. Northern boys would be given jobs on the huge fleet of cabs that Tyrone Taxis used to operate. That has changed. Guys come out here now who are trained for jobs that the GAA can't get them anymore. They don't always come to the GAA first.

They are glad to see the stars today, but players who have never been emigrants themselves can't know the heightened sense of Irishness which exile brings. Anthony Daly and Liam Doyle are heading out the gate already, their thoughts on home and the good night ahead. The stars come for the money and for the fuss that will be made of them. They are welcomed for the touch of home and their ability to make a displaced community feel as if it still matters.

New York, Boston, Chicago, Philadelphia, Cleveland, San Fransisco. A good player can see America and put a few dollars in his backpocket at the same time if he wants to. The emigrants are aware of that cold fact, but choose not to think of it. In Gaelic Park, Dilboy Field, and in the other little embassies of Gaelic games, the sport and old Ireland are still seen through the prism of the 1950s.

It's a sad trade, built on sentiment and loneliness, but time away from home is hard time for some. Gaelic Park wipes away the miles and turns back the clocks for those who dream that, one Monday, they might just hop on a plane out of JFK with the lads and head for the Ireland they left behind, just hop aboard and never come back here.

The Grand Union Canal slips by in silence at the dark side of the pitches. The towpath is treacherous with mud. At the far end of the pitches, there is a huge growth of bush and gorse. Plenty of hazards for a stray sliotar tonight, one careless puck and the ball could drown.

There are men playing rugby out on the two floodlit fields. In the darkness at the back of the Ealing Rugby Club Pavilion, two voices make a connection.

'Tis you.'

'Aye.'

'Jaysus. And I thought I was fucking late. I'm the first here.'

'Who ya trying to impress then, boy? Can't hurl, but you're first here. That'll do ya on Sunday.'

'Yerra. Fuck off. Like anything that could hurl in Limerick would be getting flown home to Limerick on Sunday, not to play for London in Roscommon.'

Tommy Harrell arrives presently. Just as well. The boys are getting restless, shuffling about in the cold of north London, talking about home.

'Anybody see *The Independent* on Monday?'

'No.'

'Christy Heffernan is still hurling for Glenmore.'

'Go on.'

'How old can that man be? How old? He was a Minor in 1974 I'd say. Jaysus he's still going. The paper said he was brilliant. I'd love to see him hurl again. Big Christy.'

'We'd love to see you hurl just once. Big waster.'

Jimmy Kennedy arrives, bearing nothing but apologies. He's done his leg in playing squash. Jimmy isn't sure if he'll be all right for Sunday. Bad news is that the doctor won't be down tonight.

'I'll take a look at the leg for you, Jimmy,' says Noel Hanley.

'Well, Noel, the way it is when it comes to fixing legs you'd best know a bit about what you're doing.'

'Like playing squash, is it, Jimmy? Complicated?'

'Come back to me when you've learned a bit about hurling, then I'll explain squash to ya.'

'Ah, lads, ah lads, ah lads.' Tommy Harrell claps his hands. He is standing in his vest and underpants half way through the transformation from civil servant to hurling coach. He loves listening to the chatter and the crack, but the county board is paying £40 a night to the rugby club for the use of the pitch. They can't stand here all night. 'Ah, lads, c'mon. We've work to do.'

Things get a little more serious. The concrete dressing-room floor is freezing underfoot. They get down to the business of changing quickly. The jerseys they pull out of their bags advertise their station in life. Sean Treacy's London Champions. A couple of faded green London jerseys. Two or three Down jerseys which they swapped and kept as trophies after they lost the All Ireland quarter-final last year. Otherwise just T-shirts and soccer jerseys and sweat-shirts.

They have come from all over the place – in the general and specific sense. Seven of them are from Tipperary; three from Limerick, two from Galway, one each from Offaly, Clare, Kilkenny, Wexford and Dublin. More specifically tonight, John O'Farrell has made the long trip from Northampton, Noel Hanley has come up from deepest Surrey, and a couple of the boys have been on the tube for two or more hours from East London.

Out on the rugby pitch, they make a fine stew of accents as they needle and encourage each other. When first they came here, there was a bit of trouble with the rugby boys – all these mad Irishmen driving sliotars over the heads of nervy scrum-halves. It took the rugby men a few nights to get used to the hurlers and their ash weapons, then another few nights before they stopped wondering at their skills and co-ordination.

Now, on this the twenty-first night of hurling training here, the hurlers can go about their business practically unnoticed.

This is their second year thrashing about in the backwaters of Division Three hurling. Some of the boys were born to better things than this. John Farrell and Mick Cunningham both won Under-Twenty-One All Ireland, playing for

Tipperary; both made the Senior grade for a while before emigrating. Dan McKenna hurled at Under-Twenty-One level for Limerick, and young Kevin Grogan picked up a Minor All Ireland playing at mid-field with Kilkenny in 1993. Back home, Brian Minoguie played for Clare in the Minor championship of the same year.

They were born to better things than Division-Three Hurling and it is beginning to show. First year out, they won six and lost two narrowly. This year, they have won their first three games, and play Roscommon this Sunday to go into the Christmas break unbeaten and on top of the league. Come next year, they could be playing Division-Two Hurling against some of the big guns. London needs that.

'C'mon, lads. Some of ye are messing. I know some of ye don't care, but c'mon. Get your heads right for this Sunday.'

London needs Division-Two hurling if only to justify its existence to the doubters and the begrudgers. Hardly a week goes by, but somebody in the GAA in London accosts Tommy and accuses him of wasting good money on putting a London team into the national league, hiving off free trips for twenty good hurlers and nothing for the rest.

'It's so unfair,' says Tommy, now animated about the whole business as the boys head off on their laps of the rugby pitches, 'so unfair. It costs about £15,000 year altogether to keep us going between the hurling and football teams. The amount of work that goes into that, you wouldn't believe.'

Tommy has an impressive array of figures to add strength to his arguments. The effort which the London Irish community puts into hurling and football is best represented by the teams which bear the city's name.

'Sean Hennelly gives £5000 a year towards the footballers, Gerry Feeney gives the same amount towards the hurlers. Then Setanta, the television crowd, give another £3000 to have their name on the jerseys. When we go away, people always do us favours. We went to Derry for the last game and got there for £84 return, and bed and breakfast plus evening meal for £28. We're not costing anybody. All these lads come from all over London with not a penny in expenses. Next year, if we're in Division Two and we have big teams coming out to Ruislip, then people will be glad of the London hurlers. We'll get good gate money as well.'

Ah, Ruislip! Out at the end of the Piccadilly line, you can trace your finger along the dark blue tube route until you come to the centre of Gaelic games' activity in London. Years ago, all the adventure happened down in New Eltham until somebody had the brainwave to sell New Eltham to the developers and put some work into Ruislip.

Now New Eltham's planning permission is trapped in the maws of local government, a million pounds had to be borrowed from Allied Irish Bank to put some bricks and concrete into Ruislip. £100,000 a year goes on repaying the debt. Until the New Eltham business goes to appeal with the Department of the Environment, and the eventual sale puts an end to all debts, money will be tight and London will have need of the big hurling names from Division Two making its way to Ruislip.

Tommy is an old-fashioned coach. In fact, at heart, he isn't a coach at all. Football captures all the glamour and all the numbers in London. There are forty-five football clubs compared to twelve hurling clubs. When applications were sought for the position of London football manager, six men wanted the job. Nobody put in for the hurling position, figuring that it would lead to nothing but heartache and abuse. So Tommy Harrell, as county secretary, took it upon himself to look after the lads. And here they are, top of the league.

'Into rows of three now,' roars Tommy. He seems half surprised that they do what he tells them. 'Pulling the ball along the ground. Accuracy is what I want to see, lads. Find your man. That's important, lads. Find your man. Oh, my God, Declan that's way off. What are you thinking of?'

It's cold now and Tommy walks around briskly, clapping his hands and shouting encouragement. Ostensibly his role is supervisory but, in reality, he is the warm central figure who pulls them all together. He barks out an order and is buried under a hail of wisecracks before everyone moves to obey. They are here not because anybody is afraid of Tommy Harrell, but because they know that Tommy Harrell cares.

He has been in London since 1960. He arrived not long after wrapping up his Leaving Certificate in New Ross CBS, planning to stay for a year perhaps before coming home. He fell in with a few Wexford men in a flat in Victoria, and found the crack to his liking. Before he knew it he was working for Middlesex County Council, playing hurling for Father Murphy's, married to a woman from Kildare and settled.

'Do you know what?' he says suddenly as the boys head towards the clubhouse and the great big sunken bath which will restore some heat to their bones. 'It's like I've two lives over here. I go to work and I talk soccer and rugby all day because that's all that any of them know about. The rest of my life is hurling then. Talking GAA and meeting GAA people. That's what's kept me happy in London.'

In many ways, he is typical of his generation. Tommy knows hundreds of people who swear they'd never have stayed in London, never have stayed sane if it weren't for the GAA and the huge network it lays down across the city.

'The GAA introduces people to work and accommodation. People meet their wives and their husbands through the GAA over here. If you fall on hard times, the GAA has funds to help you out. I go home every year and I hear people talking about the GAA as a sports' organization and a cultural organization. For emigrants, for people like us who have come away, it is those things but it's a welfare network as well.

'My phone is always ringing with people from Wexford telling me that so-and-so's son is on his way over, can I fix him up with a job and a room? I get on the phone, somebody else calls somebody else, and by the time the lad arrives he's set. If he can hurl, he's set long before that I can tell you.'

Tommy gathers up all the stray sliotars in a Metropolitan Police Five-a-Side Football bag. Equipment is always a problem. Some of the lads like their hurleys to come from Kilkenny, other like them from Tipperary. Tommy keeps a small stock of each in his house, and whenever any of the boys are travelling home he orders a bundle in the hope that these'll see him out to the end of the year.

The lads are washing and changing and preparing to head out into the London night. One of the boys is drinking a can of beer in the hope of winding Tommy up. A couple of others are smoking cigarettes, a relief from all that fresh air. Most of the others are chewing on the sandwiches and cakes which Tommy's wife, Deirdre, makes for the team every training night. Tommy carries the fare in on a big tray after every session.

Now to the cruel business of management. Tommy hates this part of the hurling cycle, the last training session before a big match. He beats around the bush a little.

'Now, lads, Heathrow on Saturday. Flight is at ten-past-four and I've had enough trouble getting the tickets out of the Board for any of ye feckers to go missing it. Be there at half-past-three and we'll have dinner in Roscommon at eight-thirty on Saturday. Travelling home to London straight after the game. Remember if the plane is late, Aer Lingus has to get you a taxi. Now the team, lads.'

He hates this. He tells the boys he picked the team sixteen times before he came to the right one, tells them that the boys who are starting have fifteen minutes to prove themselves before the men on the sidelines start warming up.

'Sorry,' he says to the lads who aren't picked. 'Ye're the most important part of any team. Now in goals, John Farrell, full-back line, Dan McKenna, Tony Lohan and Noel Hanley ...'

He calls out the team and subs. Liam Wyer has arrived late from work, just to say hallo and pick up the arrangements. Tommy has forgotten his name.

'Tommy. What about Wyer over there. Sacked, jacked and fired, is he?'

'Oh, Liam. Sorry, Liam. Sub on Sunday, Liam. Sorry, Liam. Didn't see you there.

'Lads. D'ya ever see anything like the face on Wyer standing there and the dribble of shite running down his leg? Nearly left behind, Wyer boy.'

Tommy hushes the lads down. He talks to them about London and hurling and the need for couple of points on Sunday. Lot of people depending on this. London hurling needs to be in Division Two. Want to see a bit of pride in the London jersey. This is inter-county hurling. This is what you dreamed of growing up – not in a London jersey, perhaps, but this is where you live now. You represent that and you represent our community. C'mon, lads, get your heads right.'

He finishes his speech and the lads give him the reward of a cloud of applause. His face brightens. The boys are grabbing their bags and heading out into the London air. 'See ye on Saturday, lads. See ye all on Saturday.'

'Ah,' he says, 'they're a good bunch, aren't they. Hurling people stick together. We're very close-knit in the hurling here. Just twenty-two of us going to Roscommon on Sunday. It's great for boys to be travelling home to play a few times of year. Makes it easier to be here. Not a penny in it for any of those boys. They won't be home till after midnight.'

He picks up his bag, his tray and his notebook, and heads out into the November air. Home to Harrow, his wife and children, and the two-dozen hurley sticks he keeps in the garage – the paraphernalia of his double life.

Boston on a cold January morning. Gerry Culloty picks up a fare in South Boston heading for Logan Airport. South Boston. It's a good guess that the accent will be Irish. The passenger sees Gerry's crew-cut, listens to the gregarious banter and the connections are quickly made.

'Do ya follow the football?'

'The Gaelic football?'

'Of course, the Gaelic football.'

'Yeah.'

'Do ya know Danny Culloty?'

'Yeah.'

'Nephew of mine. Captain of Cork. Danny Culloty, that's my nephew.'

Gerry likes to get across the Atlantic when time and exchange rates permit. For, a long time before he actually met the most celebrated Culloty of the entire clan, Gerry had been hearing about him. 'Danny talks the same way as you do, Gerry,' they'd tell him in their impenetrable southern Irish accents.

Finally they met, Gerry, the crew-cut taxi driver, and Danny the big-time Gaelic football star. 'Well,' says Gerry, 'if the big fella didn't talk just the same as the rest of them! Like trying to learn Japanese.'

The bones of the yarn are familiar to most everyone by now. It's over a dozen years since big-boned Danny Culloty began making an impact in inter-county football, breaking through, rather incredibly, on to the Cork Under-Twenty-One side before he'd even learned to kick a ball properly. These days, he says his accent is about fifty per cent west-coast American and fifty per cent Cork. To the Dublin ear, though, Cork is gaining ground rapidly. Rest assured that when Danny Culloty watches mid-field partners fetch down high ones, he doesn't embarrass himself in his excitement. 'Hey, all right! You're the maaaan! Way to go!'

Danny bears the same name as his father. Dan senior left Cork in the early 1950s keen for travel and adventure. He settled in San Fransisco, married a native and had two sons and a daughter. With his roaming done, the longing for home-place soon manifested itself. Dan had played football for Newmarket before shuffling off to the New World. When the need for wandering left him, it was stuff like football for the parish that he missed.

His two sons, Danny and Sean, were to learn to the fundamentals as a basic rite of passage. Dan, an emigrant father passing on a strange game to a couple of American sons. Tutorials took place on weekend afternoons in Golden Gate Park. Two brawny and athletic youngsters learning to catch against each other, practising their hand-to-toe solo runs, scooping the ball from the ground with their feet.

Practical lessons took place every other summer. Dan senior, a gardener on a west-coast golf course, would hoard his holidays so that every second summer might be spent in its entirety in Newmarket.

So every second year, his two sons would fit entire underage championships into their holidays at home. Gaelic football was a supplement to a normal American childhood. Danny played soccer, baseball and basketball. The Cullotys watched the San Fransisco Giants play baseball in their draughty stadium above the Bay. Danny's older brother, Sean, had the pro baseball scouts sniffing around for a while.

The Cullotys were raw, but they were game. San Fransisco's Irish community mustered three teams at the time. The Cullotys played with Shannon Rangers. Their fixture list was short. Two games with Sean McDermotts; two games with The Gaels; perhaps a game (the very first he can remember, in fact) with a visiting team from LA.

The standard equated to Junior football. Lots of hardy old football dogs on the way down, a few bright lights on the way up, taking the tough knocks along the way.

From the time he was fifteen, Danny Culloty was playing with men. Always a mid-fielder, big-shouldered and keen. 'Some people wanted to hit you, but there were plenty of people there to look after you.'

It was a good school by all accounts. The Culloty family moved home to Newmarket, county Cork, in August 1982, and the following summer Danny played with the Cork Under-Twenty-One side for the first of the three seasons he would enjoy at that grade. It was a remarkable elevation for Culloty to be playing among the cream of the county, with players who had been making their mark in front of county selectors for years and years.

'It was hard in one sense. My kicking was very poor. It was shocking – still is, some people would say. But the game in the US was played on a very small pitch in Golden Gate Park, a pitch called the Polo Ground. Any time you got the ball there was a lot of heavy physical contact, so you got rid of it quick. At home, in Ireland, you had more space and you were expected to use the ball better. I was still in the habit of hoofing it anywhere.'

Bob Honohan, the county Under-Twenty-One manager did a little work with the big fellow, although not sufficient to prevent him being dropped for the Munster final in 1983. It was Billy Morgan's influence some years later which was to make the crucial difference.

Young Culloty was no stranger to Morgan. In the 1970s when the All Star tours were still a carrot at the end of every season, the Cullotys were among the west-coast families who took in All Star players every autumn. Not just any old stars for the Cullotys either. 'Well, we had Ray Cummins and Jimmy Barry Murphy, and one Billy Morgan,' says Danny. 'There was always footballers around the house and always people talking football.'

One Billy Morgan. The man with the magic touch. He recognized the abundant promise in the big Newmarket player and sought to straighten out this Russian roulette business of his kicking.

'I don't know if Billy had to do the same with other players, probably not,' says Danny, 'but he took me aside and had a couple of long chats about the problem of my kicking. It was going all over the place like and was embarrassing. Billy forced me to lay it off soft and short all the time. I wasn't allowed to stray outside of the area between the two fifty-yard lines for a long time. I'd get the ball and lay off short passes to guys around me. They'd know to make themselves free.'

There was homework, too. Every evening involved inveigling his brothers-in-law or brother out to the Newmarket pitch to kick and catch for an hour or two. Head down, eye on the ball kicking. Travelling, head down, eye on the ball, kicking. On and on, until the self-consciousness went away and the accuracy arrived.

Football is a confidence game. It took him, he thinks, until about 1989 or 1990 to catch up with his team-mates. Through all the years of learning, he disguised his deficiencies. 'I'd lay it off soft always. I'd hardly ever go on a solo run, no matter how much space I had.'

It was a strange and curious devotion. Young Culloty would have been forgiven for resting on the ample laurels that a place in the local club side afforded him. Here was a guy who arrived from the States, aged eighteen, and he was holding down a mid-field spot for Newmarket. Over-achievement already. The red jersey of Cork, though, was a residual obsession from childhood.

'We'd come home every other summer and we'd play for Newmarket and be brought to see Cork play in the championship,' says Danny. 'We'd watch the All Star games in the States when the teams were over. We were Americans maybe, but Gaelic Football was what I always wanted to play. The family always talked about coming home to Ireland for good. It was something we always wanted to do, so it wasn't strange for us to think about playing for Cork. Sean, my brother, came home two or three years before the rest of us and was doing well at football. I knew that when I came home I wanted the chance to be as good as a I could be.'

So it was. Dreaming beneath the Golden Gate Bridge in San Fransisco through the tyrannous years of the great Kerry team, Dan Culloty senior could never have dreamed of such a streak of Cork successes, or that his younger son would be an integral part of it all.

Danny Culloty's Cork side have lost more All Ireland finals than they have won, but Cork has been the most consistent team of the post-Kerry era: seven Munster titles and two All Ireland wins.

Emigrant fathers dream of having sons like Danny Culloty who grow up to catch high balls in Croke Park. There have been some great nights in Hourigan's pub, in Newmarket, since the big man returned from the States. In 1991 and 1992, Dulhallo, the divisional team, won the county championship for the first time in fifty-four years, with Danny in mid-field. They've poured towards Croke Park almost annually, hoping that one of their own might give them another night of celebration.

In the Gaelic Parks of New York and Chicago, in Dilboy field in Boston and Kezar Stadium in San Fransisco, in Ruislip and in Glasgow, and in every spot where a few emigrants meet to tip a ball around and think of home, there are men and women dreaming of just such a scene. From miles away, big-boned boys fetching high catches on sunny days in Croke Park can seem like the essence of Ireland.

London hurling an old tradition

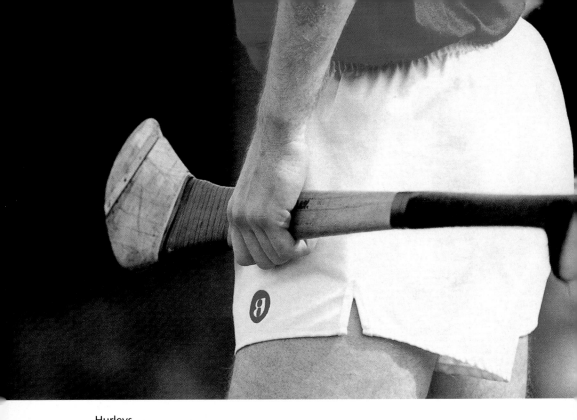

Hurleys

Another broken wand

Antrim v Clare, hurling league 1994

Clare v Galway, All Ireland semi-final

All Ireland final 1995, Clare fan with traditional bodhran

(*right*) Munster final day Thurles

Clare hurlers, All Ireland semi-final 1995, big day match parade

Tubber score the winning goal in the 1995 All Ireland hurling final

All Ireland final 1995, more Clare fans

After All Ireland final, Clare fans heading to Dublin for first time in decades

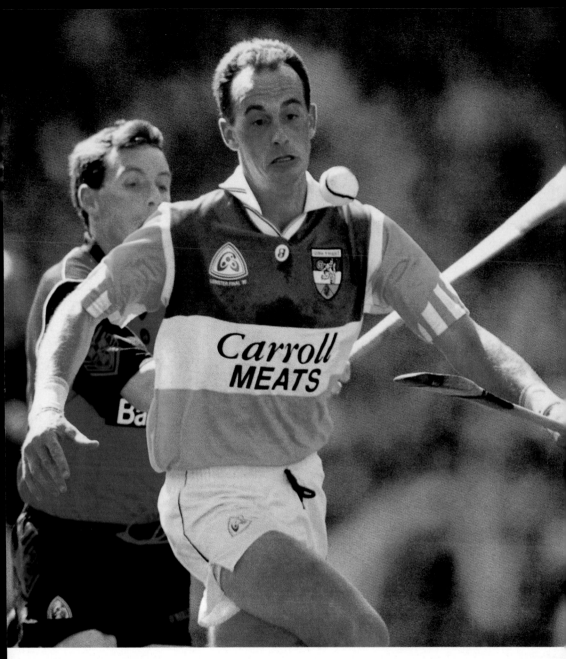

(*above*) Offaly v Down, All Ireland semi-final 1995

(*left*) Clare boys hurling

(*left*) Pre All Ireland training (*above*) Clare hurlers with Ger Loughnane
(*below*) Wexford v Offaly, Leinster championship 1995

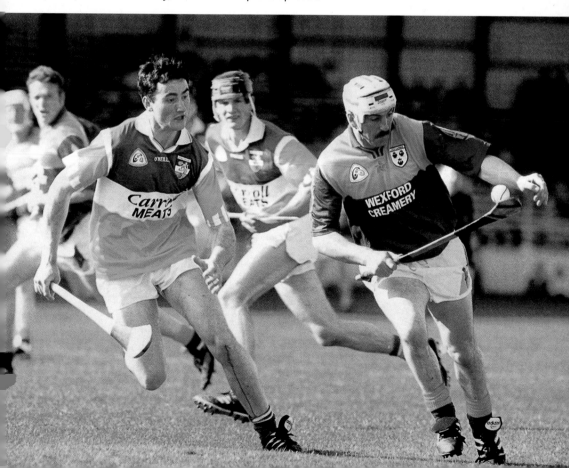

(*above*) Offaly fans day out (*below*) Croke Park people

CHAPTER FIVE

1969: Two lives

Antrim 1–8 Roscommon 0–10

Outside vocational schools' football and camogie, Antrim succeeded in winning their first All Ireland title at Croke Park yesterday, but they may still be wondering how they managed to beat Roscommon in this Under-Twenty-One football decider, considering the amount of possession they conceded to the Connacht champions during the hour.

Irish Times *15 September 1969.*

On this summer's evening, the sunlight has all but filtered away and the path to home is littered with burning cars. The Falls Road and, further on, a part of the lower Andersonstown Road have become chicanes of flaming vehicles. The concrete-and-tar surfaces are charred and oily. The ribbon of the West Belfast roadway is strewn with burning tyres and sharp flakes of shattered windscreen glass. Smoke thickens the air. To drive to Michael Colbert's house from Casement Park, you have to mount the pavement a few times. Michael hardly thinks twice about it. His mind is wrapped up in hurling and the Ulster final.

The posters tacked to the lamp-posts and pasted to the walls come in two varieties. The most common one looks like a traffic sign and depicts a bowler-hatted Orange Order man. The Orangeman's head is encircled by a red band, and a red line crosses through his face. No Orange Order marches through our piece of turf, thank you. This is the hurling season and this is the marching season. One community's history shall not infringe upon the others.

The second poster bears a simple legend: 'Clegg Out. All Out'. Private Lee Clegg, the British Army soldier who shot a teenager dead not far from here, has just been released from prison courtesy of the British Home Secretary. His short sentence and politically-motivated release is a strange and wounding insult for a community doing its best to hold a fragile peace together; a difficult test of nationalist discipline at a time when bowler-hatted Orangemen are seeking to march triumphantly through beleaguered nationalist areas. The evenings are warm and frustrations are boiling. Tonight, there are cars burning in West Belfast streets.

Michael thinks he has the Antrim boys just right for Sunday's game. They've put down the nights on the training field, from the frost-bitten sessions in early January, right through the dregs of the league campaign and into the lengthening evenings of spring. The lads from Dunloy, who make up the backbone of this young team, seem in good form. Dominic McKinley, who manages the side, has picked the right fifteen. Antrim will be going to Croke Park this summer, Michael thinks. Big time.

He's sure of it in fact. Tomorrow, he could be heading away on holidays to America with Monica, his wife, but the question just never really arose. So long as Antrim is in the championship, Michael will be in Casement Park putting them through their paces three or four times a week. Maybe he's making up for lost time. Maybe he's compensating. Who knows? Casement Park is where he belongs on summer evenings; where he's always dreamed of being.

To this day, he doesn't know why Dominic McKinley called upon him to train the team. One night he got a call from McKinley, a quiet and complex man from the tight little hurling community up in the Antrim glens to the north of Belfast.

'Can I come and see you?' asked Dominic.

'Aye, sure,' said Michael, baffled.

An hour later Dominic was at the door. Michael has a certain curiosity about how his name came to be lodged in Dominic's mind, but he's not the type to ask and Dominic isn't the type to offer explanations.

Michael Colbert knows that the buck stops with Dominic and the knowledge feeds his loyalty to the man. 'Hurling is in Dominic's bones,' says Michael, a victim of the same syndrome. 'We'll all be sore if we let him down on Sunday.'

If Michael doesn't have the boys right and fit on Sunday, it is Dominic who will feel the heat from the county board, from the people in the glens, and from the hurling folk of west Belfast. Antrim versus Down. Hurling means a lot here. Places. Politics. History. The GAA is a well from which people draw their pride and identity.

McKinley is a hero of Ulster and Antrim hurling, the pivot of the first Antrim team, the first Ulster team to play in an All Ireland hurling final since the 1940s. Michael fondly remembers that day in 1989 when McKinley's team made it to the final. It was a warm August afternoon when they beat Offaly in Croke Park. The beaten Offaly boys formed a guard of honour to clap the Antrim team from the field. It was a day no Antrim man could ever forget – tears and laughter, whooping and roaring. Sure, the whole jail erupted, man.

Niall Buckley is crying. Dermot Earley offers the lad a few whispers of comfort and drapes an arm around the player's shoulder. It's an evening in May and the boys in the lily-white jerseys are shell-shocked. As Niall Buckley and Dermot Earley stand beside each other in this dank dressing-room in Newbridge, the summer of 1995 has already been drained of its promise. On live television, Kildare has just been dumped on its backsides out of the Leinster football championship.

It was never meant to be like this for Dermot Earley. Or for Kildare. Both parties have been bulging with promise since the decade began. Kildare began the 1990s with a new high-profile manager, Mick O'Dwyer, from Kerry, at the helm, and the wind from an affluent and busy fan-club in its sails. Briefly it threatened to become the team of the decade. The lads trained forever, stringing together evening after evening of hard sessions until their fitness became the core of legend. They seemed about to steamroll all before them. A county starved of success for decades prepared the tickertape.

Kildare went to Croke Park in May of 1991 and filled the place with its hungry flag-waving fans and noisy enthusiasm. It lost a high-quality National Football League final to Dublin by a dastardly fluke of a goal. Nobody cared. The bandwagon rolled on into the summer and the fever-pitched anticipation of championship success grew by the day. And? First time out, Kildare went to Drogheda and caused a national sensation by losing to Louth. Every summer after that, brought a crushing disappointment with it. Mick O'Dwyer, the messiah on mileage, resigned in 1994, the silence of disappointment broken only by the clanking of the last wheel to break loose from the bandwagon.

As for Dermot Earley? Back in 1992, he had come home to county Roscommon. The man who wore the primrose-and-blue colours of the county with such easy grace and distinction had been away for too long. When times went bad and the county needed a saviour, Dermot Earley's name had always been top of the shortlist of saviours. Now, at last, the favourite son was home again to manage the county team. Driving to Roscommon from his home in Kildare a few times a week, he'd figure out ways to bring a little swagger back to the west.

In the end the job was too big for him, or he was too big for the job. Hard to say which, but, somewhere in the gulf between his own cerebration and his charges' raw-blooded awe of him, Roscommon's revival was lost. There were a few contributory hitches along the way, little fissures in the structures of authority which he could scarcely understand let alone countenance. His full-forward rang him up one day and asked to be excused from a Sunday league match because he was suffering from sore feet. Earley wished him a speedy recovery and was surprised to read in his Monday morning paper that the same full-forward had lined out in goal for a League of Ireland soccer team the day before. Changed times.

In 1994, he packed in the Roscommon job, walking away while his own people's affection for him was still intact.

So, for nine months now, he has been quietly working on this Kildare team. Kildare has been a home to him for quite a while, his son David wore the county colours at Under-Eighteen level and now hovers on the fringes of the Senior team. Here, in Kildare, Dermot knows how to tune into the whispers regarding form and favour on the local club grapevine. Things have been quiet, the hype has gone, but hopes have been high.

Now the team has crashed in flames on a May afternoon, losing to Louth again on an afternoon when the whole country has been watching. Nobody told him there would be days like this. He offers a few quiet words of hope and consolation to the lads and braces himself to face the media. Sometimes a man can miss the Lebanon!

Maybe hurling is bred into Michael Colbert's bones, but, many summers ago, he made his name wearing the county colours as a footballer.

All the tight little back-to-back houses in Bombay Street where he grew up were burned to the ground in the same summer, the summer that Michael won his All Ireland medal. It was 1969 and nationalist communities from Belfast right across to Derry were announcing that they had had enough of the bad times. Housing, employment, politics, all the traditional areas of discrimination, were being held up for examination. Growing up in Clonard, on Bombay Street, was to know the insulating effects of a community which held together as tightly as a closed fist, and to know also the sharp edge of bigotry and discrimination.

Bombay Street backs on to Cupar Street which touches the little hard-faced streets which run to the heart of the Loyalist Shankhill Road. In times of trouble, these little streets are the funnel for violence. Bombay Street and Cupar street always bear the brunt of Unionist furies, by virtue of being the first nationalist-occupied areas a rioting Loyalist mob will arrive at. The combined weights of history and geography, and religion, press down on the small community, always have done.

Since the turn of the century, there has been a thriving monastery set here in Clonard, founded in a small church with a corrugated iron rough – the 'tin church' – and its more sturdy successors have traditionally lain at the heart of West Belfast's spiritual life.

This stretch of nationalist Belfast blooms westwards from the city centre out, beginning with the Lower Falls, or the Lower Wack as residents know it, and shifting south-westerly down through Ballymurphy, Turf Lodge, Andersonstown and Lenadoon. Clonard, however, bucks the geographic trend and juts upwards from all this, running north-west between Dunmore Street and Cupar Street until its progress is halted by the canyon of understanding at the Shankill Road. History weighs out in different measures here.

Street names around here make jagged juxtapositions with local politics. Bombay Street, Kashmir Road, Lucknow Street, and others, took their names before the fading of the British Empire and commemorate the Indian Mutiny. Elsewhere around here, streets are variously named for the Crimean War and the Balkans. (Strangest of all, perhaps, is Amcomri Street, built with contributions from the American Committee for Relief in Ireland in order to rehouse evicted Catholic families in the 1920s. The street takes its name from an acronym of the same committee.)

The GAA has old roots here. The first hurling club in Ulster, Tir na nóg, had its beginnings here in west Belfast, playing in Shaun's Park, which later became McRory Park, which later still ceased to be a GAA park and became a British army base.

In 1920, for instance, Loyalist leaders became exasperated by the recent election of twelve Labour members (one of whom topped the poll in the Shankill Road) to the city council. Edward Carson, in particular, feared that a new wave of class-consciousness among Protestant workers would drive Loyalist constituents towards Socialism or, worse still, towards Sinn Fein. Carson raised temperatures by giving a speech to an Orange Rally at Finaghy, just outside Belfast, where he attacked both Sinn Fein and Labour and told the British Government that: 'We will take the matter in our own hands – and these are not mere words. I hate words without action'.

Not many days after Carson's speech, the Divisional Commissioner of the Royal Irish Constabulary was shot dead in Cork one month after assuring a group of his men in Listowel, county Kerry: ' – no policeman will get into trouble for shooting any man'. With Carson's incitement still fresh in the memory, the occasion of the RIC man's funeral in Banbridge county Down triggered off a pogrom in the workplaces of Belfast. The extremist Belfast Protestant Association drove all Catholic workers from the two shipyards, from the four engineering works, from the halls of the major linen manu-facturers, and the yards of the building firms. Some 11,000 catholics were driven from work.

Not surprisingly, rioting ensued and Bombay Street and Cupar Street burned for the first time. A religious Brother and five civilians were killed by a mob in the monastery in Clonard. Michael Colbert's grandmother was burned out of her home in Cupar Street during that summer of 1920, just three years after losing her husband to the British army. It isn't hard to understand how events have chiselled personalities and sculpted lives here. The last IRA man hanged (officially, that is) in Belfast Prison was a Bombay Street man, Tom Williams. His body still lies within the prison.

Forty-nine years after Bombay Street burned for the first time, the summer of 1969 brought more grief. When the Loyalist backlash against the Catholic civil rights movement began in earnest 1,505 Catholic families were forced from their homes around here in the space of three months. History came echoing down the road. On Friday 15 August 1969, Michael Colbert's granny was burned out of another home – this one in Bombay Street.

'We had two family homes burned out the same night,' says Michael. 'Both my grandmothers' homes. In Belfast, you grow up in your grandmother's house. That's the way it is. Oddly enough, I had a granny and a grandmother who lived six doors apart. I was reared in and out of their houses and schooled in St Gall's a stone's throw away. I went down Bombay Street on the Saturday afternoon and there was nothing left. Smoke, smell and nobody. Granny had wanted me to go down in the morning, but there was still sporadic shooting. By the afternoon, the street was as quiet as a ghost town.'

Michael remembers the tense tough times that followed. He was nineteen, a talented footballer, and life had suddenly become serious.

Earlier that summer, life seemed more carefree, young men a little more feckless. He remembers, for instance, missing the Ulster Under-Twenty-One final against Down just to go hitch-hiking and hostelling around Ireland with Monica, his girlfriend. It was easy then, people always gave lifts to strangers. So he just took off without a word to the team or to Tommy Hall, the manager. He was in Dublin on the weekend that Antrim beat Down by a late score. Michael went into Eason's on O'Connell Street on the Monday morning, bought the *Irish News*, and noted approvingly that his team-mates had won their Ulster final. Something good to go home to.

However, when he arrived back in Belfast, the city had become fraught with ancient anxieties. Bombay Street burned in mid August. By the time Antrim was due to play its All Ireland semi-final against Cork on the last Sunday in August, the country was buzzing with talk of troops massing at the border, of all-out war. It was deemed too dangerous for a Gaelic football team to travel by train or bus from Belfast to Cork, so it was arranged with the help of the Taoiseach of the day (former Cork footballer and hurler Jack Lynch) that Aer Lingus would fly the team down from Nutts Corner to Cork.

Flying! Free – *gratis*. A team of twenty-year-olds being flown the length of the country to play a football game. Dizzy confusing times. The Antrim boys were fêted and treated like kings down in Cork – saturated in glamour. In the Athletic Grounds on the Sunday afternoon they won with the last kick of the game. Michael Colbert, benched for the day after his unscheduled holiday, came on as a sub and played well. Din Joe McGrogan scored two goals. Gerry McCann had the winning point in injury time. Strange days, indeed.

The St Gall's club had moved its clubhouse out of Bombay Street and down to Milltown by the summer of 1969, but the club still drew its players from the little streets all around the area.

Michael came from an old St Gall's family, a Bombay Street family. His father had played for the club and his uncle had been club secretary. A brother of Michael's had died as an indirect result of playing for the team. One day he got a bad leg injury, but, it being the fag-end of a season, he paid no attention to it. The wound turned ugly as it healed and eventually turned cancerous. Michael remembers, two years later, the family bringing his big brother, Patsey, home to die – home to die from a football injury that turned bad. Michael was seven and packing a headful of questions. Patsey's death became something of a taboo subject within the family. Michael kept his questions to himself.

Michael hurled and played football. He can't remember a time when he didn't do these things. Playing hurling and football was how the community drew its breath and took its ease. Bombay Street was a Republican area, but for those growing up in the early 1960s the IRA was just an abstract borrowed from recent history. Nobody could have known that before the end of the decade, the street would have been burned to the ground at the initial stages of a grinding twenty-five-year war.

Here he was, though, on a Saturday morning, shortly before the All Ireland Under-Twenty-One semi-final, walking up what remained of Bombay Street, with his whole perspective on the world suddenly and strangely jarred. He poked around in the smoking ruins of the old house. Nothing to retrieve, except a few pots and pans. Two men appeared in the frame of the doorway, alerted by the clinking of metal in the scullery.

'Who are you?' demanded one. 'What do you want here?'

'You know me as well as I know you,' said Michael. 'I was reared here.'

'Ach, it's you. Sorry.'

So it went that Saturday morning. Frantic bewildered people casting around for some sense of purpose. Two men keeping looters away from the smoking ruins of their old street; Michael Colbert picking out the pots and pans from the debris of his old family home; an All Ireland semi-final just two weeks away. 'Very formative,' says Michael.

He could be the poster-boy for positive thinking. Matinée idol looks and a stride that knows no hesitation. He has a handshake which would bruise a statue; a mind so steeped in army ways that he must dream in khaki. He processes options and makes decisions with a computer's efficiency. Click. Whirr. Click. Whirr. Click. Whirr.

In life, he has factored in football as part of the big equation. More important than mere leisure, less important than breathing maybe, but in overall terms just as essential. Just as essential.

It could scarcely have been any other way for Dermot Ealey. Reared in a fold of the Roscommon countryside, in the lyrically named little townland of Gorthaganny, Gaelic football was in his bloodline.

The wee place had no Gaelic football club when Peadar Earley moved to Gorthaganny to teach school in the mid-1950s. So Peadar founded a club and called it Michael Glavey's after the young man who died trying to blow up an RIC barracks in 1920. Peadar's son, Dermot, became the club's greatest star. If Gorthaganny shows up on maps it is because Dermot Earley, the schoolteacher's son put it there.

A lifetime within the GAA, Dermot Earley organizes his football memories in a clear and precise manner – essentials to the front, other stuff to the back. The detritus of that day in 1969 has long been permitted to slip away, there were better football days before and after. The nuts-and-bolts of the game remain on file, however.

Asked out of the blue, what traces of 1969 remain, he pauses, then from somewhere in the back of his mind, whisks a concise account of exactly why Roscommon lost to Antrim in 1969.

'I remember the goal scored against us by Andy McCallin. It was kind of a deflection, the ball palmed past the goalkeeper by one of our defenders. It was a good shot, but these things seem worse than they actually are when there is a deflection.

'It wasn't a great day for the weather. A bit wet. I remember getting a whole series of free kicks towards the end of the game when we put pressure on Antrim. We didn't convert any of them. They were all difficult kicks which dropped in close to their goal, but which they cleared. I remember it as if it were yesterday, the frustration of all that happening. I can still feel the frustration of not converting those free kicks.'

His recall is remarkable – Andy McCallin's shot *was* deflected to the net by the palms of Wille Feeley. The final minute of play was recorded by the *Irish Times* as follows:

With a monopoly of the midfield play, due to Dermot Earley and Mick Cox, Roscommon were presented with three feasible chances for the equaliser in the last minute but the sequence of misses read: John Kelly's fifty two yards free scrambled away for a fifty. A Mick Cox fifty just wide and then with the second last kick of the game Mick Freyne was barely wide with a thirty five yards free –

In Croke Park that afternoon, Antrim and Roscommon played their final as the meat in the sandwich of a triple bill of games. Wicklow beat Kerry in the All Ireland Junior Football final to start the day off. More significantly, Offaly beat Cavan in the replay of the All Ireland Senior Football semi-final. Cavan, who had won thirty-two of the previous fifty Ulster championships, haven't been back to Croke Park on a big day since.

The baton was changing hands in the north and in Connacht. Despite their narrow defeat, it seemed that the auguries were good for the Roscommon team. Having watched its triumphalist neighbour, Galway, swan to three All Ireland titles in succession in the mid-1960s, the county had to endure the sight in the summer of 1969 of a Roscommon Senior side scoring just one point in an entire championship match with Galway.

Earley was the leader of the Under-Twenty-One team beaten by Antrim. Already a Senior inter-county player, he had won an All Ireland Under-Twenty-One medal playing with Roscommon three years earlier, and also possessed a Connacht Minor championship medal won with Roscommon in 1965. He had won his second Railway Cup medal playing for Connacht earlier that year. Earley was the greatest prospect among the waves of youngsters emerging in Roscommon football at the time.

He had made his Senior début in 1965, 'not old enough and not strong enough, but keen enough' when he was still a seventeen-year-old with another year's eligibility ahead of him in the Minor grade. That year, he made a little piece of history becoming the first player ever to represent his county in Minor, Under-Twenty-One, Junior and Senior football in the same year. High expectations in Gorthaganny.

In 1965, too, he joined the army, shifting away from Roscommon to the broad green acres of the Curragh to put flesh on a boyhood dream. Some years earlier he had chosen to attend boarding school in St Nathy's of Ballaghdereen on the Roscommon-Mayo border. The decision was predicated purely on the fact that Nathy's had a luminous reputation in the west as a good Gaelic football school, having been beaten in the 1959 All Ireland final by St Joseph's of Fairview. With his football-schooling taken care of he turned his thoughts to a career.

'It was the publicity that the army received when I went to secondary school that swung my mind. The United Nations' peace-keeping trips to the Congo had begun. There was an air of mystery about the whole thing, and this word balooba (a tribe upon whom peace was being imposed) suddenly entered Irish culture. I remember a photograph of all the officers of the battalions being hosted by the President Eamon De Valera. That photo was posted on the front of the paper and I can still see it clearly. I stared at it for weeks.

'Then JFK died in 1963, and Jackie Kennedy invited the Irish Cadet School to form the guard of honour at his graveside. That got huge publicity in Ireland. I saw it on the television, and it just added to the whole mystique and glamour of the army for me.'

Lastly and inevitably there was the hand of the GAA.

'Jim Fives, who played hurling for Waterford, Roscommon and Galway, was the training officer for the FCA in our area. I knew him well from the GAA in Roscommon and, one summer, I went to FCA camp with him. I remember loving the organization and the order of it all. They had a good football team, too, which attracted me. I joined when I was fourteen, which wasn't legal but was common enough. I didn't even bother applying for anything else when I left school a few years later.'

Two decisions: the direction of Dermot Earley's life was set.

Michael remembers little about the final, just the oppressive noise of 51,000 people in Croke Park, the dreaded drudgery of being substituted late in the game, and the constant threat from the lowering clouds. Another St Gall's man, Gerry Pollock, took his place on the pitch late on when Roscommon was starting to turn the screw. Antrim held on, the third game in succession which it had won against the tide.

That's the residue of the great day which is left now. In the intervening years, he's had other things to think about and the embers of his footballing memory need plenty of poking before they get glowing.

He remembers Liam Boyle getting the cup and the team trekking out to a hotel in north county Dublin as the evening darkened and a slight sense of anticlimax set in. The following morning the team was taken on a tour of the Guinness factory and fed free drink before the lads high-tailed it back to Belfast. That Monday evening the Antrim boys arrived home to the city in triumph. Well, home to half the city in triumph. The other half was indifferent. There was a ceilidh (informal social gathering) in St Theresa's Hall. The entire

GAA population of the city was present, correct and emotionally charged. Antrim football was on its way at last.

On the edge of the 1970s, Ulster seemed destined to control Gaelic football for years to come. Down had won the 1968 National Football League and All Ireland championship. The province had won the 1968 and 1970 Railway Cup competitions. Derry had won the 1968 All Ireland Under-Twenty-One championship, and now Antrim had succeeded them as champions. Things were bubbling at schools' level also. Antrim had been the 1968 All Ireland Vocational Schools champions. St Malachy's and St Mary's, both from Belfast, went to successive All Ireland Schools finals (The Hogan Cup): in 1970 and 1971 with St Mary's winning in 1971.

In the summer of 1970, Antrim played in the Ulster Senior Football final at Casement Park. Eight of the previous year's Under-Twenty-One team played in an Antrim side that lost by four points to a Derry outfit containing seven of that county's Under-Twenty-One team from two years previously. It was a tussle of two strong young teams who looked set to dominate football in Ulster and beyond. Then the war began decimating northern football in general and Antrim football in particular. Casement Park staged its last Ulster football final in 1971. In 1972, the pitch itself was occupied by the British army for an entire year.

In the twenty-five seasons since the Ulster final of 1970, Antrim have won just four Senior Football championship games, the last victory coming in 1982. Despite Belfast being the largest centre of population in the province, no Antrim school has made an impression on the McCrory Cup provincial football competition for schools, apart from St Mary's Belfast whose last triumph came in 1986.

'Back in 1969, we thought that there would be a Senior All Ireland coming along in a few years. Instead the whole thing just disintegrated. There's hardly anything left of Antrim football now except the pride. The GAA is totally embedded in our culture here, but I'm afraid for it. We haven't had the success and, meanwhile, the working-class streets and communities that the GAA was built on in Belfast are breaking down. Young working-class people have less identification with the GAA. People are moving out of the Lower Falls and areas like that, moving off to the suburbs.

'The relationship between the GAA and the social classes is a very complex thing. There is always a trade off. In the old days when I was growing up, the GAA had its strength from the community and from the people involved in education who taught the games as part of the culture. The GAA has been a victim of the political situation, not just in terms of harassment of players, and trouble with pitches and club houses, but right down through the sociology of the thing.

'Over the last twenty years the policy in this part of the world has been for the authorities to load working-class children, in nationalist areas anyway, into big poor-quality schools. Kids lose the sense of place, teachers don't want to know, and soccer is the lowest common denominator in terms of it being easy to play and organize. Kids put coats down and play soccer because all the pressures make it easy for them to turn to soccer. The council reflects the political situation. By and large, it builds soccer pitches in council parks not GAA pitches. I'm happy to see kids playing soccer, but it's a shame to see part of our identity being eroded. The political situation and the education policies imposed on us have diminished the GAA as part of the process of marginalizing the working-class here.

'There is the trade-off, then, with the universities. More kids go to third level now because of the grant system and because the authorities feel the need to build showpiece colleges. The GAA has never been stronger in northern colleges. That reflects a trend. People move to the suburbs and become more middle-class in their outlook, the GAA gets stronger in colleges than in working-class schools, the whole organization can tilt away from the working-class, community-based structure. If the GAA goes that way, nationalism will follow. Nationalism is becoming more like it was in the days before 1969. People are talking about culture, and the games, and the language. Nationalism spreads out culturally and the GAA spreads with it, but people become less passionate about it and less political about it.'

Times have been hard, pickings have been lean, and the GAA people in the hardest hit areas turned in on themselves for a long time. Soft southerners never could get a grasp of the realities of life in Belfast, and Derry, and other places, whose names became synonymous with bad news.

'There hasn't been success here in Antrim, but the GAA has survived because it is part of our identity and we have struggled to assert our identity and to hold on to things which demonstrate our identity. Because of our history and our politics, I would say the GAA means more to people here in west Belfast than it does to people anywhere else in the country. I would also say that here in west Belfast we are probably the most highly politicized community in Western Europe. Those two statements are linked. We've depended on the GAA for political reasons as much as anything else.'

Becoming politicized. Michael Colbert remembers that, quite early in the 1970s, he changed his habits when travelling to hurling games. Instead of carrying his hurley freely in his hands as he had done from childhood onwards, he tied his boots to the bottom of the stick. On a dusky Belfast evening, a hurley could look sufficiently like a rifle to justify somebody taking a shot at you. A pair of dangling boots removed one excuse.

'Subtle things changed – stuff like that. You adapted and got on with life.'

In 1973, his employers in the Civil Service offered him promotion and the chance of a move to England. Belfast and the GAA had its pull, however. Depression hadn't yet set in on the inter-county scene. Michael had bought a house. He declined the move and, not long afterwards, took a job with St Patrick's training school.

'Sometimes I think that if I had done this or that, or if I had lived on the other side of my street, life would have been different. You create your environment and you are a product of it as well. You choose the GAA for a reason. You shape it and it shapes you. I didn't want to leave Belfast. And there's no point in having regrets about that.'

Football marks the boundaries of time. A year ends when championship football ends. After that, time is in thrall to the demands of the grey quotidian and young men have only the following season to look forward to. Training, on some field consisting only of muck, puddles and crunchy hoar frost, starts a little earlier each year. Rumours arrive from across the border concerning new outposts of physical fitness and self-discipline being reached in other rival camps.

'P.J. has been off the drink since Christmas. They did eighteen nights' running up until last Thursday.'

Football fences off the significance of each year. Take some Roscommon summers that Dermot Earley knew.

The team reached a Connacht final in 1970 and embarrassed themselves in the company of Galway, having surprised Mayo earlier in the summer. Shame, but worse to come. Lost to Sligo the following summer. Still hard to believe. Sligo? At home? It happened. GAA history seemed to crowd in against them. On Easter Sunday of that year, in the Whitla Hall in Belfast, the GAA dropped the decades-old ban on its members playing 'foreign games'. Sligo was perhaps the most dramatic beneficiaries, filching two stars, David Pugh and Gerry Mitchell, from the soccer boys at Sligo Rovers. So Sligo beat Roscommon.

That was 1971 and the football world was leaving Roscommon behind. Andy McCallin of Antrim won an All Star that year, in the company of Galway and Mayo men and a Sligo man. Dermot Earley had been playing Senior inter-county football for seven years by then and still not so much as a provincial medal.

That changed in 1972. Roscommon beat Mayo in the Connacht final on a day when the sun was splitting the stones. The next month the team travelled to Dublin for the All Ireland semi-final and got a tutorial from Kerry in the business of big-time football. Being trimmed in Croke Park was distressing, but at least the freightload of talent that had been delivered at the doorway of the Roscommon Senior team was beginning to turn a profit. The county rubbed its hands.

So it went. Many of the bright young things whom Dermot Earley had grown up with in Roscommon football had too much of the county's hopes thrust upon them too quickly. They were neither strong enough nor experienced enough to achieve their potential. After the trip to Croke Park in 1972, the following three seasons were losing seasons. By the time Roscommon took its exit in the 1975 championship, having lost to Mayo, Dermot Earley had taken the decision to put his career in front of football for a couple of years and accept a posting abroad. The Middle East beckoned.

'Going away is part of an army career. From Ireland, battalions had been going to the Congo. When this stopped, the Irish went to Cyprus. When this stopped, there was a short run of trips to the Sinai Desert. At the time when I was selected there were only observers going overseas. I was lucky to be going to the Middle East.'

Dermot Earley found himself in the Golan Heights policing the war-strewn strip of volcanic rock which stood between the Egyptian and Israeli armies. The United Nations Troop Supervision Organization deployed its observers on little outposts across the Heights, each observation post being manned by personnel on four day shifts. Between the heat, the loneliness and the tension that the possibility of danger brings, it might have been possible to forget Gaelic football entirely for a while, but Dermot Earley wasn't made that way.

The GAA has a pull as definite and as constant as gravity. For those reared within its pale it is a constant in life, even when involvement has eased off and interest is low. To have played football or hurling at almost any level is a social passport. It was impossible for Dermot Earley to leave the country without having an entire county fret about the date of his return. The question of never playing again didn't exist in his mind, wasn't really allowed to exist, by himself or the Roscommmon GAA world.

'There was this immense sense of sadness about the prospect of missing football. I had received an injury playing at home for Michael Glavey's early that year and it was bothering me. It seemed to heal for the championship in 1975 against Mayo. I was picked in the half-forward line, but was substituted before the end of the game. I blamed it on the knee, although I knew I was playing badly. I accepted then that a break or being away mightn't be a bad thing. I was on my way regardless, so it didn't matter what conclusion I came to, yet I framed the trip in terms of Gaelic football and what its impact would be on that.'

At home, Roscommon and indeed the rest of Connacht were just beginning to suspect that perhaps the future wasn't as silver lined as the past had been. Dublin and Kerry had pulled a sneaky trick in an amateur game and improved their fitness to professional level. They had better, faster and fitter players. Bigger, too. In 1975, Sligo escaped from Connacht only to get mowed down in Croke Park by an absurdly fit and fast Kerry team. The west, which was becoming a backwater economically, was beginning to have doubts about itself in other respects.

'Going out to the Middle East, I made up my mind that I would play football when I came back. That was what I was coming home to Ireland for. I kept in touch with results and events through letters and the odd phonecall. The army had a system at the time of informing all those who were abroad of events at home by means of a newsletter which always gave the GAA results. That was my contact.

'The newsletter on Sunday night was always of particular importance to me.

I would receive a result and be able to picture the ground the game was played at and the colours of the teams, but I would have to wait for a letter from home before the details of a game could be filled out for me. I passed a lot of hours imagining games at home, many Sundays wondering how Roscommon was getting on.

'There were guys at home, GAA men like Donal Keenan, Michael O' Callaghan, Shay Gannon and others, who would write and tell me what was happening in great detail. It was always a case of being physically in the Middle East with my mind on Roscommon and football for big parts of the day.'

Michael Colbert was arrested for the first time in the summer of 1977. He was held on a three-day warrant and badly beaten up in Castlereagh Interrogation Centre, in Belfast, before being released. Castlereagh was just reaching the peak of its reputation as a centre for oppression and brutality.

Michael was working as a social worker in St Patrick's School at that time, a job which brought him in and out of RUC stations on a regular basis. In a naive attempt to demonstrate how trustworthy and upstanding he was he told his interrogators about the nature of his work. The news that a GAA man from Bombay Street was flitting in and out of its premises sent alarm bells ringing in the RUC. On the night before his release Michael was informed that he would be 'dead or out of the country' within six months. Either way, he wouldn't be doing the same job.

Bruised, shocked and unnerved he arrived home to find Father Denis Faul in his living-room. At that time, Faul and another Catholic priest, Raymond Murray, were in the process of compiling a report which would become The Castlereagh File. The report would cite 1,612 allegations of brutality relating to Castlereagh for the years between 1972 and 1978. Michael Colbert was the newest piece of grist to have been through the mill.

Denis Faul sat looking at the latest victim. He examined the bumps and bruises, noted the testimony and, within a few days, Michael, Denis Faul and a senior staff member from St Pat's were sitting at the desk of an RUC inspector in Dunmurry Barracks filing a formal complaint. After that, things started moving quite quickly.

'Denis Faul took my case to Amnesty. We were waiting for something to happen when I heard on the radio one morning that the Reverend Ian Paisley had announced in Parliament, in London, that there was an IRA man, whom he believed had shot a UDR man dead, working as a training officer for St Pat's and that he wanted him removed from his job and charged. He announced he was going to name the man the next day. He could only have been fed this line by the RUC.

'My bosses at St Pat's exchanged hurried dispatches with the Northern Ireland office. I had done nothing. If I had been named in Parliament I would have been shot surely. The next day, Roy Mason got up and announced that I was not a member of the IRA. If I was a member I would be charged as such.

Two months after that I got a letter from the RUC inspector, in Dunmurry, telling me that there was no substance to my allegations.'

Three months after that, Michael Colbert was arrested again and charged with the murder of a UDR man in Lisburn. This time, he was to be held for seven days of questioning. His previous visit to Castlereagh had achieved some notoriety. This time he was treated with wariness. No blows this time, not for Michael anyway. Just all-night interrogations and the denial of the right to sit during questioning. No physical terror for Michael, but troubles none the less. Brian Maguire, one of two other men also arrested and questioned about the same charge, was found hanging in his cell a few mornings after Michael's arrival in Castlereagh. Within two hours of the discovery of Brian Maguire's body Michael Colbert was charged.

'It was alleged that I had confessed verbally in the middle of the night,' says Michael, 'and that I made another verbal confession just to clear things up that morning. Obviously somebody panicked when they found the body. There were still two-and-a-half days of the detention order left to run. The alleged statement was later the basis of my conviction in the Diplock Court.'

The creation of the Diplock system of justice had created a conveyor-belt judicial system in the north of Ireland. The Diplock courts (one judge and no jury) were empowered to convict defendants on the basis of a confession, unless it was obtained by 'torture, or inhuman, or degrading treatment'. Proving such treatment, or disproving the authenticity of alleged confessions, was the problem of the defendant.

Disquiet was widespread. In November 1977, thirty solicitors working in the Diplock Court system wrote to Roy Mason, stating: 'Ill-treatment of suspects by police officers with the object of obtaining confessions is now common practice and – most often but not always takes place at Castlereagh RUC station – '

In 1977, Michael Colbert found himself in the maw of the Diplock system. Kafka comes to Belfast.

'I can't describe the trial. I'll give you an example. In court, my barrister enquired about the questioning of a suspect all through the night. The RUC man stood up and said that some people feel claustrophobic in custody and need company. They were doing me a favour.'

A decade-and-a-half later, the regrets provide Michael with constant company.

'At the time of my trial and appeal, the ESDA handwriting tests (Electrostatic Deposition Analysis) which freed the Birmingham Six weren't in operation. When I look back now, I often want to do something about it, go back and fight a civil case, drag up all the details. Often I think about contacting Gareth Pierce, but I know the situation in Castlereagh would be different to anything in Britain. You could go back there, but you won't find the files. Not now. I remember, that morning, watching them writing out a statement again and again till they got it right – tearing out the pages and starting again. I lost fifteen-and-a-half years as a result.'

The third man lifted and questioned with Michael Colbert was freed after proving torture while in detention in Castlereagh.

After nineteen months on remand in Crumlin Road jail, Michael Colbert entered Long Kesh prison on 13 December 1979. He remembers being asked his name and occupation, giving out the second part of his reply and then waking up in a cell.

'I just said the words "social worker" and, BANG!, I was out cold. Lights out.'

Through fifteen-and-a-half years Michael Colbert protested his innocence. His case was highlighted and pushed by Amnesty International for several years up until the early 1980s. Long Kesh was to become famous for things other than imprisoning Michael Colbert.

In the Middle East, his celebrity as a footballer was unescapable. Irish army personnel would introduce him as such, entering into all manner of tortuous explanations to convey to foreign colleagues a sense of the game of Gaelic football and its cultural importance in Ireland. For those who could not understand, Earley provided practical demonstrations on a daily basis, his solitary devotion to this strange game making him an object of curiosity in another world.

'I brought a football with me to the Middle East. I wanted to be able to come home and slip straight back into the business of football with Roscommon. I knew I could do that if I trained on my own.'

Earley had left Ireland in 1975, as an All Star footballer. He left behind a county which persisted in the belief that it was on the threshold of reaching the big time again. Returning home and breaking himself gently into the football scene would scarcely have been permitted. By then, with ten years of Senior football under his belt, Earley had become an icon of Roscommon football, his play and demeanour standing for all that Western football believed to be good about itself. Returning home was going to mean pressure and demands and phonecalls. So he lived the life of a displaced footballer, first in the Golan Heights, moving later in his tour to the Sinai Desert.

'Typically, I would be posted with an observer of another nationality and soon became a well-known eccentric among them. I was the fellow with the football. A couple of times during the day, I would head out on my own with the ball. Where we were on duty in the Golan Heights there were high blast walls to protect the local population against gunfire and shelling. I would find a flat area, or clear an area for myself, and kick the ball against the wall. Low. High. Hard. Soft. Just myself and the ball. Catching it, kicking it, blocking it down.

'Then other times I'd go off on solo runs across the countryside on little tracks we knew to be safe. The Israelis would stop me from time to time to enquire what I thought I was doing. There was an element of danger, but I understood when to go and when not to go. They got used to the sight of me as well, I suppose. I looked so strange, I must be harmless. My only worries were being mistaken from a distance as a threatening figure, or taking a tumble on the rough ground.'

It was a strange period, odd to be removed from a culture of which he was a linchpin and a hero. Home-things clung to him like barnacles. He lost his football once and scrabbled half-way down a scrub valley to retrieve it. The football was more than a tie with home, it was the key to the playing fields of his imagination. Battering the ball against the blast walls, or running through the little pathways amidst the scrub, he could be anywhere he wanted to be, playing in any position he liked.

'If I have a good memory for games it's because of my army training and because I replayed them all in my head at times when I was away. When it is just you, a wall and a football, you can recreate anything from games gone by.'

This ability to escape to the green fields of Gortahaggany, or the playing pitch in St Nathy's, or the sward in Hyde Park, served him well later in the stint abroad when his sphere of duty shifted to the Sinai Desert. Instead of a physical buffer-zone created by the UN, the armies of Egypt and Israel were separated here by the peninsula of nothingness that is the Sinai desert. Playing Gaelic football was difficult here, but on breaks to the cities of Beirut or Cairo other possibilities opened up.

'The Irish are everywhere, of course. I was known as a footballer and the talk would be about Gaelic football, but we never had enough people to play Gaelic properly. Soccer or rugby was all we could manage. At one time, when I was out there on the 1976 stint, we had an Irish rugby team called the Irish Rovers and played against teams around and about.

'We couldn't play in Beirut, so we operated mainly against teams in Israel. We got quite good at it. At that time apartheid was becoming a world issue and South African sports' teams couldn't go anywhere. But a South African university's team came to tour Israel because, well, that was the only place it was allowed to tour. This caused some excitement in Israel and the team was keen to do well. When the Israeli rugby authorities picked the team, there was half of the Irish Rovers on it. This was quite a situation for those of us working for the United Nations. We had to wriggle out as diplomatically as we could from the possibility of representing Israel against South Africa. It would have been quite a story, us being seen to represent one country in which we were intervening against another country which was being boycotted on the sporting field. I think South Africa won by about ninety points to three in the end. The Israelis might have been a bit sore about that, but it wasn't worth starting another war over a game of rugby.'

Days and weeks passed. Roscommon lost the 1976 Connacht final in a replay to Galway, opinion in the county being that, with Earley at mid-field, they would have buried the issue the first day. Dermot Earley was lost on duty somewhere in the Sinai at the time. As Earley took time out to see the great sites of early Christian history, his stock as a messiah in Roscommon soared. The county drummed its fingers waiting for him to return.

'I was notified before I came home from the Middle East that I was required by Roscommon for a challenge game in January 1977, practically as soon as I got home. They actually sent my notification of selection to the Middle East. I still had problems with the knee, so I missed that game. I played in a league play-off against Mayo in Tuam in February 1977. I think that was the first time I saw Tony McManus play and it was certainly my introduction back to the GAA. From the Sinai Desert to a wet winter Sunday in Tuam. We were badly beaten and I played poorly, but that's what coming home is like. I knew this was it as soon as I got returned, back into the GAA.'

A hunger-strikers' breath smells like nothing else. Not bad. Not foul. Sweet. The smell of nothing. The smell of cleanliness. The exhalation of a system that is shutting down.

Michael always had the cell next to the hunger-striker's cell. The screw had his desk in cell one, the hunger-striker would be next door in cell two, and Michael would be in number three.

He remembers the day they took Frank Hughes from Bellaghy away to the hospital. Frank had been on hunger strike for twenty-six days. Michael heard the door next to his opening. Terse words.

'Right. You. You're away to the hospital.'

There was a slight kerfuffle and next thing Frank Hughes was at Michael's door, whispering urgently through the gap. Michael caught the sweet unnatural smell of Frank's breath but little else; just the knowledge that he wouldn't be seeing Frank again. Michael started shouting down the wing and soon everyone was shouting farewell as Frank worked his way down the wing on his crutch, pausing occasionally to wave the crutch like a machine gun at the backs of the warders.

Not many weeks afterwards they would say farewell to Raymond McCreesh and Martin Hurson in the same way. Frank Hughes was from a GAA town, but he never took much interest in the games. Michael and Martin Hurson could talk GAA for half the day, though. 'A great GAA man.'

In prison, the GAA wrapped itself around its members just as it had outside. As Whitehall escalated its policy of criminalization in the north all political prisoners, sentenced after 1976, had lost political status and the rights which come with it. Rather than wear a prison uniform, those prisoners wore blankets in what was termed the 'blanket protest'. Through a series of incidents, this protest soon escalated to a 'no-wash protest', to the end-game of the 'hunger strikes'. With so much taken away, prisoners fell back on those intangibles which were outside the prison remit – the culture that spawned them had the GAA woven through it.

The hunger strikes of 1980 and 1981 were a difficult time for the GAA in the north. Traditionally, northern GAA clubs have looked after their members in prison, sending in jerseys, collecting money to alleviate hardships, organizing Christmas parties for prisoners' children. All this springs from local loyalties, however. History has taught the Association that, on a macro level, a vague non-party political form of nationalism has been the most pragmatic stance through the decades. To avoid internal strife, and splits on a national level, the GAA often says one thing and turns a blind eye to its members doing something entirely different on a micro level.

The GAA's difficulty lies in the fact that, historically, it has bound itself up with the aspirations and passion of communities and places to such an extent that it often finds it difficult to disentangle itself and act like a mere sports' body. St Gall's, for instance, isn't composed of a group of people who have chosen Gaelic games from an extensive menu of leisure pursuits available to them. St Gall's, the club, the colours, the teams, represent a community, an area. Generations pass the club on to each other. What affects the community, affects the club.

In the early 1970s, when the Republican movement in Belfast sundered itself into the Provisional and official wings, several clubs sundered themselves, too. The hunger strikes were to present an equally difficult situation.

Casement Park was the assembly point for most rallies and marches from the Falls Road during that long and bitter summer, yet the GAA hierarchy would not grant permission for its members' rally inside the ground. At a grass-roots level, football and hurling clubs in the north were unavoidably caught up in the passion and emotion of the times, some even had members dying in prison. Kevin Lynch, from Dungiven, had captained a Derry Under-Sixteen team to an All Ireland hurling title, and had later played for Hertfordshire. Bobby Sands had kicked a little football in the Belfast of his youth. Raymond McCreesh had played with Garrick Crudden's in Armagh. Some clubs suspended all fixtures as the bodies started coming out of Long Kesh, others maintained an official silence. Neither course was easy.

As the tension grew and positions hardened, all Belfast GAA clubs were asked by the prisoners to place notices registering their dismay in the newspapers. Most did. Some, including St Gall's, declined. In St Gall's a club banner was created. The new banner was made and carried. After all Patsy Sheehan another St Galls man had already entered the hunger strike. The club committee refused permission for the banner to be carried. The question arose as to who actually owned the club. The Dublin GAA hierarchy? The Committee? The Members? The banner was carried.

On the outside, it was a tense and bleak time, a summer of pervasive depression and lingering sadness. Inside Long Kesh, despair was more acute. News of each death came to the prisoners over the tiny crystal radios they operated off the piping in the jail. The protests and the death impacted on morale. Privileges were lost. Visits denied. Right to association was taken away. Cells were bare, cold and dirty. Prisoners were stripped of everything except their sense of self and their own culture. Some semblance of normality had to be retained. Some vestige of sanity salvaged. Michael began learning Irish.

* * *

September 1980, life was sweet. For those few moments when Roscommon stood on the cusp of fulfilment, with a breeze at their backs and a crowd roaring in their ear, life was sweet. Roscommon and Kerry. With his first touch of the ball, Dermot Earley blocked down a free kick and passed creatively to young Tony McManus who sets up John O' Connor for a goal.

Imagine what you could spare yourself if you could only stop an All Ireland final by the force of your will, freeze the clock and look back forever after on a game that finished with you three points ahead. No introspection. No gloomy homecoming. No lifetime of being told that you were the best footballer never to win an All Ireland senior medal.

Michael remembers it as a bad day, the wind strong enough to make mischief for those who aspired to precision in their football; a day when the hopes of the entire county weighed on him; a day when a man might buckle. Yet on the brink, Earley felt nothing but strength in his legs, strength and a frisson of shock and pleasure when he saw a stadium full of Roscommon blue-and-primrose as his boots hit the turf. Fifteen years of Senior football had prepared him for some reward.

'I remember not being intimidated by it. I was a Senior player and players looked to me. I got out there and enjoyed it. After fifteen years of playing Senior football, this was an All Ireland final at last. It might be the only one I would play in. In fact, I knew it probably would be the only one.

'I remember the two boys Kerry had at mid-field – Jack O'Shea and Sean Walsh. I saw them there. It was their third All Ireland final together at mid-field – three finals in three years. I shook hands with them, stood for the anthem, and then a shock of adrenalin went through me.'

Twelve minutes later Roscommon led by five clear points and all was well with the world. Sweet dreams are made of this.

In the aftermath, Roscommon never really got to mount a case for the defence. It was beaten, Kerry won its third title in a row. Roscommon was castigated for its tactics. Much of the stone-throwing was done by Kerry men.

The frustration, as that early five-point lead evaporated and Kerry metamorphosed into the giants who strode the popular imagination at the time, gave a little edge to the Roscommon play that day. A team noted for its almost prissy devotion to clean football came away with a convict reputation.

Kerry shook some salt on to Roscommon's wound. Some of the players at the core of the Kerry side had been involved in the Under-Twenty-One final of two years previously when Roscommon supporters had assaulted a couple of Kerry players as they came off the field. Kerry players freely floated the idea during the postmortem to the 1980 final that Roscommon would have won if they hadn't been so physical. The opposite is probably true, but Kerrymen took some pleasure in Roscommon's discomfort.

The game marked Dermot Earley's last major achievement on an inter-county football field. Roscommon football declined quickly into chaos and disorganization; defeats in the championship to Sligo and Galway sending a virus of disillusion through the squad. Earley, thirty-four years old now but still refusing to countenance the thought of placing a full-stop at the end of his inter county career, hit the road again in 1982. He departed for the Lebanon on a nine-month tour of peace-keeping duty.

'I knew there would be plenty of years for regret if I gave up football too soon.' He was right. Folk heroes are seldom taken to task for hanging around for too long.

During the blanket protest, Michael became the results' man for all the GAA men in the jail. It was not an easy task, but one which earned him the affection and gratitude of many.

'There's not many county coaches who could say they've done what I've done for the GAA.'

Not many. On Tuesdays, Michael would take his visit late in the afternoon. Visits for prisoners in the process of appealing their sentences were still allowed. Through the medium of a greeting kiss, a small pellet, smuggled in any one of a variety of ways into the jail, would be passed from mouth to mouth. Michael would swallow it. Later the fun would begin.

'The results could be got in, in two ways – up or down! Up was quicker, down was easier. It was fingers down the throat, eyes bloodshot and watery. Always hard. Rotten. One of things I hated. In jail you were always under pressure to get the pellet out quickly. On those Tuesday evenings it was back to the cell at four-thirty or five in the evening and straight to work at getting the pellet out of the system before grub came around. If you didn't get it before grub, you'd never get it. Half the prison would be waiting for it. That's pressure.'

When the pellet was eventually propelled from his system, the small bundle wrapped in cling-film would unfold and become the GAA results' page from the previous day's *Irish News*. When the warders packed it in at about eight-thirty and the still of the night descended, the process of transferring the results around the jail would begin. One by one, club by club, the results would be passed in whispers from cell to cell, down one leg, then shouted across to the opposite leg on the H. One prison unit, H Block 6, was in isolation some two-hundred and seventy metres (three-hundred yards) away. When the traffic from the M1 was quiet, prisoners would shout the results across. It only took a breath of wind, or the scraping of a table leg somewhere in the night, for the messages to be lost.

'I'd be up to the top of the H and call the results across slowly. It was all supposed to be quiet, but sometimes a fella would get a big championship result from home and there'd be a big roar out of him. We'd be quiet for a while and then it would start up again. It wouldn't take more than fifteen minutes maybe to read them all, but the result would be going up and down the wings of the prison in whispers after that for quite a while. It was a big thing for the boys.'

So, one by one, the results would go out and, in the darkness as men heard the results from their home pitches and beloved parishes, little half-suppressed exclamations of happiness or despair could be heard in the stillness of the prison night. On one level, football seems a trivial business to have taken such risks for. On another level, the results brought a piece of home into every cell.

Saturday evenings. Visiting time over. Soccer results were somewhat easier to come by. Orderlies, usually prisoners serving sentences for non-political acts, would slip notes with the English soccer results under cell doors. These would then be hollered around the jail in Irish.

'Aontaithe was United; Col Ceathar Aontaithe (literally Cousins of United) was Manchester City; then you'd have Caislean Nua (Newcastle), or, if a prisoner followed a certain team, just Fhoirean Mick (Mick's team). That was a strange set-up, all those English teams getting nicknames in Irish so Republican prisoners could find out how they were doing without the screws catching on.'

From the hunger strikes, the prisoners seemed to win everything except bragging rights. The prison regime loosened perceptibly and continued to do so, even after the successful escape in the autumn of 1983. The essential loneliness and claustrophobia of prison life, however, continued.

By that time, Michael Colbert was well into his time in jail, resigned to staying there for the duration of his sentence. He turned his mind to life afterwards, putting together bits and pieces of hope. Having entered Long Kesh jail without a word of Irish, he walked out the gates on 8 October 1993 as a fluent speaker, ready to teach the language to a new generation around Belfast.

In one sense, Michael Colbert had a right to feel abandoned by the GAA. That feeling is common throughout west Belfast where the Association breathes different air and runs into different problems than the nabobs in Croke Park, Dublin. Yet the broad spirit of the Association stayed with him. In his latter years inside, a prominent northern hurling man sent official GAA coaching manuals into the prison to Michael. He broke the game down into its nuts-and-bolts' components in his head and built it up again while reading through the pages. Things that maybe would have been taken for granted once became catalogued and specified in his brain.

Often he thought of the duality between Irish culture and Irish Republicanism, the manner in which they have overlapped through the decades. One night when he was in prison, there was a knock on his hall door up in west Belfast. Michael's wife Monica answered and a man presented her with a parcel. Inside were two jerseys from the Kerry football team, one signed on the collar by Jack O'Shea, the other signed by Mikey Sheehy – two special heroes in the Colbert household. The jerseys had arrived as a gift from Joe Keohane, a noted Kerry full-back in the 1930s and 1940s, a free state soldier and, later, a noted Republican. Thereafter, a card would arrive in the Colbert household every Christmas time: 'Thinking of you. J. Keohane'.

In honour, the Colbert family dog would be named Jacko, and would be presented to a bemused Jack O' Shea one afternoon in Casement Park.

'In Lebanon once,' Dermot Earley said, 'some grenades were thrown at our compound. They bounced off the wire harmlessly and exploded on the road. Our commanding officer went out to negotiate. You wouldn't often be scared, but you would be in situations occasionally that you knew were scary. There had been threats of RPGs being used that day. I remember watching our officer through the binoculars as he haggled. Suddenly two Israeli jets flew overhead. I never saw them coming, but the sonic boom they made well near killed me.

'There was another time at the end of the Iran-Iraq war when I was negotiating the safe passage of prisoners and dead bodies. The problem at such times is war debris. There were mines everywhere. I established two pathways about two feet wide through the minefields for each side to drag their dead bodies through. An argument broke out and I remember standing on one of those paths with ten people around me, all waving maps, all very excited and all pushing. My heart was galloping. It would have taken just one of them to brush off an anti-personnel mine. He would only have blown his own leg off if he did that, but, as sure as eggs are eggs, he would then have fallen on to an anti-tank mine and blown the rest of us away. Football seemed a long long way away at times like that.'

Footballers seldom escape their reputations. Dermot Earley's playing career hit the twilight years, then the lights went out. He turned his attention to that which he was paid to do – army life. In Ireland, this other dimension to his life remained almost a secret. The only question to be asked, regarding Dermot Earley and his life after football, was when he would be taking over the management of the Roscommon team, when would he be resuming the thrice-weekly drives from Kildare, westwards to Roscommon?

Earley's second peace-keeping tour, that is 1982, had taken him to the Lebanon in the wake of an Israeli invasion of that state's southern territory. He performed well in a difficult situation.

In life, reward arrives more reliably than it does in football. In 1987, Dermot Earley, from Gortahaggany, county Roscommon, became the assistant military adviser to Javier Perez de Cuellar, Secretary General of the UN. News of this prestigious appointment was greeted with great joy in New York. The joy was no greater anywhere than it was in the heart of the Bronx. Within days, a notice from the New York Roscommon GAA Club arrived in the UN. Training schedules. The GAA expects.

'In New York the Irish population is huge. It's a replica of what happens here, but maybe twenty years behind. They want to recreate the Ireland they left behind. They want to freeze Ireland. From a social point of view, you had an acceptance straight away. You were a sportsman and a GAA person, regardless of what you worked at or didn't work at.

'In New York I was immediately swamped by Roscommon people. As soon as the news broke here in Ireland, I received a telephone call telling me to be sure and pack the gear. On the second Sunday I was there, I played in Gaelic Park.

'My reputation preceded me in New York. I was known as a sportsman. Irish people there would introduce me as a footballer. They would attempt to make comparisons between games of whoever they were speaking to. I would be introduced as somebody who had played for Ireland or had played in the equivalent of the Superbowl.

'On one Monday, attending a meeting in the Secretary General's office, I had a number of small scars and cuts on my face where I had slid along the sand in Gaelic Park the previous day. There was concern as to whether I had been mugged. I explained what I had been doing and the next Sunday a senior UN official came up to Gaelic Park to see this game. He is now the Special Representative of the Secretary General in Cyprus. He knew the area well because his father lived up there near the Bronx. He also knew of the Irish activity there. It must have been a curious sight for him.

'We won the Junior championship the first year I was there, and we played Senior for the next three years. The handpass rule was frowned upon. In the first game I played I remember being made to feel like an imposter on a GAA field for the first time in my life: "If you are coming out here you won't do that".

'Inter-county players were coming out for weekends at that time. It was a regular form of traffic. I remember introducing Gay Sheerin, our goalkeeper in 1980, to his auntie who lived next door to me in Long Island.

'I had only been out there twice as a player, back in 1973 when I went out to assist Roscommon. When I was with the UN, I played for the four years almost constantly against many fellas who came out from Ireland. I remember a very wet day in New York, when Cork had been beaten in the All Ireland final the week before. I saw a fellow coming towards me wearing this new pair of Cork socks. He was playing centre half-back for Donegal and I was playing centre half-forward. I looked at the socks and my eyes rose to meet his face. It was Anthony Davis whom I had watched on television playing in Croke Park the week before. I knew I was in trouble.

'I was wearing multi-stud boots. He looked at me and said "God, you're not wearing very good boots for today". I remember the ball broke just after the throw-in, and off he went like a bolt of lightning and cracked the ball over the bar at the other end. I knew I was in trouble.'

'Do ya wanna be in my gang, my gang, my gang? Do ya wanna be in my gang. Oh, yeah.'

From the dressing-room next door, the sounds of the 1970s are seeping. The hurlers of county Down, the little tribe of obsessives who live out on the Ards peninsula, are singing. These boys have beaten Antrim in the Ulster hurling final replay.

It means so much to them. Almost forgotten down on their little limb of land, the days when they win big like this, when they earn the right to travel down to Croke Park for an All Ireland semi-final, these days provide them with a sense of self-ratification.

Down is an old team, a bunch of lags who have been around the block quite a few times in the previous decade. They should have been seen off the premises today. Antrim had it all going for them – youth with a backbone of experience, a new manager with a portfolio of ideas. They got out-foxed and out-scored. So it goes.

It's a sore defeat for any Antrim team when they lose to Down. There's an old story about an Antrim manager sending a team out to play Down in the years not long after the IRA split into its Provisional and official wings in the early 1970s. 'Go boys,' said the manager, thumping a fist on the table, 'those are the bastards that stole our guns.'

Much of that heat has gone from the games now, Down players and Antrim players hurl in the same club league for most of the winter. Still, though, the passion is unrivalled. The dream of representing Ulster down in Croke Park on All Ireland semi-final day warms many an imagination through the winter.

In the little arterial corridor which leads to the Casement Park dressing-rooms, Dominic McKinley is standing and shaking his head. Dominic is a stoical reticent man. He has just stepped into the Down dressing-room to congratulate the boys. When he crossed the threshold, the Gary Glitter songs stopped just as if a gramophone needle had been lifted. As he walked out again, having said his words, the first bars were ringing in his ears.

'Did you miss me? YEAH. When I was away – '

In the corridor, he speaks of his disappointment, his bafflement that the path he had mapped out for his team had been forgotten at the first crossroads. This is his first year in charge. Defeat burns his heart. His eyes had been on Croke Park, on bringing some honour to the county after a series of heavy defeats down there. Now this. Harsh things will be said behind his back in the hive of politics that is the county board. That's not a road Dominic likes to travel. He's a hurling man.

In the little dressing-room you can hear yourself breathe as you walk among the beaten players. Fifteen minutes after they have come off the field most of them are still sitting on their benches, the sweat and the rain drying into their backs, the defeat eating into their heads. Nobody has a word at times like this. Later, the brave talk about how next year will begin. Tables will be banged and somebody will say 'never again'. Now, though, they have to head off to their hurling communities up in the Glens of north Antrim and feel the weight of their people's disappointment. No trip to Croke Park in August. Not this year, boys.

Michael Colbert makes himself busy with the small silent rites that need attending to at a time like this: collecting bits and pieces of gear, gathering the team's belongings, a whispered recommendation here to see a physio, a murmur of condolence there. In his head, perhaps, he's thinking of the afternoon in Long Kesh in 1989 when he saw Antrim qualify for an All Ireland final, the afternoon when they beat Offaly and the whole jail erupted.

Sometimes he wonders if all this re-immersion into the GAA is a reclamation of lost time, an attempt at an accelerated version of what might have been. Today he just knows that the dream needs another year before fruition.

'Next summer, we'll go at it again,' he says, moving away among the players.

One evening in the winter of 1992, Dermot Earley was driving along the poor road from the Curragh Camp in Kildare to Hyde park in Roscommon, commuting between the two satellite stations of his life, when he tuned his radio to news of Angola. That September, elections had been held. In October, Dr Jonas Savimba had refused to recognize the outcome of those elections. In November, a UNITA official was shot dead. Dermot Earley had known him well. Angola was sliding back into chaos.

Estoril. Dermot Earley spent more days than he cares to remember in a complex outside Estoril, teasing out the end to a sixteen-year civil war in Angola. That was 1991. Not long ago. He can remember nothing as satisfying, as deeply rewarding as seeing that peace accord come to fruition in May 1991. Not the high-fives, porter-drinking, back-slapping rush of joy that football brings, but something deep and lasting. That night in May 1991, he wished he could be in Luanda, the Angolan capital, walking amidst the celebrating people, absorbing their relief. Memories.

'There was a dinner in Lisbon with Secretary of State James Baker, Perez de Cuellar, Eduard Shevardnadze, Dr Jonas Savimbi and President Eduardo de Santos. As the UN official who had negotiated the peace accord in Angola, I was asked to say a few words to mark the occasion. Going back to my dressing-room days, I suppose, I made a passionate speech about what we had achieved together and what the future held for Angola. Afterwards a Portuguese professor, who had been studying the peace process, handed me a slip of paper upon which he said he had written a synopsis of my speech. He had just written the words: "You have it. Don't fuck it up". I suppose that would be in line with my basic philosophy.'

Dermot Earley drives on through the night, into the west. He puts faces to the names he hears on the radio and wishes he could return to that bleached concrete complex outside Lisbon and knock their heads together again. Just sit down and tease it all out. He puts the boot to the floor and heads for Roscommon. Angola is unravelling again. A long way from the war, twenty-six footballers are waiting for him. A long way from the war is a good place to be this evening, amidst the constants and certainties of football.

Roscommon will unravel, too, and, finally well into his forties, he will stop making that drive westwards three times a week or more. Football will lead him to a losers' dressing-room in Newbridge town, with Kildare boys all around him, shocked and beaten. There will be hope, too, as always. His son will play for the team next year, spring will bring its championship promise. Football will always bring its warmth.

'I liked the other life, but in Ireland I'll always be Dermot Earley the footballer. There are worse things to be remembered for.'

Twenty-five years later the boys of 1969 had a get-together. A man took some photos and the county board presented some nice polished glass mementoes of the twenty-fifth anniversary of it all.

Michael Colbert was there. The other boys showed the years on their faces and across their guts. A strange evening. Life had taken them so far apart since they flew on the plane to Cork, since they were fêted in Belfast, since Antrim football bulged with promise.

Ray McIlroy, the goalie, was there of course. He lives right across the road from Michael. He sees Ray everyday, sure. Other guys? Donal Burns is a butcher in Glengormley. Seamus Killough, who won a Sigerson Cup with Quenns in 1971, is a dentist now and a good amateur golfer. Martin McGranaghan? Marty is in business down the west – Galway or somewhere.

Jimmy Mullan? Jimmy disappeared. His life brushed up against tragedy. Remember Danny Lennon, the IRA man, who was shot dead at the wheel of a car in Belfast by the British army? His car careered across the road and killed the Maguire children and, out of this incident, the Peace People were born. Well, Jimmy was driving a car with Danny Lennon's sister in it when tragedy struck. The girl died. Jimmy just disappeared. He was never seen in Belfast again.

Billy Millar emigrated to Toronto, got involved in communications over there. Still knocking about with the GAA, too.

Liam Boyle was the captain. Liam served something like eighteen years in Long Kesh after being apprehended with a rifle in his car. Played football through the prison years inside, in the cages, and came out with dodgy knees. He tried a bit of over-forties stuff last year, but his knees wouldn't wear it.

Terry Dunlop is still knocking about Belfast. Aidan Hamill became Dr Aidan Hamill, Head of the Northern Ireland Education Board. Gerry McCann lives up the back of Michael's place. Michael and Gerry play football together for the Antrim over-forties team. Gerry is a body-builder – for tourist coaches, not himself.

Gerry Nellis is still involved in the GAA, too. He's living in county Down, involved with club football. Andy McCallin had a good inter-county career afterwards. He's still managing a club team. Works as a surveyor. Doing well.

Din Joe McGrogan, the corner-forward scored the goals that put the boys in the All Ireland final that year. Din Joe was killed by a Loyalist bomb in 1975 outside the White Ford Inn, just across from Casement Park. He was going on holiday that day, and took a little time out of the house just to get out of the way. Was nipping between the bookies and the pub with one of the kids when the bomb killed him.

The manager, Tommy Hall? Tommy is still a GAA man. This year he has the Antrim Under-Twenty-One footballers under his charge. Again. With one of Michael Colbert's sons to look after also.

Quarter of a century of life in the real world, good times, bad times and hard times. Gaelic games entwined through it all.

'Next summer, we'll go at it again,' says Michael.

Eternal as the seasons.

CHAPTER SIX

Fourth field

The first match kicked off in March 1981 and a local DUP councillor who grabbed the ball received a black eye. Violence ensued. DUP supporters broke bottles on the pitch in an attempt to prevent Gaelic football being played and council staff refused to carry out maintenance work following threats from the Ulster Defence Association.

C. Knox, Unpublished thesis on Local Government Leisure Services:
Planning and Politics in Northern Ireland. University of Ulster 1989.

A quick dart of tension passes through the men and women gathered in the pastelled ballroom of the large Dublin hotel. They have come here for the weekend from the deepest pockets of rural Ireland, from the streets and suburbs of the big cities, from Britain, America and from Canada. They have come here to argue the toss about the GAA.

The Association's Annual Congress, the arena in which ordinary members can potentially mould and shape the Association's future has fallen into disrepute in recent years. As the administration of the games, the making of deals, and the hawking of wares, has become the streamlined business of qualified men in pinstripe suits, so Congress has become an anachronism, a throw-back to the early days of a great demotic organization. The GAA still spreads itself out into a myriad of largely self-governing entities, but, as a showpiece of democracy, its Congress is largely stage-managed and occasionally asinine. There are moments when the arguments from the floor threaten to capture the flavour of the national mood.

Right now, a delegate from Dublin is on his feet arguing for the right to open a debate on Rule Twenty-One. At the press table, reporters flick to a fresh page of their notebooks and crane their necks forward. At the back of the hall, the last stragglers squeeze in. On the podium, there is much shuffling of papers and a few hasty whispered conferences.

Rule Twenty-One prohibits membership of the GAA to members of the security forces in the north of Ireland. This overt reference to the political *status quo* is a tricky thing for the Gaelic Athletic Association which, as an organization, aspires to the political goal of a thirty-two county republic.

So ticklish is the matter of the 'severed six counties' that when Down regained the All Ireland football title in 1991, becoming the first six county team to do so since the outbreak of the troubles in 1969, the GAA was at a loss to describe the significance of the event. The team was sent off from the Burlington Hotel on the afternoon after the game with the congratulations of the Association's president on becoming the 'latest team to bring the cup across the ancient border which divides Ulster and Leinster'.

Now, some four years later, in the same ballroom of the same hotel, the GAA is still grappling with its own identity, still coming to terms with the philosophies of its past and the realities of its present. In Dublin, and in other parts of the south, Rule Twenty-One is nothing but a hindrance in marketing the games of football and hurling. Move northwards, however, and resentment of the security forces in the six counties grows deeper.

Cross the border at Aughnacloy, for instance, and there in no-man's land, framing the little white monument dedicated to the memory of Aidan McAnespie, are the goalposts of his local GAA club. In 1988, while walking down to a game in this field, Aidan McAnespie was shot in the back and killed by British soldiers. 'Murdered' is the word inscribed on the roadside monument. Aidan McAnespie was buried with his Gaelic football jersey draped over his coffin.

Wander around the six counties and politics infringe on sport everywhere, not just metaphorically but literally with bruising impact. The results leave scars. In South Armagh, the British Army has chosen to shield itself from attack by buildings its helicopter base on ground requisitioned from Armagh's most successful club, Crossmaglen Rangers. The occupation of Crossmaglen's premises is almost as old as the Troubles themselves. Helicopters swoop over the pitch as games are being played, balls disappear into the military compound and never reappear, players are harassed as they go about club business.

The club has always endeavoured to make the issue one of property rights, but the implications raised, and the emotions stirred, are purely political. Crossmaglen Rangers, an outfit of pinched resources, has fought its battle through the courts for two decades. Meanwhile, the local community of 2,000 people has pitched in some £5 million to build a new community hall for the club.

In county Down the club houses of the small hurling community on the Ards peninsula have been repeatedly burned out. Further north, in Belfast, the St Gall's club pitch lies cheek by jowl with the sprawling maze of marble that is Milltown cemetery. In the course of a few crazy days here in the mid-1980s, two British soldiers apprehended by the mourners at a Republican funeral were dragged behind the stands at Casement Park on the Andersonstown Road and killed.

Casement Park itself had been occupied by the British Army in the early 1970s, denying the community access to its principal leisure facility. In August 1978, the mood of the north had been inflamed further when Provisional IRA men displayed weapons at a rally inside Casement Park. The ground itself is named after a Republican hero, the British traitor Roger Casement. Just one pitch drenched in so much history and emotion.

In the north, GAA people know the feel of saw-toothed steel on flesh that being a minority can bring. In Craigavon, the local club was for many years denied the right to develop a Gaelic games' complex because, it was claimed, the sight of those games being played on a Sunday would be offensive to the members of the Royal Black Perceptory, whose headquarters in Brownlow House stood nearby. The club, St Peter's, appealed its case and won. Lord Chief Justice Lowry pointed out in his judgment that he was imposing a heavy financial penalty on the local council because its actions had been motivated by sectarianism.

Other areas aren't so lucky. In Derry city, the GAA has long struggled to make an impact. In 1980, two council pitches were built in the Waterside, a largely Unionist area of a largely nationalist city. Unionist political opinion united in condemning the council. The very stability of the local council was threatened as Unionists announced their intention to withdraw from a power-sharing arrangement. The pitches were moved, but the Unionists remained unhappy. In March 1981, the first match kicked off and ended in violence after a DUP councillor grabbed the ball. Glass was broken on the pitches. The pitches fell into disuse.

Everywhere one travels in the north, the stories of the troubles mesh with the stories of the GAA. Clubs who have lost members through death or imprisonment play against clubs who have lost property through arson, or under the auspices of the Northern Ireland Emergency Provisions Act. Everybody has a tale to tell. In some areas the GAA has thrived, blossoming as a source of local identity. In other areas it has been driven underground or out of existence.

The cultural totems of Republicanism, the claim to place and the seizing of history and language, are the totems of the GAA also, and separating the two has been too delicate a task for the Unionist community in the north.

'It's recognized as a sport with political connotations,' said Chris McGimpsey of the Ulster Unionist Party to the *Irish Times* in April 1994.'The flag, the tricolour, the refusal to let RUC men go on crowd-control duty. There is a feeling of a state within a state.'

McGimpsey's views reflect the more moderate shades of Unionist opinion. At the other end of the spectrum lies the odd Loyalist splinter-group which has denounced the GAA as a 'pan nationalist front of which all members are legitimate targets'.

There is another dimension, too, a complicating layer of inconsistency. The GAA has built a political qualification into its membership rules, yet the despised British administration in the six counties has been the source of plentiful grants and financial aid for ambitious GAA clubs and county boards. The Ulster Council of the GAA has filled its coffers by playing off the competition between the two British-owned television companies in the north. Young northern players have advanced quicker than their southern counterparts by means of their access to the north's comprehensive third-level education scheme.

Through all this, Rule Twenty-One and its prohibition on northern security force members being members of the GAA has survived. The Rule has its genesis back at a time near the foundation of the Association, and was designed for an era when paranoia made good sense, a time when GAA men worried about spies from Dublin Castle and informers from the garrison.

Decades later, the rule survives, its last chance for disappearing into history having come and gone with the GAA Congress of 1971, held in Belfast, when the motion mysteriously disappeared from the agenda at the last minute.

Now, in a Dublin hotel, a Dublin GAA man, detached from and baffled by The Troubles, seeks to give Rule Twenty-One another airing. Eight months into the ceasefires in the six counties, he feels his voice carries the essence of reason, feels he can walk unimpeded through the middens of hypocrisy, double-think and paranoia which surround the issue. The nabobs at the top-table know different. The men and women from the northern counties know different. He is treading all over a raw nerve.

In the era of sponsorships and lucrative television deals, the GAA can't afford an ugly and emotional dust-up here. The top table bids to buy some time, proposing a Special Congress on the entire issue during which the question of Rule Twenty-One can be examined in the broader context.

And that is it. The gathering backs away. Nobody truly expects to attend a Special Congress. The broader context is code for the litany of worst injustices and grievances which members, north of the Border, have endured and can't yet forget. 'Special Congress,' mutters a delegate from Derry, 'aye, that would open a few eyes around here all right. Let's have it up where I come from.'

Bellaghy on a hot summer's night, the sun dipping down behind the trees at last. Here on neutral turf, Ballinderry and Glen are hammering out their differences in the county football championship. The roars of the faithful carry up the hill and on through the town as Ballinderry pull away to win easily. When the game ends, an excited knot of Glen people surround a couple of county board officials to complain excitedly about the standard of the night's refereeing performance. Plenty of steam is let off before the sour reality of defeat is absorbed.

Meanwhile, Ian Milne is up the road feeding his pigs and minding his own business. The commotion reaches his ears, but pigs – well, pigs make no allowances for county championships. Ian will content himself this evening with listening to the cheers and finding out the result later. Bellaghy might yet meet the winners of this game in the county final. The commotion reaches his ears again and he smiles to himself. Were Ian Milne to get down among the tight little knot of red-faced partisans just now berating the county officials,

All Ireland trophy in Offaly

Munster, final afternoon

Limerick play Tipperary

(*above*) Limerick v Tipperary, Munster Championship 1995, Limerick's Dave Clarke breaks free (*below*) Antrim v Limerick Hurling

Limerick and Kilmallock, 1995 Munster final, ball to hand Dave Clarke

Cork v Kerry Munster Hurling Championship 1995, 'keep on keeping on' Kerry Hurlers v Cork

Kerry v Cork, Munster Championship 1995, perservering Kerry hurlers

(*above*) Get your county colours

(*left*) Defeat

(*left*) Boom! Boom! Boom!, Croke Park (*above*) All Ireland final day (*below*) Artane boys band, traditional accompaniments to big match day

Another year wearing the colours

Close finish

(*above*) Corporate Gaels, new Cusack stand (*below*) Croke Park, Dublin under reconstruction

(*left*) Home (*above*) Emigrants and exiles, London hurlers v New York
(*below*) Hurling, placed ball

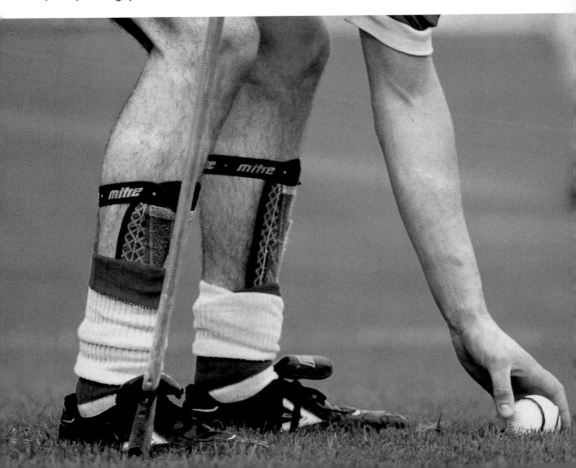

Young and learning

he knows what he would tell them, knows some advice they might usefully listen to.

'I see fellas bickering and fighting over games and I tell them not to bother. The good years are too short for that. I regret not having gone as far as I could have gone with it. The football is an escape from all the hassles. There's no need for shouting and fighting with each other. No need for that bother.'

He knows the nature of regret and the subtlety of it carries in his lilting south Derry accent, the complex mix of feelings and sadness with which the past is freighted. He is politicized now, he says, educated to the causes and effects of the struggles with which he has been associated down through the decades. It wasn't always so. Clarity came later.

Twenty-four years ago now, he was just seventeen and seeing the inside of Crumlin Road jail for the very first time. It was 1971 and Ian Milne was by no means unique, just a young south Derry boy reacting violently to the events he saw unfolding all around him. If the troubles hadn't come along, if south Derry had been, well, south Kerry say, he might have been a good senior inter-county footballer, might have had his name in the papers all the time, and gone to Dublin for big games, and All Star awards, and got himself fixed up with some cushy job where his name alone sold the goods.

Instead, for over twenty years, life was a series of jail-terms and court appearances interspersed with brief colourful and event-filled periods of life lived on the run. Mainly, though, the years have been marked down in different jails around the country, long spells of hard time.

The summers of his late adolescence were clouded by the eruptions of boiling hate and steaming bigotry which would turn into the twenty-five year war which we call The Troubles. You'd have to have lived somewhere else not to have been in someway shaped by the whole business. Near the epicentre Ian was shaped by it – shaken and shaped by it – his life poured into a mould. Clarity and politics, as he says, was something he learned later.

In September 1971, not long turned seventeen and still really just a boy, he entered Crumlin Road prison for the first time. He was released in February 1973. The following summer he wound up in Portlaoise prison where he remained until escaping along with eighteen others in the summer of 1976. Recaptured a year later, along with another Bellaghy man, he was sentenced for the murder of a UDR soldier in Lurgan and served a fourteen-year stretch in Long Kesh, a term which he finished just three years ago.

Years of hard struggle and turmoil. For a time in the mid-1970s, Ian Milne's face appeared on 'most wanted' posters along with those of fellow south Derry men, Frank Hughes and Dominic McGlinchey.

Ian is the only one of the three still alive. Frank Hughes was the second hunger striker to die within the walls of Long Kesh prison in the dark summer of 1981. Dominic McGlinchey was murdered towards the end of a long and bitter feud within the Irish National Liberation Army. Ian and Frank had grown up together, playing and pucking around here in the fields around

Bellaghy. Ian and Dominic had been friends also. Somehow the fates of the three of them seemed linked, tied together. Now Ian is the only one still alive. Dominic and Frank lie in the little graveyard in Bellaghy.

The strength of both the Republican movement and the GAA in south Derry aren't entirely unconnected, not in the realms of emotions and symbols anyway, and certainly not when you talk about place and cultural expression, and the self-confidence of a people. In South Derry, all these notions are carried in the breeze.

Ian Milne's mind runs through the playing membership of Bellaghy Wolfe Tones back in the days when he went to prison for the first time. He estimates that perhaps a dozen of those boys ended up in prison at some time or other during the troubles. Most of the others were touched in some way or another by the events unfolding around them.

The causes of this harsh disruption to the rhythms of rural life are complex and embedded in the geography and history of the place. The outsider needs to grasp those reasons before throwing stones of judgement around Bellaghy.

In 1971, for instance, the old Bellaghy Wolfe Tones' club house on the Castledawson Road was burned to the ground. One crazed and malicious act that removed the focal point of the community. A little earlier than that, Ian Milne's friend, Frank Hughes, was badly beaten by a UDR patrol after a dance in Ardboe in county Tyrone. Shaking and shaping all the time.

Ian Milne himself had an older brother interned at a time when stories of repression and torture of internees ran like wild-fire through the Catholic areas of the north. Men would come home and tell how they had been hooded and bundled into helicopters, then beaten and kicked and told to say their prayers, then tossed out of the flying helicopter. No blind-folded man could tell that the helicopter was hovering just a few feet above the ground.

The little community braced itself for hard times and people responded in different ways. Some poured their energies into the football. Ian Milne's club were champions of All Ireland in 1972, his brother played on the team. Others took to the fields, hedges and ditches in the cause of the Irish Republican Army.

It was hard to be indifferent. Ian Milne remembers how, as a fifteen-year-old boy, he sampled the excitement which ran through Bellaghy on the announcement that the great civil rights march of 1969 was to pass through the town on its way from Belfast to Derry. Bellaghy had always been a predominantly nationalist town. The cutting edge of Unionist supremacy in the cities, the discrimination in housing and employment didn't have much impact in the small country town. In Bellaghy, nationalism sprung from different more visceral things, a sense of place and pride which couldn't accommodate a vision of Bellaghy as part of the United Kingdom. Bellaghy and the areas around have a quiet self-sufficient grasp of rural nationalism – principles and philosophies rooted as firmly as oak trees. If a civil rights march was to pass through town, then the banners would be out and the numbers would be swelled.

Ian Milne also remembers the boiling sense of frustration which united the nationalist populace when the RUC refused the marchers entry to the town on the pretext that a prominent local Unionist, whose house occupied the vantage point on a hill on the outside of town, wouldn't like the sight of marchers passing by on the road below. A long stand-off ensued at the Ballydermot crossroads. The march never came through Bellaghy.

'I think in south Derry not everybody was politicized back then,' says Milne. 'It was a reaction to what happened at first. I wasn't fully aware of the whys and wherefores. It was reactionary. Things like internment brought it to a peak. Around here we got houses and jobs if Protestants didn't want them. It all came together. You react and the reaction builds into an understanding. You become politicized. I believe in what the struggle is about now. I think for boys from Bellaghy it was easy enough to come to that understanding.'

After a year of fragile peace, it is counter-productive to attempt to unravel the whole knotted ball of causes and effects. Too much history and blame there. Impossible to sort out who to bless and who to blame. Some in Bellaghy, south Derry, Belfast, and other spots beyond, responded through the gun; others expressed their defiant nationalism through football, hurling and culture. For others, the areas of resistance and cultural self-expression overlapped. This is their story.

Ian Milne recounts the impact of Republican involvement on the other constant thread of his life, Gaelic football. Two strands running through one life. In each existence he can hear echoes of the other.

'I went to jail too early,' he says in the living-room of his little Bellaghy home. From the wall, the photographs of two dead hunger-strikers (his fellow Bellaghy men, Frank Hughes and Tom McElwee) gaze down on him as he speaks. Frank and Tom were cousins. Together, with another friend and future prisoner Seamus Bradley, the boys and Ian passed through childhood together.

'Too early. Back in the sixties and seventies, Bellaghy was *the* club around the county. I had a brother who played on the team that won the All Ireland club championship back in 1972. I was playing Minor around that time and played a bit of Junior football, too. I had a couple of games for the Seniors. I'm not blowing my own trumpet, but it was hard to get on the Seniors back then. A good hard settled team, do you know that road? That's one of my regrets. I often say that to the boys in the club. I'd like to have seen how far I could have gone with it.'

Aye. A few Senior games back in the days when Bellaghy was the king of Ulster and beyond. He remembers playing a Junior match in Ballinderry one Sunday afternoon and scoring 1–5 from full-forward, a performance impressive enough to merit including him in the Senior team for the game which formed the main part of that afternoon's double bill. He was small for full-forward, but quick enough to stay out of trouble. Accurate, too, and good with his hands. A young man still in the Minor grades. The whole club was waiting for him to mature into a star of the Senior team. Ian Milne was going to be good, Ian Milne was going to be in the vanguard of championship wins for a decade or so to come.

He reaches up to the shelves above him in his living-room and, from amidst the heavy wooden Celtic crosses and harps which he carved for himself while in prison, pulls down a little plaque upon which are set three silver medals.

Two of the medals are for football and one is for hurling. 'Gaelic League, Belfast Prison, 1972' says the legend carved beneath the medals. Back then, when the bite of the troubles was still fresh and the numbers piling into prisons were growing exponentially every month, prisoners played prison leagues on full-scale pitches. Clubs, especially those from Belfast and south Derry, would send in gear to equip entire teams. Men from Ardoyne could line out in their own club colours against men from, say, a Falls Road club. A slightly distorted version of normality was created.

In the north's crowded prisons during the early 1970s, logistics were a nightmare. For the sake of simplicity, Loyalist inmates and Republican inmates would be allowed out of their cells on alternate days. During late summers, when television would show the concluding stages of the All Ireland championships, unlikely deals would be done between the two groups of prisoners to facilitate Republicans getting out of their cells on the afternoons of big-game broadcasts.

'It suited them and it suited us,' says Ian. 'We'd change for them when they had a reason.'

The stories of the football and hurling games, played in the Long Kesh cages during the years of internment, are legendary in the relevant parts of Belfast, Derry and beyond. Entire leagues and championships were played out for the Jimmy Steele Memorial Trophy – Jimmy Steele was a legendary IRA man of the 1930s, 1940s and 1950s, whose deeds included escaping from Crumlin Road jail in 1943. While briefly on the run, Steele facilitated the escape of another twenty-one prisoners from Derry Jail. His memory lives on among Republican prisoners today.

Ian Milne's memento of his playing days in Crumlin Road is augmented by many trophies won playing football since his release in 1992. He captained Bellaghy's reserve team to the Junior championship in 1993 and lined out for the Senior team several times. Although he isn't playing at the moment, he hasn't quite put all thoughts of it away.

Inside prison, however, with the turbulence surrounding the fight for political status in the late 1970s and early 1980s, and with the increased pressure of public opinion being turned on the British authorities, Gaelic football and hurling went underground. For a period before and during the hunger strikes, Republican prisoners were on twenty-four hour lock-up. Milne never again played Gaelic games within the prison system on the same organized basis as back in the early 1970s.

Later in the 1970s, when things got bad in Long Kesh, the remand prisoners, who were enjoying the comparatively luxurious freedom of association while awaiting trial, would stuff large socks with other items of clothing and play rough-and-tumble Gaelic football games in the yards, but the practice was frowned upon by the authorities. Football and hurling, like the use of the Irish language, came to be regarded as symbols of Republican resistance and were outlawed within the jails.

'It was driven underground. When political status went in 1976 and the blanket protests began, it was harder and harder to organize football. We'd talk about it all the time inside, though. Who had played with who. Which lads knew each other, what games they remembered, fellas from different counties slagging each other.'

When the prison authorities clamped down on the playing of Gaelic games, they unintentionally glamorized them. Like the Irish language, the games came to be seen as weapons of Irish self-expression. Beginners' Irish classes started in jail, one wing eventually becoming totally Irish speaking. Prisoners who had never even played before on the outside took up the games in jail. Prison authorities recognized the point that was being made. Prisoners, becoming politicized, were seizing the symbols of nationalist culture and replacing their weapons with them.

'It's eased off again now in the past few years,' Ian Milne says, of the suppression of Gaelic games. 'There'll always be GAA inside in the prisons because there is such a strong connection to Republicanism. GAA is about being from your parish and from your county. When you're inside, where you are from and your politics are the main things you carry with you. They can't be taken from you.'

So when the six-a-side games started up in the little concrete yards around the H Blocks, Ian Milne, in the year after the hunger strikes ended, had a Bellaghy club jersey and a Derry county jersey sent inside to him and played away.

The jerseys spoke as eloquently as any speech. Clubs sent in their own colours and county jerseys to prisoners. The jersey was a badge of sorts, a sartorial means of expression and identification. You could see a prisoner a short distance away and not know him from Adam, but know where he was from by the colour of his jersey.

It seemed so natural that, when the prisoners were planning their great escape of 1983, the heavily symbolic date originally fixed for the break-out was that of the All Ireland football final of that year.

'That would have been in mind all right,' says Ian, 'a big GAA day down in Dublin, the boys busting free in the morning, thinking of the news spreading about the place. That would have been the thinking.'

Another Sunday evening. Sunday is the butt-end of the week and a lazy day within Long Kesh prison. No visits allowed, no post in or out. Prisoners write letters and read papers. Time weighs heavily on Sundays.

This afternoon, Derry are playing Tyrone in the 1995 Ulster championship and around the various exercise yards the Republican prisoners are lolling in sun and shade. Ears are welded to small radios. As Derry pull away in the first half, with two Tyrone men being sent off, great roars issue from the mouths of men in white jerseys with red bands across them. During the second half, Tyrone men reassert themselves with demonic passion and the roars flow from different quarters. Across in the Loyalist wings, all is silent. Prisoners whose politics come with a different hue have gotten used to these strange Sundays when the Republicans get high on GAA.

A bus with no windows carries the weekday visitor from the search-and-wait area to visiting areas within the H Blocks. For long minutes the bus sits idle in security vacuums between gates. The sun bakes the women and children inside. A head pops in and counts the occupants. The bus proceeds to another security vacuum.

The visiting conditions have improved down the years. The prisoners meet their visitors in little visiting areas with walls that slant downwards towards a central walkway. Fourteen cubicles to a room, maybe seven or eight people can sit together in a cubicle. The warder doesn't sit and listen to every word anymore. The prisoners can bring stuff out, but not back in when they are on visits. One by one they arrive out, each escorted by a warder, each carrying a little bag from the tuck shop for consumption by their guests. Cans of Coke, Mars bars, sweets.

Martin Molloy is a Strabane man serving fourteen years for possession with intent. He began his sentence in 1986, having been free for the previous three years. Before that, he served another stretch in Long Kesh for the same offence. His prison time began back when he was eighteen years old. The only Senior football he has managed with his club Sigerson's was during three years of intense GAA activity between 1983 and 1986.

Tony Gillen is from Belfast and was arrested six years ago in the company of Gerry Adam's brother, a circumstance which can't have helped either of them. Like Martin Molloy, Tony Gillen was sentenced for possession with intent. A month previously, he had stood on Hill 16 and watched Antrim achieve a little bit of history playing in the All Ireland hurling final of 1989. The tickets had come from Sean McDermott', the club he had helped revive with a couple of friends of his in the late 1970s and early 1980s.

The fine afternoon when Tyrone beat Derry this summer was one of the better ones put down during Martin Molloy's time in prison. Molloy misses the GAA passionately, and the pull of home and Tyrone is especially strong this month with the wings humming in anticipation of another northern victory in the All Ireland football series. Tyrone is playing Dublin in the final. If Tyrone wins, it will be Ulster's fifth consecutive All Ireland on the trot. A hard thing for Martin to miss.

Prisoners are already busy making red-and-white flags for their cells. In the week leading up to the game, they will be busy preparing the heavy prison concoction that is the staple fare of celebrations inside – biscuits, Mars bars and custard are laid down in layers to create the heaviest most calorific cake known to man. 'No yard's football for a week after eating a bit of that stuff. It just lies there inside you,' says Martin.

Now that the internal rivalries of the Ulster championships are subsiding, most prisoners are pulling for another Ulster win. Ulster is a unique GAA province in this regard. Local rivalries disappear as soon as the fight for the right to represent the province ends. All the boys are pulling wildly for Tyrone now. Most, not all.

'Well, I've tipped Dublin from the start of the year,' says Tony Gillen. 'I've a few bets down, so there's quite a few bars of chocolate (the currency of prison gambling, if a man doesn't smoke) coming my way if Dublin wins. That and a heap of abuse.'

On this particular afternoon, however, the prison is buzzing with rumours that Patrick Mayhew, The Secretary of State for Northern Ireland, is about to reintroduce the fifty per cent remission for prisoners that was abandoned in 1989. Republican prisoners express annoyance that their fate is being used to distract attention from the lack of progress on more substantial issues central to the peace process.

The adjustment in remission times will make a material difference to many men, however. Molloy will serve the same time he was sentenced for. Tony Gillen will lose two years of his sentence. Both are politicized in the manner of most prisoners. They view the concession in terms of the overall political picture rather than personal gain or loss. Down on the micro scale of individuals and their lives, however, it means for some a return to the things they miss most from the outside. The mind can't but wander off the political footways occasionally.

'I'll definitely play again on the outside,' says Martin Molloy. 'Watching Tyrone going on this summer gives you the hunger for it. The football is going all right in the club at the minute. We keep in contact with each other. I always know the results from club games, and who's playing well and who's going badly.'

'I'll have a few years playing yet,' says Tony Gillen. 'I think our football side is going well, but we're doing badly in the hurling. We'll come again through.'

For clubs, the question of contact with members in prison is a tricky one. Some ignore entirely the fact that IRA men have sprung from their midst. Other clubs, usually in Belfast, Tyrone and south Derry, where the nationalist communities are tightest, have the reputations for maintaining the strongest links, sending in jerseys and footballs and coaching manuals, looking after wives and families on the outside and making sure kids are catered for at Christmas with parties and presents.

Saoirse, the prisoners support organization on the Republican side of the house, is a common sight at northern GAA games collecting money for the welfare of prisoners and families. For those in attendance, their presence is merely another part of the jigsaw the community laid down within the GAA grounds. To the apolitical southerner, the sight of Saoirse collection boxes inside GAA grounds seems stridently political, seems to send out all sorts of green messages. In Belfast, Derry and Tyrone, it is what people expect of the GAA, their GAA.

One south Derry club abandoned all activities for the five or six months during which the hunger strikes were in progress in 1981. Others tailored their schedules to facilitate marches and demonstrations. The expressions of solidarity, and the maintenance of contacts with imprisoned members, causes little remark in tight-knit communities. Prisoners, in a curious way, are both central to the history and future of the north and a sacred side issue. The treatment of prisoners and conditions within jails are an issue for both sides of the community. The support structures on one side are duplicated on the other. In prison, nobody looks like the demonic terrorists who lurk behind the ritual condemnations on newspaper front pages. Everybody is somebody's brother, son or husband. Everyone comes from somewhere.

They all come from somewhere. Inside Long Kesh, meanwhile, the yearning for Gaelic games never ceases. Coming from somewhere is the foundation upon which the GAA is built. They wear their jerseys, advertising where they come from and what they stand for. This month, August, is a busy month in the prison's GAA calender.

'There's something about August,' says Martin Molloy. 'It does funny things to people in the north of Ireland – inside the prison and out. We raise money for Gaelscoileanna in here through sports days we hold in August. A big part of that would be the yard's GAA league which is going on at present.'

The yard's, concreted exercise areas of about thirty-six metres (forty yards) length and eighteen metres (twenty yards) breadth are used for six-a-side games between teams selected from various wings around the prison. The concrete was marked out years ago for use as basketball and volleyball courts, but prisoners asked the painters to add a couple of little goalposts against the walls and to lay down a small square for the protection of goalies.

They have been repainted regularly ever since and football goes on in its mutant prison form, with the authorities turning a blind eye. Sometimes players form their own county teams to play against each other in the county colours. It's patchy and unreliable, though. Wing teams are the usual form of representation. In prison you come from the wing you sleep in. The games are intense, but different in character from football on the outside. The environment dictates the style of play.

'We use a light ball because a heavy ball kicked hard from close range is impractical,' says Tony Gillen. 'The games would be mainly hand-passing, partly because of the size of the pitch and partly because of the lines hung over the yard to prevent helicopters landing. You can't kick high. Challenges have to be easy enough because of the concrete, but tempers run high. I've seen a couple of badly twisted ankles and a couple of broken noses from boys running into each other.'

Long-term prisoners who play regularly throughout their term inside often come out with bad knees and dodgy ankles from all the afternoons of jarring their joints along the concrete surfaces.

For many years now, the battle has raged to be allowed use the prison's all-weather pitch over near H Block Seven. The argument goes to the core of the clash of cultures which has sparked the northern turmoil, and is one which makes the GAA turn and look back within itself.

'In the late eighties,' says Martin Molloy, 'there was a lot of action on the use of Irish language within the prison. We lost a court case challenging the right for the prison to outlaw a minority language, but, out of that, I think through development in the EC, we were allowed to organize Irish classes in the prison.

'The next step culturally seemed to be Gaelic games. There is an all-weather pitch in here which isn't in good condition and we asked to be allowed use it for Gaelic games on our once-a-week visits to it. Permission was refused.'

The reason provided by the prison authorities for the ban on Gaelic games related to insurance policies. The prisoners themselves are inclined to the view that cultural bigotry lay at the core. The suspicions which all sides of the triangle have of each other are probably at the heart of the problem. The GAA, the prisoners and the prison authorities was always going to be a difficult relationship to settle down.

All exercise within the prison is supervised by Prison Training Instructors (PTIs). Prisoners playing games on the all-weather pitch near H Block Seven are subject to the same rule of supervision. The GAA's own Rule Twenty- One prevented the PTIs from becoming qualified referees or coaches, so the prison refused to countenance the playing of games under the guidance of PTIs who weren't qualified to supervise them.

It was argued that, as teachers come into the prison to teach both Loyalist and Republican prisoners a wide range of other subjects, the impasse could be avoided by bringing in qualified GAA people from outside the prison. Permission for this initiative was refused. Prison Training Instructors aren't banned from participating in any other cultural activity which might find an outlet within the prison. The GAA's own paranoia was being turned back on itself.

Eventually the argument reached its hub.

'It was agreed by the GAA,' says Martin Molloy, 'that Rule Twenty-One would be waived to permit a PTI to become a qualified referee within the GAA. It seemed that would be the solution to the problem, but then the individual involved came back and said that if he was going to train and receive this qualification he wanted to have the right to train other PTIs in GAA courses and issue qualifications himself. Nobody could agree to that – the GAA couldn't at any rate.'

Paranoia. The thought of one Prison Training Instructor breeding a new strain of GAA man in the north made the GAA baulk. Huge embarrassments would surely follow as the newspapers chronicled the PTIs' supervision of the annual Derby game between the British Army and the RUC, while the GAA looked on.

So the stand-off between two cultures continued and the campaign for the right to organize Gaelic games fell away. If the issue of prisoners' exercise, and what games they play, appears peripheral in the face of the history of the struggle in the north, the principle at the core is central to all that has happened in the last twenty-five years.

Times have been harder in the past for prisoners than they are now. If the fight for the right to play Gaelic games isn't as sharp and as passionate as it might once have been, it is because other greater battles have been waged and an uneasy impasse reigns now.

When political status was withdrawn from prisoners in the mid-1970s, and the campaign to regain them started and quickly escalated into the blanket protest which, in turn, culminated in the grim end-game of the hunger strikes, prisoners forfeited all their rights and lived locked up in their own cells for twenty-four hours a day with their own dirt and their own thoughts. Ten of their number died eventually.

Back then, it was the responsibility of one prisoner to ensure that all the Republican inmates received news of their club's activities over the weekend. News of club games came into the prison the hard way, through the 'comms' which female visitors would pass orally to boyfriends or husbands during the quick kiss – the only bit of physical contact permitted during those heavily supervised visits.

Most 'comms' carried IRA instructions, or personal letters written in tiny handwriting on cigarette paper and wrapped in cling-film for protection from moisture. In the event of trouble, they could be swallowed and reproduced later. On Mondays, however, the GAA results came in.

At night, then, when the prison was quiet the results were passed around the H Blocks verbally, through a series of shouted whispers called scorching.

The risks were great and to the outsider the pleasures of Gaelic games seem of small importance when set against the sea of troubles and regrets which a long prison sentence involves. Yet the assertion of one culture, one set of rights within a system established by the ruling power of another culture, seemed crucially important. The right to play and to follow their own games is vital to prisoners, something which they can't countenance being without. 'Place and politics are the only things that prison leaves a man with,' says Ian Milne.

'Over the past few years,' says Martin Molloy, as he prepares to be escorted back to his wing of the prison, 'with northern teams winning four All Ireland titles, we have all felt as if a bit of focus has been turned on our troubles up here. We feel as if nationalist culture has been taken some notice of – the positive parts of it. Contrary to what people think, Republicans don't have a great opinion of the GAA and what it has done nationally over the troubles. Clubs and families have been tight, but nationally the GAA has been as apathetic as anyone else. Winning the All Irelands has been good for confidence. We've felt we are from a place that people in the Free State dismiss very easily and that we are winning something that is important to the culture of most of the island. That has been a good thing for us.'

Within the prison, attitudes to Gaelic games have softened – especially since the intense heat went out of the political situation. Some warders take a passing interest in the games, and prisoners and warders alike take an interest in English soccer so there is an uneasy common ground to share. One warder plays soccer for Crusaders with Dublin footballer, Mick Deegan, and has described the player's speed and balance to prisoners. The curious cultural connection between prison and Gaelic sporting celebration has one more strange link in a Dublin footballer turning a few bob at weekends by lining out with Crusaders.

Later, on the third Sunday of September, the prisoners will celebrate the All Ireland final. From where they live and exist, the act of 70,000 Irish people standing in Croke Park, turning to the tricolour and singing The Soldiers Song is a resounding gesture of Irish self-determination.

Even those Republicans indifferent to the game will wander into wing canteens for the couple of hours of the live broadcast. Perhaps, as happened when last Tyrone played in an All Ireland final back in 1976, one of the sweating post-match players will dedicate his performance to all the 'boys in the Kesh', and the great guttural cheer will ring out, baffling still further the Loyalists in their three blocks of this shared prison. More diversion as they while away another quiet Sunday, waiting for the long war to truly end.

The first time Ian Milne was in Croke Park was the year after he got out of prison for the last time. He stood on Hill 16, the mound named after the rubble of the 1916 Easter Rising, and watched Derry win its first All Ireland Senior football title. The feeling of pride and joy was unbelievable. The experience of seeing a Derry team, which sprang from his own place and his own culture, beating all of Ireland at his own sport amazed him.

'I think that around here a lot of people who wouldn't express themselves politically through armed struggle or anything like that expressed themselves through the GAA and their county flags and colours. That was a great day. To see Derry going and doing that, was important for us all.'

He also remembers that summer of 1993, which culminated in the All Ireland final win, for the fact that Derry flags were removed, torn and burned in nearby Castledawson and in other places. The confident expression of one culture was too much for another to handle.

He's getting on with life now, making up for the missing years by striving for the things that most twenty-year-olds have to strive for. He went straight to the GAA club when he was released, keen for the activity and the expression of normality, eager to see if he could learn to judge once more the timing of a leap for a flying football, to see if he could guide a football between the sticks again with some beefy defender breathing down his neck. He wore Bellaghy's blue-and-white and, after all the years away from them, he felt part of his home community once more, part of the place where his Scottish father had settled down so many years before, immersed with his own people, participating in his own culture.

Twenty-six years after he watched Bernadette Devlin standing down the road arguing with the RUC about the right to take a civil rights march through little nationalist Bellaghy, he watched another flash-point come and go as Loyalists endured a stand-off on the edge of Bellaghy, facing down the RUC for the right to parade triumphantly through the same little nationalist town. Ian Milne has spent seventeen of those intervening years in prison and sometimes wonders if much has changed.

He notices that players work harder at the game now, that there is more pride and more importance attached to it. There is less fist-fighting, too. Ulster teams don't dissipate like southerners, football and hurling are more than just sports to them. One culture has learned to express itself. Neither culture has learned to stop fearing the other. Almost a year into a kind of peace, they are still waiting and watching. Football is still more than mere sport around here.

'This is the real world,' northerners like to say to soft beery southerners sounding off about Ireland's problems. 'Come here and see what it's like, then get back to me.'

At the sharp end of the real world, people know that the existence of Rule Twenty-One means more to them than the abolition of the Rule means to the soft under-belly of the GAA. In a world where so many things are morally indefensible, Rule Twenty-One exists for them as a shield and not a weapon, a comfort and not an insult. They know that Special Congresses and 'broader contexts' are things that only a politicized community has the stomach for.

Men and women with good dinners in their bellies, debating in hotel ballrooms down in Dublin, won't dig in for the long fight.

Here in the north, in the places where nationalism turns a darker green and emerges as Republicanism, they will have to evolve a long way and for a long time before their sharp political senses desert them. Troubled circumstances have given them an understanding of what mere games can mean – their games with the perfume of history and the feel of home about them.

CHAPTER SEVEN

Big time, small town

Coming home to Tubber with history in their pockets, young men can hardly grasp the meaning of it all. Here is the communal prize, the well-spring of joy for the entire county. It is the eleventh day of July 1995, two days after Clare have won the Munster hurling final for the first time in sixty-three years. The team is approaching Tubber. Eamonn Taaffe, the home-boy in these parts, warns his team-mates not to expect too much. No Beatlemania, no screaming girls or crying old men. Not in Tubber.

'Lads,' he says to the boys who have absorbed the adulation of an entire county in the past forty-eight hours, 'we haven't enough people in Tubber to make a crowd.' He is right in a sense. His home-place is just a scattering of 200 or so houses. They've never known a rush-hour in Tubber.

Eamonn, however, hasn't factored in the heartbreaking history of hurling in Clare. He hasn't allowed for all the years of yearning and longing, for the hunger which has infected the imagination of every soul in the district. He hasn't allowed for all the bitter tears which have swelled the appetite for this day.

All the way to Tubber things have been the same – through Shannon, Clarecastle and Ennis, and so on. Young people singing, old people crying, mothers holding up babies, men embracing. The county of Clare is in rapture.

So, of course, Tubber surprises Eamonn Taaffe, rocks him right back on his heels. Every man, woman and child for miles around has congregated here to gaze upon the Holy Grail. Days like this don't come around too often. The last time any hurling silverware was paraded through these parts was when Clare won the Oireachtas Tournament back in 1954. The Oireachtas? The very name seems cobwebbed with quaintness. Here's the real thing, and Eamonn Taaffe is holding it above his head, half-shy, mostly proud.

Among the beaming faces in the crowd, when a Munster cup comes at last to Tubber, are those of the neighbours from just across the border in south Galway. Tubber and its neighbouring parish, Beagh, have rubbed shoulders for so many years now that it is only the hurling which separates the two communities. In fact, the very thing that unites them separates them – hurling.

Beagh looks to Galway for its heroes. Tubber draws its lifeblood from Clare hurling.

'See that tree,' says George Taaffe, standing outside his shop in Tubber on a fine August day not long after his son, Eamonn, has brought the Munster trophy home. He is pointing to a tree a short distance away.

'That tree is in Galway. See, just over that hill? The Gantleys live there – Galway hurling people. Famous Galway hurling people. See, out this direction?' And he points northwards along the sun-soaked road. 'When you get to the fourth house along there, you are in Galway.'

Galway. The county and the province of Connacht lie just a stone's throw from this little oasis of Clare hurling. Galway – whose hurlers lie in wait for Clare at the end of this week.

There is no seam in the land, or change in the colour of the acreage, to back up George here. You have to take his word for it, that just over the hill, is Galway; that not far up the road the little stone walls will begin to proliferate, and further north the land will get appreciably worse but appreciably more beautiful, too. Galway looks pretty much the same as Clare from where we are standing. Then, as if to prove George's argument, Mary Gantley walks into his shop and the gentle slagging begins as George slices the ham for her. Galway and Clare. Galway and Clare. Galway and Clare.

'How many tickets have ye?'

'Tickets? Oh, plenty, George. Galway people are used to going up for semi-finals.'

'Ye'll be kicking yourselves if ye miss the only chance to see them play in Croke Park this year, Mary.'

'Well, we'd be interested in the novelty of that now, George.'

Mary's husband, Finbarr, played hurling in the maroon of Galway in the years before and after the breakthrough came. Her sons, Rory and Finbarr, have been wearing the maroon jersey for the past couple of summers now, biding their time in the Under-Age grades before shifting into Senior where they will bring more lustre to the name. They both played starring roles when Galway won the Minor All Ireland title last September. Finbarr has moved on to play Under-Twenty-One this summer; Rory is having another crack at Minor.

Meanwhile, George Taaffe's son, Eamonn, arrives up the road in his overalls, atop some colossal piece of farm machinery which looks as big as most houses around here. While the Gantleys stroll on towards destinies filled with medals and glories, Eamonn looks like being the hard-luck story of Clare's magical summer. A young full-forward of invention and promise, he has had the heart torn from his season by a treacherous hamstring.

Clare is on a roll right now, making history with each outing. This summer it has risen to altitudes where air is rare. Sean McMahon won a crucial line-ball against Cork while playing with a broken collar-bone. He just refused to leave the field while there was hurling to be played. He won a line-ball late on, and from it the winning goal came. History. Onwards to a Munster final. Clare had lost the previous two finals and a disinterested nation averted its eyes from the mauling which was about to happen. But more history came raining down. Clare is on its way to Dublin to play Galway in the All Ireland semi-final. Eamonn Taaffe's hamstring has ripped. He's just along for the ride.

Just last Wednesday week, Clare went up to Croke Park in the evening time just to get the feel of the place. No Clare team has played championship hurling there since the 1930s. Things had been looking good for Eamonn. The hamstring was healing and had been for several days. Then, out on the green grass of Croke Park, beneath the empty echoing stands, without warning he felt the ripping pain in his upper right leg. So close. It was a long lonely journey home to Tubber that night.

So, this weekend is All Ireland semi-final weekend. Eamonn will fly to Dublin with the team and keep his fingers crossed. If Clare's season ends, Eamonn Taaffe will have taken less from the summer than anyone else in the team. If it wins, he has a chance of making the final. Three weeks or so, sitting on top of the exercise bike in the room at the back of the shop, might just make the difference. Who knows? Fingers crossed.

In the Gantley's house across the border, fingers are crossed too. Clare is playing Galway this Sunday. Driving down to Tubber, through the county of Galway, the maroon-and-white flags which seem to decorate every house suddenly cease to exist at Tubber where the more exuberant yellow-and-blue of Clare begins. The change is startling.

The little neighbouring parishes of Beagh and Tubber will empty themselves out this Sunday, the respective populations pouring in the direction of Croke Park, one tribe in maroon-and-white, the other decked in yellow-and-blue. For the moment, though, they wave their flags at each other and enjoy the slagging. In a long hot summer that threatens drought, the weather has been banished from conversation.

Around here, if you have men in the house, the odds suggest that you have hurlers in the house, too. In the back of the shop, for instance, the Taaffe's mantelpiece is about to surrender under the weight of all the silverware it carries. The winning of it has been the joint responsibility of the Taaffe men.

George himself is an old county full-back, having put down a year with Clare in 1964, one of the many periods when it was neither profitable nor popular to be a Clare hurler.

'We lost in the first round of the championship,' says George. 'I suppose I didn't put enough effort into it all.' His voice still carries a little regret.

'Tis all hurling around here,' says young Eamonn, the parish's most prominent hurling ambassador at the minute. 'There's not much else to do.'

Eamonn is right. Not much else to do. Today the August sun is bleaching the land. Dogs are lying baking themselves in the heat outside the little houses all the way down here. From the Taaffe's shop, looking northwards, the little national school marks the forking of the roads a short distance away. Scarcely a breath of air ruffles the leaves in the trees. Eamonn went to school here, hard by his home-place – for about a week that is.

'I had a run in with the teacher.' he says, matter-of-factly. 'One afternoon a few of us were going across to the field to play hurling. A few big fellas and me. I ran across the road on my own and she didn't like it. There was a bit of trouble, I suppose, so I moved school. I was about four at the time.'

Aye. There'd be far more employment in Tubber if a boy needed an escort every time he crossed the road to play hurling in the field. After that, Eamonn went to school a short distance away across the border in Galway. He had his hurling education there. Same old story. They always go away.

Tubber has fewer than 200 houses and has been turning out hurling teams for the best part of the century. The history has been one of steadfast struggle, but the old days are spoken of with a quiet satisfaction. The club hasn't achieved great glories, but it has achieved more than its modest means should permit.

For many years Tubber men played their hurling in a field donated by the villages hurling historian, Pa Howard. Before that, they played in a field belonging to Matt Nugent. Before that, they disported themselves in a field donated by some other farmer with hurling in his blood and generosity in his heart. The itinerant history ended a few years ago when they mustered enough wherewithal to purchase their own field. No more changing clothes under the bushes, no more walking home with the sweat and the muck drying into their bodies.

They have done their best against the odds. Once upon a time, camogie was strong in the parish too, but, with the bite of emigration and the cut of harder times, the camogie just seemed to disappear. Numbers have always been a problem here in Tubber. Put it this way: as soon as you were good enough, you were old enough. Eamonn Taaffe played Under-Twenty-One hurling for the club when he was fifteen.

'I was in goal. When I got older and starting playing out-field on the Under-Twenty-Ones my younger brother started off in goals. He was fifteen, too. That's the way for us. When we were smaller the Under-Twelve team would be the Under-Thirteen team as well. And so on. I played Under-Fourteen hurling from the time I was nine years old.'

As Eamonn grew older and numbers continued to be a problem, Tubber even fielded a girl, Noelle Comyn, on its Minor and Under-Twenty-One teams. Perhaps Noelle started out by just being a solution to the numbers' problem, but she earned her place and performed with excellence and influence at centre-forward. She plays full-back for the Clare women's football team now.

Despite their scant numbers and their decades-long search for a pitch of their own, the Tubber clubmen have given exceptional service to Clare hurling through the years, pitching in with a player here and there on most of the good days and lots of the bad ones: Tom Burnell in 1932, Matt Nugent from 1945 onwards, Donal O'Grady from around the same time. O'Grady's nephews, Pat and Enda O'Connor, played for Clare from the late 1960s to the mid-1970s and won national league medals for their troubles. Johnny Lee, now working as a doctor in Dublin, hurled with distinction for the county from the late 1970s onwards. Now Eamonn Taaffe flies the flag for Tubber, and people expect that his brother, Oliver, will follow him on to the county team some time soon. If you have a hurling name in Tubber, people expect a lot.

Tracing a finger back through the tangled Tubber bloodlines, the same names keep cropping up on the Senior hurling teams: Taaffe, Clancy, O' Connor, O'Grady, Scanlan, Lee. This year alone, three Taaffe brothers will wear the black-and-amber jersey when Tubber go into championship battle with Eire Óg at Ennis. If you have men in the house in Tubber they will be hurling men.

Tubber is a unique little place. Not only does it mark the end of Clare territory as the traveller passes northwards past the Burren and on towards Connemara, but it also marks the apex of Clare hurling country. The ash stick is used to the east from here, down through Corofin and Kilmaley, and on to the Shannon estuary. West of the county belongs to the football folk. This little dot of houses and farms might have fallen to football, might have fallen to Galway, but it's Clare hurling territory and fiercely proud of the fact.

Geography, demographics and tradition have put hurls in the hands of the Taaffes. They and their neighbours, the Gantleys, hurled together on national school teams made up of Tubber boys and Beagh boys. Eamonn Taaffe and Finbarr Gantley hurled together in mid-field for a season or two. The team had middling success, but when secondary school came around the Taaffes and the Gantleys went their separate ways – Finbarr heading for the vocational school in Gort, Eamonn settling into Our Lady's school in the same town.

In hurling terms, Eamonn got the best of the bargain.

'We had a run of success all the way up. We beat Finbarr's team in the championship in first year. After that, we won every year all the way to Senior. We lost to St Kieran's of Kilkenny in the Hogan Cup final of 1993.'

All that, though, was schools' stuff. Eamonn Taaffe might have had his hurling education in Galway, but at home he was always a Clare man. There will be no thought for that little school in Gort this Sunday as Clare plays Galway. The sense of territory and the sense of pride in place don't die so easily. Away from school, matters on the borderlands have always been much the same.

'Always we played together,' says Eamonn of the Gantleys from Galway. 'If a few of us were pucking around of an evening, the Gantleys would come around and play with us in Pa Howard's field in Tubber or sometimes we'd be up in their house playing hurling. We always supported Galway in anything that Clare weren't playing in and they always supported Clare. When we played together, sometimes it would be Galway against Clare. We always knew they were from Galway and we were from Clare even though they were neighbours and friends.'

'There was always great support for the other county,' says Finbarr Gantley junior, a scion of one of the other great Galway hurling families. 'The only time when we were growing up that I can remember any rivalry between us was for the 1987 league final (Galway 3–12 Clare 3–10). There was a bit of slagging then. All the rest of the time, though, the Taaffes would come and see Galway play or we'd go and see Clare.'

This week, of course, there is an edge to all the slagging. Clare and Galway in an All Ireland hurling semi-final in Croke Park. Who would have dreamed of such a thing, that two rare cycles of prosperity could intersect at just the right moment?

Beagh, where the Gantleys live, work and play, lies slightly uphill from Tubber, the two parishes tied together forever on this lovely parcel of rich rolling farmland, speckled with lakes and contoured by gently rolling hills. It's agricultural territory here, fields and farmers, teachers and labourers, men and hurlers. The nearest big town which, in itself, is hardly a metropolis, is Gort. In the countryside, however, the only thing that stops people emigrating and leaving the towns to ruin is the quality of the land and the love of the hurling. Even those who go away are usually drawn back to play for their clubs when the call comes. The county line divides the two villages, everything else unites them.

Here on the Clare and Galway border, the hurling provides the means for identification. What tribes feel about each other is defined by what the they have achieved on the hurling field.

Clare watched Galway break through to an All Ireland in 1980 and goodwill turned to admiration. In Galway the *nouveau-riche* took to offering Clare their sympathy.

The Gantleys live in a couple of houses just across the hill from where the Taaffes have their shop and house. Hurling tradition runs back a few generations in the Gantley households. They are the heart and soul of hurling in these parts.

Joe Gantley, father to Finbarr senior and grandfather to the boys, moved here from Ardrahan as long ago as 1943. He stopped just short of the Clare border. '"You've gone far, shaggin' far enough", they said to me "you've gone shaggin' far enough".'

Well into his seventies, Joe is a big sturdy man from whom life and good humour still flow freely. He pours a visitor a whiskey and begins turning out the memories in his head. He, himself, claims that he found the hurling 'a bit rough', but if he did that's news to anyone who ever played against him. No Gantley was ever a shrinking violet on the hurling field.

'I didn't hurl much, but I crippled men who did,' says Joe laughing. His brother, Paddy Gantley, can't get away with making such claims. Father Paddy Gantley was canonized many years ago as a fully-fledged legend of Galway hurling, his reputation mossed long since with anecdotes about the days when he passed himself off as a variety of other individuals in order to escape the old church ban on priests immersing themselves in Gaelic games.

'One day,' says Joe, as soon as the subject of his illustrious brother is raised, 'he was playing against Waterford and Bishop Brown raised an objection and he was out on the pitch ready to play. After that, he played for a time with St Finbarr's in Cork as Paddy Gardiner, and then a bit later he changed the name to Gallagher. There was a great hurler at the time called Josie Gallagher. Then I think Paddy went out as Ignatious Gallagher for a while!'

Paddy played on the first Connacht team ever to have won a Railway Cup final in 1947. He left Ireland to work as a missionary in Nigeria in 1949, strolling down to the docks and boarding a cargo ship immediately after playing for Galway against Dublin in Croke Park one Sunday afternoon. He returned to train the Galway hurling team in 1953, taking them to an All Ireland final. Eventually he became chairman of the Galway County Board and the most illustrious so far of the hurling Gantleys.

Meanwhile in Beagh, however, hurling wouldn't have survived without the family's input. Back in the early 1970s, Beagh almost dissolved itself as a club. One season, eleven players were lost to the Senior team through emigration. Then Joe's son, Finbarr senior, returned home after a long stint of work in England and began playing for Neagh and Galway. Life returned to the club.

Steve Mahon, another hero of the era, switched clubs and began hurling for Beagh. Things improved still further. Gantley and Mahon won a famous All Ireland together with Galway in 1980. They reached a county final with Beagh a couple of years later and the losing of it is still a matter of contention all these years later, Finbarr having been withdrawn from the action late on when things were going well in order to provide a run for a long-serving sub. A five-point lead evaporated in the last eight minutes. Joe remembers that only the field-mice were left in Beagh or Tubber that afternoon. Sure, the gable-end of Steve Mahon's house lies in county Clare. What option had Tubber people got, but to go and roar him on?

Besides the support was always reciprocated. Wherever the hurling was good, the Gantleys would be willing to travel. Joe Gantley swears the best club hurling he ever saw was the 1971 Clare county final between mighty Newmarket and the Magpies of Clarecastle. The first day was a draw, and for the replay Joe went along on crutches having managed to break his leg between times. And? 'I enjoyed every puck of it.'

If Tubber's cheek lies by Beagh's jowl, then naturally the hurling histories of both parishes intersect every now and then. To mark their closeness, they both wear the same black-and-amber colours into battle. Liam Gantley, another of the sons, works in the Taaffe family's silage business and last summer he played a little tournament hurling in Clare wearing the Tubber colours. Just goodwill stuff.

Way back in the 1970s, Finbarr Gantley senior played in a Clare Under-Twenty-One final for nearby Crusheen, although debate is still hot as to whether or not his presence in that game was entirely legal. Certainly, he had to be introduced to his team-mates beforehand.

Down through the years, the rivalry between the clubs has sustained them when nothing else could. Who knew when disaster would strike? In 1946 Tubber reached a Junior county final. The following year they were unable to field a team. In 1948 they put out a team, but then Matt Nugent and Donal O'Grady moved away and began playing for St Joseph's in Barefield. In 1949, 1950 and 1951 Tubber had no team at all.

Beagh has fared slightly better on its own turf, a brief period of uncertainty in the early 1970s notwithstanding. Furthermore, Beagh has always held out the hand of friendship across the border. In the days when the season is young and the light is stretching, there will often be full-blooded challenge games between the parishes as they gear up for the summer. In the days when Pa Howard's field served as a pitch, there would be two county tournaments played out over the course of a weekend. Gort, Ardrahan and Beagh from Galway would joust with Tubber, Crusheen and Ruan from Clare.

Today, at teatime, the Gantleys are hurrying about the place. Joe is preparing to head into Gort to talk on a radio programme about the great days of Galway and Clare hurling. Finbarr Junior has just disappeared to Athenry for training with the county Under-Twenty-One team. Rory is gathering his sticks and gear and heading off with the Minors who play Cork in six days time. Finbarr Senior is finishing another summer's day on the farm, the dust of the fields still in his wiry hair. He's wondering about tickets for Sunday. What tribes feel about each other is reflected in the hurling around here.

'Oh. Have to go to Croke Park on Sunday,' says Finbarr. 'Sure t'would look bad if we didn't bother going up.'

Hurling has laid down a deep seam in the folklore here. From some place in Joe Gantley's head, this seam can be mined and retold. The place is suffused with the history of the GAA and that history is enmeshed with the history of the country. Michael Cusack was a teacher here in nearby Lough Cutra before he founded the GAA and, to this day, the local and much-neglected football club is named after him.

In both parishes, in Beagh and in Tubber, the older folk still talk of the days when the Black and Tans infested the area. Pa Howard in Tubber can remember the talk of a county final which Tubber played in as long ago as 1919. The game was to be played in Newmarket, but the Royal Irish Constabulary (RIC), identifying the hurling game as a small expression of national self-determination and pride, entered the ground and the game had to be held up. A stalemate developed with the hurlers refusing to play and the RIC refusing to leave. Eventually, through the intercession of the local clergy, the RIC was persuaded to leave. The match continued. Tubber lost.

Tubber lost the game, others lost their lives. Take the Loughnane brothers of Beagh, both of whom were instrumental in halting another game on another afternoon when the RIC entered a GAA field. The brothers insisted that their teammates ceased playing. For their trouble they were picked up by the Black and Tans some days later, tied to the back fender of a Crossley Tender lorry and dragged around the district until their bodies hung limp and drained of life on the road. They were then dumped into a nearby pond and some oil was poured on to the surface of the water to obscure the sight of them.

There is a footnote to this dark story, a touch of magic realism almost. In the days that followed the killings, the search for the brothers' bodies became feverish. A cousin of the Loughnanes 'who had never travelled beyond Gort in his life' dreamed one night of seeing the brothers lying in a dark pond. The ponds of the locality were duly dragged and searched. The bodies were recovered. 'You can go back to Dublin,' says Joe Gantley, animated at the end of his story, 'and tell them that dreams do come true'.

Joe is right. Dreams do come true. This week, the old man is pleased as punch to see his neighbours in Clare escaping from their long period of house-arrest within the province of Munster and stepping out into the big time. Joe has been an eyewitness to Clare's unlucky history. Between himself and Pa Howard down in Tubber, they could fill a book with the misfortunes of the Clare men.

Joe draws down the Munster championship of 1936 as a prize exhibit.

'I remember seeing them play Limerick. They were leading by two points with the game going towards the final whistle. The Clare full-back fouled Mick Mackey. It was a free-in and the Clare defenders lined across the goal. The Clare goalie had hands the size of shovels. Mackey knew he wouldn't blast it past him so he tipped the ball up in the air nice and gentle. The Clare goalie put his hand up to take it and, next thing, he woke up in the back of the net. Limerick won the All Ireland. Ah, they had bad times in Clare.'

The sympathy is genuine. For years Galway struggled in similar circumstances. In the nine years, for instance, when Galway toiled as guests in the Munster hurling championship they won just one game against Clare – one sunny May day at Nenagh in 1951. The rest was heartbreak.

Dreams come true, however. Joe's son, Finbarr, brought the All Ireland back to these parts with the Galway boys in 1980. If Clare reverses the grain of its own sad hurling history this Sunday, the Gantleys will travel on in hope with the Taaffes to follow Clare's journey right to the end. Beagh will row in behind Tubber. South Galway will roar on north-east Clare. The only thing that divides the two parishes will have united them. It was ever the same.

The boys are clattering around the departure desk. Ger Loughnane, more tired and more happy than any of them, can't leave go of the reins, can't abide this slide into cheery chaos. He stands in behind the check-in desk and supervises the flight arrangements of the entire Clare panel, a handful of journalists, a gaggle of blazered officials and other hung-over disciples. Clare is coming home.

Home. Ger Loughnane returned to Clare with so many losing sides on so many heartbreaking nights that he can scarcely dare to anticipate the excitement and merry mayhem that awaits the team. Twice in this long strange summer he has brought the boys home, first with the Munster title, now with an All Ireland title.

All his adult life he has quested for this day. He was nineteen and fully reared before ever he even attended a Munster hurling final. That day is etched in his mind: Cork 6–18 Clare 2–8. Nothing but the same old story. The final lesson before passing into adulthood.

He played on teams that ventured forth with the hopes of the county behind them. In 1977, they played Cork and had to struggle a man short for most of the match. Came home shaking their heads.

The following year they surfed into Thurles on the crest of a wave.

'It was a more innocent time then, not so much media, but a Munster title meant everything to Clare. It still does. That Sunday in Thurles, I have never sensed anything like it. The crowd was so highly strung. The new stand wasn't built at the time. The gates got broken down with the pressure on them and about 5,000 people got in for nothing. There are people in Clare who were at that match and their feet never touched the concrete in Semple Stadium. They were lifted in and out by the crowd. There were players on the Clare team that day who hadn't had a wink's sleep since the previous Wednesday. Worrying.'

They lost. Went back to the vigil. Lost Munster finals again in 1981, 1986, 1993 and 1994. Lost on the way to Munster finals every other year. So much trouble and woe. He remembers a wet evening a few years ago when he dropped Brain Lohan home to his house in Shannon one night after Clare had lost an Under-Twenty-One county final. Brian was an intense lad, from an old hurling family, but slow coming into his own strength. The drive was silent, punctuated only on departure when Brian Lohan turned to Ger Loughnane and said: 'I suppose I'll never wear a county jersey again'. Heartsick with defeat, Ger Loughnane hadn't got the words to answer the lad.

This year, just thirty-six months later, Ger Loughnane is about to be crowned manager of the year. Brian Lohan is already acclaimed as hurler of the year. Ger Loughnane is knocked out by the romance of it.

This summer he has tried everything and the gods have smiled on him. Ger Loughnane has seen so many bad days, and so many losers in saffron-and-blue jerseys, that he has learned to read the very grain of a man.

This year, then, he has picked fifteen single men for his team, picked them for character not for hurling. He has brought the lads out training at seven in the dewy morning in the park in Ennis, re-drawn the pitch in Ennis to the precise dimensions of Croke Park, taken the boys to Croke Park for nights of practice. With no substitutes left in his pocket, he has left a player with a broken collar-bone on the field of play. The gods have been smiling. The player has a one side-line puck, from which Clare have scored a goal and reached the Munster final. The gods have been grinning and winking even. He has stuck on a substitute late in the All Ireland final and the substitute has scored the winning goal while Ger Loughnane was looking the other way.

Now they are on the plane for home. The television people need some footage of the airborne champions. The boys are fatigued, seizing this oasis of peace before they touch down in Clare and the world goes wild. Dozing heroes don't make good TV.

'We need a song. Anyone up for a song,' crackles the imploring voice over the microphone. No takers, some grumbling.

A guitarist from the team's retinue of hangers-on is pressed into service. Under the hum of the aircraft he can scarcely be heard. The TV man with the cattle prod is undeterred.

'We need some applause,' he begs. More silence. 'Some applause.' More silence. 'How about the Clare shout then?'

Nobody is quite sure of the origins of the Clare shout or, indeed, the purpose of the Clare shout. The natives of Clare have kept their shout to themselves until now. In the week of their first All Ireland win since 1914 somebody has uncorked and patented The Clare Shout.

'This is how it goes,' croaks Pat Guthrie, the Dame Kiri of Clare shouting, 'Hooooooooooo-Hoo-Ha-Hooooooo. Hooooooooooo-Hoo-Ha- Hooooo.'

'I've heard it all now,' says Cyril Lyons, the team's oldest player. He probably has, too.

Then the boys are packed on to the top deck of the open-top bus as it pulls away from Shannon Airport. For miles all that can be seen is a sea of people. Just about every man, woman and child in Clare, and a fair few well-wishers from the counties all around, they reckon. There is music playing as there always is in Clare. Eamonn Taaffe has his arm around his girlfriend.

Eamonn Taaffe is the man, the substitute who scored the winning goal, the guy who made a guerrilla raid on history. The man who played sixteen minutes of hurling all summer, sixteen minutes of Senior inter-county championship hurling in his lifetime, damn it, and scored the winning goal in the All Ireland final. Scored the goal that brought the cup back to Clare for the first time in eighty-one years. Then got taken off again, because, in the confusion, the Bench thought Cyril Lyons had scored the goal. Eamonn Taaffe is the man whose name didn't appear in the programme, whose photo was never taken, who was known nowhere except in Tubber. Eamonn Taaffe's grandchildren will be hearing this yarn for as long as hurling is spoken about in Clare. Now, though, he's riding towards Ennis with the entire county spread out below him in an ocean of celebration. He has his arm around his girl.

The summer has been a long lonely fight against the possibility of being forgotten – riding the exercise bike in the back of George's shop, tripping up to Dublin to see sports' doctors, coming home with a new headful of routines and exercises. A lonely summer which might have ended in some poignancy. And yet –

'I was always hopeful. I was always told to keep going, to keep doing the job, and maybe I'd be used in some game. You can't ask for more.'

He gazes out at the happy turmoil below. The team has arrived in Newmarket on Fergus. Here, there is a little reminder of what Tubber might have felt had Eamonn Taaffe not resurrected himself. No stop has been scheduled in Newmarket, but a stage has been erected and decency demands that the bus takes a pause.

'We'll have to get off here, lads,' says Loughnane, rousing himself from the shelter at the back of the bus. 'It's the least we owe Newmarket.'

The least we owe Newmarket. Hurling people never forget. When Ger Loughnane hurled for Clare, Newmarket was the backbone of the county's efforts, providing the spine and the brains of the team winning two-out-of-every-three county titles. When Clare last reached an All Ireland final, a Newmarket man was captain and Newmarket men made up half the team. The parish is devoted to hurling, drenched in the lore of it, lost in the love of it. When Clare ended the long hunger, however, there was no Newmarket man on the team.

The lack of a Newmarket input into this great day hurts.

'I know this parish,' says Anthony Daly, the Clare captain. 'I know what a great hurling parish and club it is. I know because I'm from down the road in Clarecastle and nobody knows ye better. Ye'll be back.'

What wound there was is closed.

Clarecastle. Eamonn Taaffe moves to the front of the bus to see this sight. All evening the players have girded themselves for the arrival in Clarecastle.

'Wait till you see Clarecastle,' they have said. 'Wait till you see that.'

Clarecastle will be the barometer of the county's joy.

When the town hoves into view the bonfires are blazing, swelling the sky with their heat and colour. People have spilled out across the bridge and out of the town to greet the team, sirens are blaring, lights are flashing, music is playing, horns are being blown. The bus can advance no further. A deal is made with the crowd. They can have the six Clarecastle men.

If there is a moment that sums up the breadth of hurling's appeal, the way in which the game can touch an entire community and change entire lives – if there is such a moment, it comes when players arrive home in triumph. Only GAA players never move away from their audience, only hurlers and footballers live to hear the din of the thousands on Sunday, and the neighbourly chatter of the same people on Monday.

Here is such a moment. Within sight of most of their homes, the six Clarecastle men are hoisted on to the shoulders of their own townsfolk and carried across the bridge right to the heart of their town. Astonishing scenes. Old people leaning from upstairs windows crying, young women holding up babies, men hugging, people dancing. A thunder-storm of emotion.

When Anthony Daly came here on the night after the Munster final win, the town was still so shocked and unprepared that he had to give his speech from the roof of the bus shelter. Tonight, he faces the broad green upon which he grew up. He talks about Clarecastle and growing up there, about those who helped and taught him, those who built the club and the parish, all the old hurlers and heroes who walked around this town when he was a boy. He speaks of the love of hurling and the long years of silent and fervent wishing that went into making this day. He speaks of the black-and-white of Clarecastle.

On board the bus, every other Clare hurler is absorbing the words of this lovely speech. They each come from a place shot through with the love of the game, from streets that house local heroes and humble hurling men, from country roads where boys bash sliotars against gables until they have perfected their art. All summer they have beaten men who have gone home to parishes and villages just like their own.

Eamonn Taaffe, thinks of Tubber, hard on the Galway border. Fifteen years ago, they watched Finbarr Gantley bring the shining cup home on the Galway side of the border. Dim memories. Neighbouring powers. Nineteen years old now and Eamonn is Tubber's most famous son already.

Sixteen minutes of hurling isn't what it is all about – not at all. Afternoons in the field with his brothers and with the Gantley boys, long evenings bashing a ball about, the hunger to keep driving on. That is what hurling is about. Every small town knows it, knows that one of its own might one day ride the bus to the big time and come back and live among them on Monday morning. It isn't about sixteen minutes, it's about sharing the harvest of the days, about the communal prize, the common passion, about home-place and home people.

He thinks of Tubber. His name heads the list of heroes now: Tony Burnell, Matt Nugent, Donal O'Grady, Pat O'Connor, Enda O'Connor, Johnny Lee – Eamonn Taaffe.

His name is there, in the lore of his own people.

In Clarecastle, the people are singing 'The Lovely Rose of Clare'. The night is young yet. Ennis lies ahead. The week will be a series of events like this, explosions of emotion, each like the other but each one unique. Every town and village has waited and yearned for this happy day. Every place has its story, its roots tangled up in hurling and in history, its reason for deserving this golden hour. He's got his arm around his girl, he wonders if they will ever get to Tubber. There'll be a crowd there for sure.

CHAPTER EIGHT

Boom! Boom! Boom!

Padre to a young congregation in Campile, county Wexford, in the week of President Bill Clinton's historic visit to Ireland in December 1995 – also the week when Jason Sherlock presented medals in the local community hall: *'Now then, boys and girls, we had a very special visitor amongst us this week. He came to us with a message and made a very great impression on us all. He was an historic visitor. Can you tell me who that man was boys and girls?'*

CHORUS: *'Jayo. Father. Jayo.'*

High summer and Uncle Eddie is in his shirtsleeves, waiting at the newsagent's. He's a small gaunt man who seems never to be still. Nervous energy has gnawed all the excess flesh from his bones. His eyes are hooded and quick, and the only time Eddie looks close to repose is when he closes his eyes and takes the first sweet drag from a newly-lit cigarette.

Today is a summer bank holiday, and the local meat factory is shut. When the meat factory is shut, Ballyhea basks. The sun is making the tar-seams on the road look watery. Eddie, waiting and smoking, feels the heat on his back.

The meat factory and hurling are the two things which Ballyhea is known for. The actor and *bon-vivre* Oliver Reid lives close by, but it would take a greater sensation than Oliver Reid to divert attention away from the hurling in these parts. Even the publicans know that a good run in the hurling is better for business than having one of the world's most celebrated boozers living next door. The sporting summer is pregnant with promise just now. A county semi-final date lies ahead for Ballyhea's young hurling team. Maybe this year little Ballyhea will go all the way. Maybe this year.

Eddie himself devotes big parts of his life to both the meat factory and the hurling, but in Ballyhea this summer his personal renown springs from being the uncle of the nation's most famous footballer. Eddie's nephew is a national obsession just now, Gaelic football's first superstar.

'Your lad was on the telly again.' people tell Eddie. He smiles, draws them in, tells them the latest on his lad and the incredible summer he's been having.

'They haven't got the best out of him yet,' he likes to tell people. When he talks about his famous nephew he has a way of implying confidentiality, of welcoming people to an inner circle of those connected to young Jason. That's who he's waiting for right now, why he's hopping anxiously from foot to foot at the newsagent's shop by the main road. He's waiting for Jason.

Ballyhea is a parish of just 1,100 souls whose houses are scattered randomly on either side of the main Cork to Limerick road, a short distance from Charleville. You could pass 1000 times and never suspect that, between bricks and fields, this little patch of land has the makings of a tight and proud community. Ballyhea looks like the sort of place you stop in, only if you've just hit a cow on the road.

The houses are dotted around the townland, clustering together only in the tight little estate near the meat factory. Everywhere else is rolling farmland and plain sturdy houses linked by little lanes and narrow roads which spread out like concrete capillaries from either side of the motorway. If there is a focal point to the place, it is either the GAA club in its neatly fenced-off field hard by the railway tracks or the Bridge Bar, a huge cigarette smoke and leatherette pub which looms in isolation on the roadside and which entertains much the same people as the GAA club does.

Eddie came to live here some ten years ago, a refugee from Dublin and the threat of unemployment. Ten years. Sufficient time to put down roots and pick up traces of the north Cork accent. It might have been hard to fit in, what with the city-life bred into his bones and the smoke bedded deep in his lungs, but the GAA is a passport to anywhere. Soon Eddie was taking out teams to hurling and football pitches around north Cork, and talking about the prospects for each successive championship. Ballyhea was home, and, these days, Eddie's voice sings a little with the borrowed lyricism of the local countryside. When he talks about his nephew, he likes to say: 'He's Finglas, but there's a lot of Ballyhea in him too, boy. A lot of Ballyhea in him'.

It's true, too. There is a lot of Ballyhea in him. Jason Sherlock began spending summers here with Uncle Eddie as soon as he began secondary school. He remembers Eddie coming home to Dublin for Christmas and holidays, and showing him photographs of the under-age team he was in charge of down in Ballyhea. Jason remembers the photo and remembers not too long afterwards lining out with the same faces in the same black- and-white jerseys. A Ballyhea boy.

Uncle Eddie would drive them around – Jason and Tomas O'Riordan, and Mick Mackessy, and the Ronan cousins, Neil and Ian, and Ollie Morrissey. Eddie and Tim Dennehy would drive them from match to match, and what Jason remembers most is Eddie's car dawdling along as Eddie tried to roll the next smoke with his hands on the cigarette paper and his little fingers wrapped around the wheel. It could take a long time to get to games when Eddie was gasping for a smoke.

Ballyhea was an escape from the great unforgiving urban sprawl of Finglas, and an immersion into the rural soul of the GAA. Having Jason safe and sound with Eddie in Ballyhea was a break for a hard-pressed mother. The benefits spread themselves both ways, too. Having Jason Sherlock safe and sound in Ballyhea was a break of a different kind for the local GAA club.

They broke him in on hurling first, sticking him at centre-forward against Kanturk one afternoon, hoping he'd survive but content to knock a little fun out of the occasion if he didn't. There was no awkward learning process, though, no ungainly or dangerous moments as he went chopping and swiping after the sliotar with the stick. His hand-to-eye co-ordination was perfect, his speed extraordinary, his accuracy uncanny. Hey! He scored three goals that day and sowed the beginnings of his own legend. It was a couple of years before anyone thought to stick him on to a football team.

When underlining their own intimate knowledge concerning one of their own, they like to say around Ballyhea that, for those who saw him play the game, Jason Sherlock was a better hurler than ever he was a footballer. It's probably true, but they'd probably say that if it were not true. Hurling is life here, football is trivia.

They saw him every summer after that – more often, perhaps. Any big game and Jason was on the train to nearby Charleville as soon as the phonecall came. Looking back, people think that time must have been elastic then for Jason to have crammed so much in.

For a while, they thought that wearing the red jersey of Cork would be as natural a progression for young Jason as pimples, stubble and girlfriends. He might have spoken with the flattened vowels of the Dublin suburbs and borne the looks of a long-vanished father, but he got his hurling and football education in Ballyhea. The red-and-white, the blood and bandage would become him.

A Cork Minor selector came to see him kick football against Glanworth one summer afternoon. The Minor championship had already begun and Cork was motoring well, but Ballyhea people knew they had something special playing at corner-forward. Well, the Minor selector came and saw Jason Sherlock substituted after forty minutes. The substitution was a theatrical flourish, an emphatic resting of the Ballyhea case. Jason had scored two goals and ten points from play in a championship semi-final. Two goals and ten points is an impressive accumulation of scores, even if one were being marked by a traffic bollard. Jason departed and the stage was left to the supporting cast. The Cork Minor selector departed and was never heard of again.

Next summer, Jason scorched around Croke Park in the sky-blue of Dublin. In Ballyhea they still wonder about the selector, wonder if his silence was a racial thing, or a slight on their little club, or just an act of arrant stupidity.

'Toddy Cuthbert is not to blame in that little episode,' says Uncle Eddie.

'Well, somebody is to blame,' says Tim Dennehy, 'somebody is to blame.'

Jason just got on with his sporting life – indeed, with several sporting lives.

Above in Dublin, he thrived at soccer, playing first for Rivermount and later for St Kevin's Boys. Team-mates, such as Alan Moore and Darren Grogan, took the boat to try their hand at the English professional game but Jason had too many irons in the fire.

Soccer would bring its rewards later on, a scholarship to University College Dublin, an appearance for the Irish Under-Twenty-One side against Austria, a constant hiss of whispers that some big English concern was about to whisk him off to the big time.

Basketball was a passion, too. Travelling to Estonia with an Irish under-age team once, he met Magic Johnson at Helsinki airport and the five-foot-six guard from Finglas had his photo taken with the six-foot-seven guard from LA.

The stories concerning his basketball prowess follow him about like a retinue, adding to his exoticism. In Ballyhea, the basketball court in the school yard is decorative only, its hoops drooping earthwards, shorn of their nets long ago, the tarmac court existing only as surface for scuffling soccer games.

Jason could play this game, though, dribbling, faking and passing amidst the beanpoles. His GAA summers might have been passed on the fresh-mown fields of gentle north Cork, but his daydreams brought him to the shiny parquet floors of the National Basketball Association (NBA).

'People think you have to be tall to play NBA,' he'd insist when the doubters would tell him to catch on to himself, 'but Muggsie Bogues of the Charlotte Hornets is smaller than I am.'

'Muggsie Bogues of where?' they'd ask.

His school, St Vincent's in Glasnevin, Dublin, had a fine history of breeding basketball players. In his senior year, Jason carried an injury into the All Ireland schools final, but played anyway and out-scored everyone with twenty points while playing as point-guard. St Vincent's were champions. Muggsie Bogues at point-guard.

That's how life went – charmed and feckless. One summer, Ballyhea lost him for a month when he was taken to a basketball camp in Philadelphia, the sort of place representatives of American universities hang around in, their pockets full of scholarship offers. The other kids, the American kids, were in the system working their way through to the basketball Nirvana that is the NBA. Jason and four other Irish youngsters worked their way through camp by acting as bus-boys in the evenings. For two weeks out of the four, Jason was voted Most Valuable Player.

The air was thick with rumours of college scholarships, but Jason and his pals disappeared from sight – back to Ballyhea and hurling and football – as soon as the camp finished. The rumours evaporated. Even now, though, as an embryonic Gaelic games' superstar, he falls asleep at night looking up at posters of those NBA heroes: Tim Hardaway, Golden State Warrior, Die Harder.

Sport offered so many avenues. In Ireland, though, if you are going to stay at home and at the same time singe your name into the national sporting consciousness, your tool will be the GAA.

Just as Uncle Eddie had merged into the background of a small north Cork village by speaking the language of Gaelic games, so it was with nephew Jason. His dark slightly Asian features made sure that he got singled out early for racial abuse on the field of play. Nothing sharper than what the streets of Finglas had to offer, but all the more shocking for hearing it down in the north Cork leagues.

Eddie remembers the day that they broke Jason in as a Ballyhea man. It was an Under-Fourteen league game and Jason was at full-forward. Little shards of abuse were flying about and Jason was distracted and vexed.

Eddie on the sideline was agitated, furious and protective all at once. A scrap broke out and Jason's fists flailed furiously. It was decided to take Jason out of the game to let him cool down a little. On the way off, Eddie unaccountably hit Jason a slap – the only time he ever raised a hand to him. Half a decade later, standing here reminiscing in the sunshine on the roadside, the regret is still in Eddie's voice. He can't explain the stew of emotions that led him to lift his hand, and he can't forget the sight of his nephew sitting on the sideline crying his heart out.

'I gave him a flaking. Aw, too hard. As soon as I done it I knew I was wrong. Next thing was he started crying. I thought he was never going to stop. He came out of himself after that, though. I think he took a look around and said to himself that, if this was the way things were down here, that was fine. He was going to start making it. He never paid much attention to what was said after that.'

Jason was a Ballyhea boy after that. Through each successive summer he picked up a couple more medals for his collection. They won nine north Cork titles together and, by the time Jason's generation graduated from the Minor grades, Ballyhea knew good times were on the way.

Jason was part of it all – arriving down to Eddie's house more and more often as the years went by and the games got bigger – staying over at the O'Riordan, Morrissey or Ronan households. Distance was no barrier. Once he played basketball in Dublin in the morning, jumped into Tom Gleeson's car, still sweating and fully kitted out, and slept in the back seat for the trip to Cork. He arrived, played and scored for Ballyhea and jumped into the back seat again for the trip home. Jason Sherlock was the sort of kid that any coach would drive ten hours a day for.

They grew older and tighter together: Jason Sherlock, Eamon Morrissey, Tomas Riordan, Darren Ronan, Ollie Morrissey, and the boys. For a tiny parish, sundered by the Limerick-Cork road, the gang represented an extraordinary crop of talent. Ballyhea was a hurling town, but, with a postulant inter-county footballer in its midst, football served as a diversion too.

Today, Jason Sherlock is going home to Ballyhea, taking another long car ride from Finglas to Cork. His celebrity is blooming like a hot-house flower and he's keen to wipe away any perceived distance between himself and Ballyhea. He, and some of his confederates from the long summers of childhood, have crossed the border into adulthood and the achievements have continued to flow.

Eamon Morrissey and Darren Ronan have been buzzing about the Cork Senior hurling panel this summer. Jason plays in the All Ireland semi-final in two weeks against, co-incidentally, Cork. A week later, Ballyhea travels to Ring Park in Cork to play Imokilly in a county hurling semi- final. It's hard to get Ballyhea people to talk about much else this week. The summer is ripening nicely, lots of achievement already, dreamtime ahead.

Uncle Eddie has an itinerary laid out, a tour of the parish and a few quick stops for tea and sandwiches in the various houses which young Jason grew up in. By the time Jason arrives, Eddie is beside himself with pride and excitement.

'We'll do the O'Riordan's, then Morrissey's, then Ronan's, then Dennehy's, then we'll go to the club, and then we'll go to the Bridge.'

Eddie is licking the gum-strip of another cigarette paper.

'Okay, Eddie.'

And so the car is pointed down the first leafy by-road.

'Boom! Boom! Boom! Let me hear you say Jayo! Boom! Boom! Boom! Let me hear – '

Nine maybe ten-thousand throaty Dublin voices are singing the new hymn of the faithful. On the great banked terrace that is Hill 16, people are jumping up and down in a frenzied sort of unison, worshipping the new prince of Dublin football. Around the rest of the ground another 50,000 people are absorbing the implications of what they have just seen. Jason Sherlock has just plugged Croke Park in.

All summer long his legend has been growing exponentially, his fame measured by new indices. In the dark cold months either side of Christmas they heard whispers about him, and on winter league highlight programmes they caught glimpses of his energy spreading like a current through the drab cold day games. Winter brings its one-day wonders just as surely as it brings short evenings and bad weather, though. Yet, here in high summer, the kid is doing the business. The kid is born for the big time. The real thing.

Already he has scored the goal of the summer, a lovely rising shot hitting the back of the Laois net one afternoon down in Navan. Having pulled down a high ball from above his head, he has turned so quickly that he has left his boot in the hand of a flailing defender. Boom!

Afterwards, the entire Dublin team waited on board its bus, baking in the summer sun while Jason finished his rounds of media interviews. A couple of weeks later in Croke Park, Dublin have dismantled the team that has haunted them for several years, taking Meath apart piece by piece in the course of a ten-point victory. Jason's riding the wave, all the way now.

In every game, his genius pops once or twice as dazzlingly as a flash-bulb.

He runs and turns as quick as a fish. He shoots for goals every time the hint of an opening presents itself. He does more than that. The moments keep coming, and soon the TV people have strung them together with Dinah singing 'Mad About the Boy' as the backing track.

Against Meath, he kisses the referee after he is awarded a free kick. He feigns injury one afternoon to take a breather, and the TV cameras pick him out giving the team doctor a huge theatrical wink as he arrives with the magic bottle.

Now, here on All Ireland semi-final day, the game has turned on another moment of Jason Sherlock brilliance as he gathers a long ball, turns and slips a goal into the Cork net. Cork people spend the rest of the afternoon gathering themselves, and Dublin people spend the rest of the afternoon copper-fastening their passage to the All Ireland final.

In the aftermath of this game, the Jason Sherlock phenomenon takes off into the stratosphere, the hype takes him places where no man has been before. He straddles three sports, being a former Irish basketball international, a soccer scholarship boy at University College Dublin, and an inter-county Gaelic footballer. It is the Gaelic football which is burning his name into the national consciousness, however. The GAA will never be quite the same again.

Jayo. Evening papers publish serialized spreads on his life story. His face beams down from the bedroom walls of thousands of teenagers. Prime-time chat shows wrestle with each other for the rights to the first in-depth interview. Men in suits form an orderly queue asking the boy-wonder if he might consider endorsing their product. The GAA has grasped his potential, and his days are spent cruising the summer camps where some 5,000 Dublin youngsters are having the skills of Gaelic games instilled in them. The idea of Jason doing some coaching at each of the camps is dropped, instead he's just driven in, presented to the kids, and the rest of the visit is an exercise in crowd-control.

All forms of craziness. On the occasion of the Dublin team's media night two weeks before the All Ireland final, Jason appears at the head of a large posse of screaming fans. They chase him across the pitch like hounds after a hunted fox, chasing him down but never quite catching him. He arrives breathless at the spot where the team management is holding a private conference.

'Are we going to do anything tonight?'

'No, just kicking about then meeting the press upstairs.'

'Okay.'

And he's off, dodging his way back to the dressing-room where he will spend the next two hours signing autographs.

They wonder sometimes if it's all getting to him, if it isn't taking the energy and good sense out of him. He's barely nineteen and all on his own out there under the spotlight. Nobody in GAA history has ever been on the receiving end of such an explosion of adulation and hype before. Ever. One night he cries off training because he has 'wind'. Another evening, he rings the team manager from a summer camp, Bohernabreena, in the Dublin mountains. He doesn't want to train this evening. He needs to talk now. He needs his leg looked at.

'We'll take a look at it at training.'

'No. Now.'

'Why now? At training.'

'No. Now.'

So he arrives half-an-hour later needing his taxi-fare paid. The issue of his hamstring causes some contention. The story grows legs and walks of its own accord in Dublin football circles. In club houses, people pass on spiteful whispers about *prima donnas*. The kid at the centre of this great tidal wave of excitement still needs his taxi paid, however. That seems to be the point.

The madness never stops. Speculation mounts on a daily basis that he is about to be whisked off to a soccer club in England. He appoints an agent, choosing Kevin Moran, a childhood hero and another Dublin footballer, who was once whisked away to the world of soccer. Moran's years with Manchester United, and with the Dublin team of the 1970s, were preceded by an academic career which brought him a Bachelor of Commerce degree and, several stages along, the path to becoming a chartered accountant. Sherlock is the first GAA player in the history of the game to require the services of an agent. Things change quickly after Moran's arrival.

'I remember once during the summer,' says Jason, when his life has calmed again, 'and Kevin had just taken over looking after these things, just to take the pressure off me really. He asked me if anyone had been in touch for me to do commercial stuff and I mentioned the name of this big dairy firm. They had come to me and I'd got a letter saying how the fee would be. I chanced my arm when they called me up and the woman said that the figure I mentioned was no problem. I was speaking to Kevin and he said he'd look after anything I was doing from then on. He got their number from me and took it from there. Kevin got my fee and a VAT cheque. The VAT cheque was more than I'd asked for in the first place! Most of us in the GAA don't really know what we are doing when it comes to commercial stuff.'

The summer of Dublin's twenty-second All Ireland brought much change. An entire new commercial world opened up within the GAA, an Association, which only four years previously had hesitantly accepted the notion of commercial sponsorship.

The GAA has always taken a two-strand approach to the issue of money. Some would say two-strand, others would say hypocritical. The Association cherishes and polices the amateur standing of its players, and makes sure they maintain a status which keeps the stars of the game tied to the communities from which they have sprung.

The GAA is surely the only sports' association in the world where a person can sit in an executive box watching an athlete perform in front of 70,000 people, and a huge television and radio audience, knowing that the athlete isn't getting a penny of the revenue generated, and that each of the 70,000 people can enjoy the privilege of walking into the athlete's place of work the next week to tell him just what they thought about it all.

So, on the one hand, the dressing-rooms are kept free of money and the taint of commercialism, and, on the other hand, the GAA with 750,000 adult members represents the biggest sporting market in Ireland. Stadiums have to built, over 2,000 clubs need facilities and maintenance, television hungers after the rights to cover big games, and sponsors have been knocking at the door for more than a decade. The market penetrates deep into the soul of the community, cutting across class-barriers and geographical barriers. Yet these players are amateurs. How can the two imperatives be reconciled?

In the 1990s, the gulf between the players who play for the pride of the parish and the suits who shuffle the papers in head office has grown considerably. The Senior football and hurling championships at club and inter-county level are tied in to long-term and lucrative sponsorship deals. Every county team, and most club teams in the country, carry a sponsor's name on their jerseys. No sport or pastime has been soaked into the fabric of a society in quite the way that hurling and football have. The emotion, the ties with place, history and family, are unique. To keep the sport thriving in a modern world, the GAA has begun to sell shares in this heritage.

Television has opened itself up as a significant source of revenue. The Ulster championship in football and hurling are now sold as a package to television companies operating to the north of a border which the GAA doesn't officially recognize. The blossoming of interest in Ulster has been TV- and success-led. The result is that, for the first time, the GAA is in a position to auction off its wares to competing television concerns.

Money is also pouring in from other previously untapped sources. The GAA, having equipped itself with an extraordinarily ambitious new stand as the first part of an attractive and costly redevelopment of Croke Park, financed the operation entirely with funds raised from the sale of corporate boxes. The only strand of Irish life, hitherto immune to the charms of football and hurling, has emptied its pockets for the right to sup wine and munch *hors-d'oeuvres* while watching the peasant games. In that regard, perhaps, hurling in particular has come full circle having once been a game sponsored by gentry and played by plain people. At the grass-roots of the game, however, not many have grasped that irony. Skyboxes and corporate receptions seem to have little to do with the pride of the parish and the wearing of the colours.

In a world where every club is named for a place, a saint or a Republican martyr, this wash of new and easy money has been hard to absorb. On a local level, sponsorship has been merely an extension of the community support upon which the GAA has existed for decades. On a national level, the club secretary in the Junior club in the west of Ireland, who can't get a ticket for the All Ireland final, bitterly resents the snapshots of suits sipping Champagne above in Croke Park, and wonders if they have ever stuck an Under-Twelve team in their car on a Saturday morning and driven them miles.

Through all of this, inevitably, the pressures on players and managers have greatly increased, yet they themselves have been required to remain lily-white and virginal when it comes to the amateur ethos. The winning of a championship carries more romance and glory than ever it did before, but for those playing big-time hurling and football the pressures of staying on top are almost unbearable. In the weeks approaching big games it isn't uncommon to find players taking days off from work just to cope with media demands.

As the world shrinks and televisions influence becomes all the more pervasive, a tide of global homogenization threatens to wash away idiosyncratic cultural assets such as hurling and football. The GAA needs to keep running faster just to stay in the same place. Full-time youth coaches and development are being appointed around the country, the infrastructure is constantly being updated and modernized, and the top level of games have come to be seen more and more as product which must be produced and tailored to pay for the great nationwide structure which they must sustain.

As for the players at the centre of it all? All their effort, their dedication is funnelled back into the heart of the game, yet, having opened the door to sponsors and requested that the players turn their bodies into walking billboards, the GAA has ushered in a new age of commercial exploitation which it sometimes looks ill-equipped to handle.

When Dublin launched a new sponsorship deal back in the early 1990s to help defray the costs of training the county Senior teams, two players took time off work to attend the relevant reception in a Dublin hotel. Sipping drinks and mingling, they were suddenly thrown football shirts with the new sponsor's names emblazoned upon them. Embarrassed and slightly taken aback, they refused. The reality of the new age was dawning.

In the summer of Jason Sherlock's rise to the top, the rules seem to be changing all the time. The team Jason trained with to win the 1995 All Ireland was managed by a group of four men, each bringing separate professional qualifications to the task. They, in turn, were backed by the services of a sports' psychologist, a nutritionist, an exercise physiologist, a medical officer, a physiotherapist, a video services' unit and a masseuse. All this for an amateur game. Jason is clear-eyed about where he sees the future of the GAA.

'Most of the stars of the GAA have been older players who have established themselves with a job by the time they have broken through to county teams. I know I have no foundation and that I have to make something out of my life. That's why I do what I do. I took a look at what other people were getting out of me and what I was getting and took a decision. I'll put anything I can back into football and hurling, but I'm not here to put money into other people's pockets. That's separate. Other players will certainly come along after me and say "I can make a few bob out of this". It depends on the individuals. I have to do it, I need to do it. At the same time, the fact that I play soccer for a career gives me an outlet to do it. Somebody else might have to face the GAA head on.'

Not long after the All Ireland final, the discomfort felt by traditionalists at the perceived earning power of one nineteen-year-old within the game seeped out when the President of Association, Jack Boothman, delivered himself of some peevish comments concerning Jason Sherlock and his demand for appearance-money at commercial engagements.

The remarks were ill-chosen. By then, Jason had become the poster-boy for a chain of department stores, but he had also been selfless in the business of bringing the All Ireland trophy to schools all over the county in the aftermath of Dublin's win. Schoolteachers reported a huge swing in the childish imagination away from Manchester United and towards Gaelic games. In November, Jason went to Boothman's own club in Blessington and spent an evening presenting medals to youngsters and signing autographs for them. Neither Blessington nor Boothman can have seen anything like it before.

The future? For many years players have been nibbling away at the rulebook. The legendary Kerry team of the late 1970s and early 1980s appeared in the Sunday papers one morning wrapped in towels and loitering with intent around a washing machine. The deal broke down in a welter of accusations and wild rumour-mongering, but most Kerry players of that era were happy to show those who were interested just where their household appliances had come from.

There have been other deviations, rumours of All Ireland winners charging money for appearances with the Sam Maguire Cup, stories of top players waking up in the morning and finding large parcels of sporting goods and modest cheques deposited outside their front doors. What happens to Jason Sherlock in the course of one crazy summer is just the start.

'It all depends on the player or the person,' says Jason. 'Most GAA players are so affable that if somebody asks them to jump, they say no problem and jump. But there comes a time when you say hold on, I can't do all this for nothing. You are selling other people's goods for them. There must be players out there who resent having to do these things, but aren't in a position to ask for money.'

Certainly, within the Dublin GAA, as the summer wore on, the warm breezes of commercialism were felt all the more sharply with a superstar in the vanguard. Jason had a personal deal with Reebok even before the great summer adventure began. That tie-in brought responses from both the county sponsors, Arnotts (a city department store) and sports' goods manufacturers.

'Puma was the main mover really, not Arnotts so much. We, the players, talked with Billy Kelly from Arnotts after the Cork game and the problem wasn't Arnotts, it was the county board. Arnotts didn't have any obligation to do anything for the players during the year. What they did for us was out of goodwill.

'Puma came to me during the summer, though, and asked me to wear their boots. They were going to pay me to wear them for one game (the All Ireland final), but the other players on the team were going to be wearing them just because they got them for free. I should have told the lads straight out that that's the way it was, but I remember telling Puma – just to let them know – that the lads were hoping to be looked after by other companies. One pair of boots each seemed a bargain price. Lo and behold, next thing is: "There's your sweatshirt, there's your T-shirt, there's your two pairs of boots" for all the lads. So many people know they can get away with things with GAA players.

'I got some of the players Reebok gear. I was just trying to look after mates. I went to lads who I knew would be interested, fellas who it wouldn't affect to be asked. I went along and asked would they wear them and they said they wouldn't mind. As it turned out, most of them didn't wear the Reebok boots because of the conditions on the day – they didn't have the studs that suited. Most of the lads wore Puma, but I stuck with Reebok.

'I had no real intention of getting into the deal with Puma, but Kevin was anxious to test the water just to see what was on offer. Kevin just sussed it out. I was already tied into a deal with Reebok for the year. Since the All Ireland final, I've signed with them for another year. It's nothing major, mainly it means not buying boots and gear. There's cash involved, but not much.

'It would be possible to make a living out of Gaelic games. I would have to sit down and think of all the options, but the chance is there. You need some luck. An individual can be good, but it all depends on the team. The destiny is shared out, it's not all in your own hands. It would take a lot of good luck and consistent success to make a good living out of it under present circumstances. One summer you lose and, bang, you're out of the limelight for the year.'

So he continues in the limbo of wanting to make a living out of sport, but being a superstar in an amateur game. As his twentieth birthday approaches, the chances of a move to England and the world of big-time soccer appear to grow more slender. The GAA, his life in Ballyhea and his crazy summer in Dublin's blue have unhinged him slightly.

'Sometimes I wonder, even allowing for the money and the chance to make a living, if I really want to go away. I love the fact that I can walk into any place in Ireland and talk about football to somebody. There isn't a soccer culture in Ireland, just a few die-hard league supporters and a load of people who follow Gaelic games and the Irish soccer team. GAA is the real culture. I've been lucky to have a summer which means I'll always be remembered in the folklore of Gaelic football when people talk about 1995.

'I can't imagine being away, being in some English town, going into a pub and asking them to put on Channel Four and sitting there watching Gaelic football. I can't imagine being that far away from it all, thinking I could be here, knowing how much it means to people. That's one of the things I think about when I think about soccer and England. I go to places in Ireland and I know I matter because I'm a Gaelic footballer. I matter not because I'm Jason

Sherlock, but because the people think that Gaelic football matters. I could go to England and make money, and even be a star, but I wouldn't ever have that connection with people again.'

I travel down the leafy green lanes again, to Ballyhea people turning up the furrows of their memories.

They recall different things about Jason in Ballyhea. Upstairs in the little club house in the Gaels Memorial Field, Jason gazes at all the old-team photographs, a pictorial biography of himself and the boys growing up, little landmarks: Tomas O'Riordan on a St Flannan's Harty Cup winning team, Eamon Morrissey with the Christy Ring trophy, Jason throughout his teens tucked in with winning teams all the way.

As Jason browses, Tom Gleason remembers pitching him into a North County Under-Twenty-One final when he was just sixteen and hadn't yet grown into his strength. Jason was carrying an injured ankle into the game.

'He pointed to his ankle after fifteen minutes and gestured to me. I wasn't sure what he wanted, so I gestured back to see if he wanted some water. He's getting annoyed with me now and signals back "No" and points at his ankle again. I assume he wants to come off. I send a sub on and Jason comes off steaming, really fuming. He throws away the hurley, gives us all a ream of abuse, sits down on the bench, tears coming out of his eyes and hardly able to speak with the anger. Turned out, he only wanted a spray for the ankle. We were so taken aback by it that we put him back on for the last twenty minutes. We won by a point and he scored the winning goal in the last minute.'

In the O'Riordan's house he is made to come to the hall while the family phone Diarmiud who is sleeping soundly somewhere in Chicago. The next stop is the Morrisseys, whose family tradition is goalkeeping. Lack Morrissey won a county medal in goals for Avondhu in the 1950s. His son, Ollie, plays between the sticks for Ballyhea this summer. The Morrisseys remember Jason's odd habit of lying down and taking a rest before all games, no matter how trivial.

'We always knew Jason would be special,' says Mrs Morrissey.

'Well, if only he could have got a girlfriend and stayed in Cork, he might have been,' says Lack, and the place breaks down in laughter.

In the Dennehy's house, they are football people – aliens in a land of hurling. Tim, who played a few league games himself in the red of Cork, seems slightly bemused still that football never had wholehearted backing as a pastime in Ballyhea. It was Tim who put many of the finishing touches to the Jason Sherlock who has been scorching the meadows all summer.

'I kept the football from your last game for us, Jason,' says Tim. 'The one against Valley Rovers? I always said if you ever played for Dublin, that's when I'd give it to you. Do you remember that game, Jason? Myself and your Uncle Eddie here were like people on the shoreline shouting encouragement to drowning sailors.'

Onwards and down the road to the Ronans. The boys, Neil and Darren and their cousin Ian, have their photo taken with Jason in the summer sunshine out in the middle of the road. There is a slight awkwardness. Nobody here has ever felt the need to have photos taken with Jason before. An instinct for slagging and gentle insults dissolves the tension into laughter. Soon the boys are dandering about the roadway and there is no place in the world they would rather be. Cars slow down and blast their horns at the Ballyhea boys who have broken into the big time.

'I have the calendar from 1991 in work these days, Jason,' says Neil Ronan Senior who works across the Limerick border in Kilmallock. 'I keep it behind the door and any time the slagging starts up about Kilmallock, I show them the pictures of you in the three Under-Sixteen teams that year. Keeps them in their place.'

Onwards to the Bridge Bar. On the right through the door is a little shrine to Jason, a collage of newspaper cuttings and headlines concerning the boy who was never old enough to drink alcohol in here. The remaining walls are covered with pictures of old Ballyhea teams. The talk is of summers past and summers present. The years are marked out by games won and lost, by the life-cycles of teams and players.

Jason is engulfed in warmth here, gentle home-place stuff. Old men grasp his hand and won't let go, thanking him and wishing him well. Dan Flynn, an old teacher and an old hurler who won a Railway Cup medal with Galway in the 1940s, wraps an arm around him, almost squeezing the life from him. Finally, when everything settles, Jason makes a speech. He has brought his first championship jersey, framed, blue and folded, here to Ballyhea, to be hung in the clubhouse. 'Just so yous won't forget me,' he says.

He thanks them and they thank him. They remember him coming down in the early years – 'a little gurrier' from Finglas, with a temper and flashing fists, he did little damage to their prejudices. But, with his gameness on the field, he earned his place among them.

Ballyhea became his home place as much as Finglas. 'There's a lot of Ballyhea in him,' says Eddie again and again. The GAA eased his passing into this world of friendship and trust.

Later in this crazy summer, he will come down to see the boys win their semi-final game against Imokilly. He will stand in their dressing-room and they will applaud him just for being there. More awkwardness will be dissolved through humour as he looks around the little dressing-room half-embarrassed to be there.

'Jaysus, lads. It's old fellas on one side and young fellas on the other side.'

And they throw him a tracksuit and tell him to sit on the bench where he belongs.

On county final day, in September, Uncle Eddie will wait for him at Charleville Station, rosette on lapel and fag in fingers, fidgety as ever. Once again, Jason will fall in with Ballyhea, sitting on the bench in the club tracksuit as the team lose, one of the boys even when the umpires for the game come across to ask for his autograph.

That match is his last memory of the summer when he changed the face of the GAA. Many things changed, but more things remained the same.

'On the day after the match, the team went into Cork for the Man of the Match award ceremony. They met up with the boys from Na Piarsaigh who had beaten them the day before. I know how much losing that game meant in Ballyhea – it's been ninety-nine years since we won a hurling championship – but they met the boys from Na Piarsaigh and had such a night of it, they ended up staying over in their houses in Cork city.

'Then, before Christmas, all the Na Piarsaigh lads came out to Ballyhea for another night out. Put up in the houses again. That's the GAA. After all the fuss, the money and the hype, that's what you remember – the friends, the contacts, the games and the amount it means to people everywhere in the country. If I were ever to go away from home, I know I'd look back and think that that is what being Irish is all about. That's home.'

Times change, but as long as fields stay green and home remains home, the games will live on. Money will circulate, but only fear and hypocrisy can choke the games. When it comes to change, the GAA always moves with the stealth of a guilty man, always gives the impression of having dark secrets to hide.

The summer of Jason Sherlock marked a watershed and an opportunity. Players will always love the games as surely as they love home and the essential joy of playing. Reward will ease their way, but will not diminish their passion. There is no need to make them feel grubby about their own realization that they themselves are what the market is about, that it was pictures of players, not administrators, which Kelloggs chose to slip into their cornflake boxes in the spring of 1995.

Players streak across our consciousness and, before long, they are gone. They don't get many years, yet the time they are given is the part of life when others are pressing ahead, pulling down the material gains. In 1995, Jason Sherlock was the greatest marketing and recruiting tool the games ever possessed. But, by the middle of winter, he was back playing League of Ireland soccer for UCD in front of a couple of hundred people each week.

The clock won't turn back, though. Nobody will ever row across from Valentia Island, like the great Mick O'Connell used to do, in order to train with the county team. The games have to seize their commercial potential as steadily as they have exploited their cultural importance. If we have faith in the strength of the root, we have nothing to fear from the full and final blossoming.

EPILOGUE

When I was four years old, growing up in the concrete sprawl of south east London, my grandfather bought me a hurley for Christmas. It was a curious gift for a child. We were far removed from the Irish community and I was the only boy in a very small family. Yet I was much taken with this exotic thing. A boy's hurley – forty-six to fifty-one centimetres (eighteen or twenty inches) long. White tape banding the bottom part of it.

I did splendid things with that stick. Many things except hurl with it proficiently. I banged nails into wood. I assaulted friends in heated fights. I swatted bumble-bees. I sent the blossoming tops of daffodils flying through the air.

I never attained any great skill at hurling and, now as middle-age creeps up, it is unlikely that I ever will. Yet the memory of that gift warms me. It marked a continuity, the culture of home reaching out to claim my imagination.

My grandfather had played in the green-and-white of O'Toole's early in the century. He never claimed to have played well, not even the claims that a grandfather is entitled to make to his only grandson, but he played with, and knew others who played with, a splash of genius.

I grew up listening to stories of Johnny McDonnell and Paddy McDonnell, of the Synott brothers, Josie, John and Stephen (the clan had five other lesser lights as well), of Joe Joyce, Johnny Carey, Paddy Carey, and just about anybody who wore the blue of Dublin back in the 1920s. Teams – O'Toole's, St Mary's and St Joseph's – from the same parish of Seville Place, off the north strand in Dublin, won successive All Irelands for Dublin in the early 1920s. My grandfather never quite got over the thrill of that.

There were nine O'Toole's men playing for Dublin in a challenge match on 21 November 1920 – Bloody Sunday – when thirteen people, including Tipperary player, Mick Hogan, were shot dead by Black and Tans in Croke Park. Members of the Tipperary team hid out in little houses around Seville Place afterwards.

The fact that the members of the two teams fled Croke Park together, and relied on each other for support and shelter in the aftermath of that day, fascinated me more as a child than the gruesome facts of that atrocity. The story of the Bloody Sunday game was always preambled for me with an explanation of the great rivalry that existed between Dublin and Tipperary at the time.

Many of the O'Toole's and Dublin team ended up being interned during the years that followed. My grandfather's accounts of what happened to them all off the field were vague enough. Off the field, those men weren't any more exceptional than most of their generation. In times of trouble they were luminous because of their abilities in the matter of the native game. For me, the whole business of nationalism and football, and the unique inter-connectedness of GAA people, was already well mixed up in my mind before ever I played the game.

We were a watery kind of GAA family ourselves. My father hurled a little for St Brendan's, and my mother, my grandfather's only child, worshipped weekly in Croke Park through the 1950s when St Vincent's was enjoying its most glamorous era. By the time the Dublin team of the 1970s had arrived, we were living in Ireland again and I was taking up space in a solid GAA school, plodding about solemnly in a St Vincent's jersey most weekends.

As time goes by, all of this seems more valuable. If the games are rooted in our history and our culture so, too, are the experiences of those who play and watch them. There is something precious and time-worn about the games, but the spirit of them is conversation, laughter and passion. Certainly, hearing the national anthem played and sung on All Ireland final day, is different, more spine-tingling, than hearing it rendered on any other occasion. And hearing two old men argue about a passage of play from the 1920s is equally unique and usually more fun.

I'm always slightly surprised, and initially at a loss, when I meet an Irish person who didn't grow up with some involvement in the GAA. The playing of the games seemed to mark out the rhythm of the seasons for the rest of us, and it is a conversational reflex on hearing what part of the country somebody claims provenance from to pass comment on the waxing or waning of that region's GAA fortunes.

When we were kids we played soccer, lots of it, but never seriously – never for medals or glory. I followed Leeds United, but was always vaguely aware that Leeds United was a business whose fortune depended on the effectiveness of their training and recruitment policy. Leeds United would never come to my school when they won a league and make in-jokes about the teachers. Leeds United would never pack us into their cars on Sunday mornings and drive us to games on county council pitches. Great GAA men did those things, though.

We measured ourselves against each other on football and hurling fields. Some of us never amounted to much in those measurings, but merely having been there brings good memories and the regret that we didn't try harder.

There is something depressing about passing into one's mid-thirties and appreciating that the time has passed, that there is no chance to go back and exploit fully the potential you might once have had.

The pleasures left, though, are significant. Gaelic Town is a world of talk and stories. Walk into any place with a picture of a team on the wall and, if you can talk and listen, you won't be asked to leave at closing time. At times, life in Gaelic Town can be claustrophobic, almost inescapable.

The politics and attitudes are broadly green and rural, and generally conservative, and when conversation strays discomfort can set in. Yet that is just a reflection of the country at large, a country with growing pains and insecurities and deep-held fears. The games give us a chance to celebrate ourselves, to celebrate with each other, to meet each other on common ground.

Life goes on and the grip of the games seems never to loosen. This community within a community seems to endure forever. I see men and boys buried in their graves with their jerseys draped over their coffins. I see families marry into each other and becoming Gaelic town dynasties. I see entire communities consumed by the passion of a season, generations welded together in the love of the game. I see children in my home-place running around in jerseys of Dublin-blue, and no end to the rhythm of our Gaelic seasons.

INDEX